TALES
OF
CHRISTIAN UNITY

Tales
of
Christian Unity

THE ADVENTURES OF AN
ECUMENICAL PILGRIM

Thomas Ryan

 PAULIST PRESS *New York/Ramsey*

Acknowledgments

I am deeply grateful to

Fr. Michael Fahey, S.J. and Dr. Thomas Bird
of the North American Roman Catholic-Orthodox Consultation,

Fr. Antony Gabriel, president of the
Eastern Orthodox Clergy Association of Montreal,

Anglican priests William Raines, Mark Gudwin,
Douglas Hodgkinson, and William Richards,

Fr. Thomas Stransky, C.S.P., JoLee Tachney,
Fr. Ronald Roberson, C.S.P. and Mary Mooney,

all of whom read particular sections of this
manuscript and offered helpful comments;

Fr. Toby McGivern for his illustrative sketches;

The Collegeville Press, St. John's Abbey,
Collegeville, Minnesota, for granting permission
to reproduce three diagrams from the book
These Are My Rites by Edward Finn, S.J.;

Marguerite-Marie d'Avignon, Kathleen Porritt,
Rose Mackie, Juliette Gaudreau, Jessie Mellor,
and Francine Bissonnette for so generously
volunteering time at the Canadian Centre for Ecumenism
to help with the typing and preparation of the manuscript;

and Pat O'Rourke and Helen Richard
for their careful proofreading.

Heartfelt thanks!

Library of Congress Catalog Card Number: 82-60748

ISBN: 0-8091-2502-1

Published by Paulist Press
545 Island Road, Ramsey, N.J. 07446

Printed and bound in the United States of America

Maps by Frank Sabatte, C.S.P.

Contents

PREFACE   1

PROLOGUE   3

AN ORIENTAL TALE   7
Cairo   9
Jerusalem   39
Constantinople   68
Mount Athos   92

A GENEVA TALE   133

A CANTERBURY TALE   209

EPILOGUE   275

DEDICATION

To
Mom and Dad

Preface

A Minnesota-born Paulist, in his first priestly assignment as campus minister at Montreal's McGill University, decides to pursue more intensely his commitment to ecumenism. With the encouragement of his Paulist superiors, he backpacks for a year in Europe and the Middle East, eyes and ears and heart open, very open. At the end of the journey Fr. Tom Ryan claims, "I learned more in this year than in any other in my life." Books and books he has read, but he fuses such knowledge with the reflective experience of absorbing cities and towns where Christians live, united yet divided in their common calling. By no means a mute loner, he seems to meet the right folk, some well-known, or, more usually, others not listed in any ecumenical Who's Who.

In this account of that year, Fr. Ryan shares his observations of Cairo and Jerusalem, Mount Athos, Geneva and Canterbury. His remarks reveal not an indifferent vagabond journalist but a Christian pilgrim who rejoices in the signs of ecumenical strivings and suffers the burden of others' indifference and downright hostility to what he is about.

Fr. Ryan is now at the Centre for Ecumenism in Montreal. His full-time ministry for Christian unity at so many levels of the churches' life throughout Canada is already giving flesh to new tales which he or others may someday share, I hope, with the same enthusiastic commitment this book conveys.

Thomas F. Stransky, C.S.P.

Prologue

These tales are an invitation to journey. A journey through history. A journey through some of the world's great religious capitals. A journey through some of the problems that divide the Christian family and the mentalities that make us different.

The wonderful opportunity to spend a year of my life on this journey was given to me as preparation for the work at the Canadian Centre for Ecumenism. I received it as a "gift." In the middle of the year I wrote in my journal while on a retreat day:

"The silence and prayer of the weekend have been like a long drink of cool water. The imperative to write resurfaced during my prayer today, and by the end of the day had worked its way out of the shadows and into a top priority for the Christmas holidays when I will have some free time. How I wish, in a way, that I could bury it. I know from the last time around how many other meaningful things have to be sacrificed to make time to write. And in Switzerland, over the Christmas holidays, it's not hard to think of other more 'fun' options.

"The need to respond to the inner imperative to write is closely tied with a sense of these experiences as gift. And in the Church, gift is always to be given away again, used, put at the service of others. A gift is never to be kept just for oneself. Hence the imperative to find ways of putting it at the service of and making it available to others."

Over the Christmas holidays, the first of these Tales was born.

There was one particular conviction that kept me at the typewriter throughout all of them: that the weakest element in the design for Christian unity is the level of information and experience—and thus *understanding*—available to the laity and the clergy in no matter what church. There is a great gap between what goes on among the theologians who are representing our churches in the official dialogues for unity, and what is communicated to and understood by the majority of people who make up no matter what parish.

The questions I am asked whenever anyone hears I am working in the ecumenical movement set the framework for these Tales: "What is happening ecumenically today? What are the issues that are dividing us? What is the outlook for resolving them?"

These Tales are not for theologians. They are for parishioners and their busy pastors. They are for people who would not be inclined to plow through a dry text on dogmatic theology or church history. Yet they are both theological and historical.

They are liberally woven with historical yarn because there is no way around history when one is trying to grasp why we have been divided all these years. But they are spun in story form, and the stories are true. They are the experiences of my year. The stories seek to give you not only appropriate historical and theological information but a "feel" for the places where significant events in Christian history took place.

I learned more in this year than in any other of my life. These Tales are your invitation to travel along, listening to the conversations, seeing the sights, and being provoked right along with me to new discovery and understanding.

The schema of Tales presented, to be a more complete representation of the main Christian confessional communions, should have an Augsburg Tale and a London Tale and a Southern Tale which would be of particular interest to Lutherans and Methodists and Baptists respectively. But alas, a year can only hold so much. If I am ever given another gift someday, a gift that would take me in those directions, I would be happy to share it with you in more *Tales of Christian Unity.*

TALES
of
CHRISTIAN UNITY

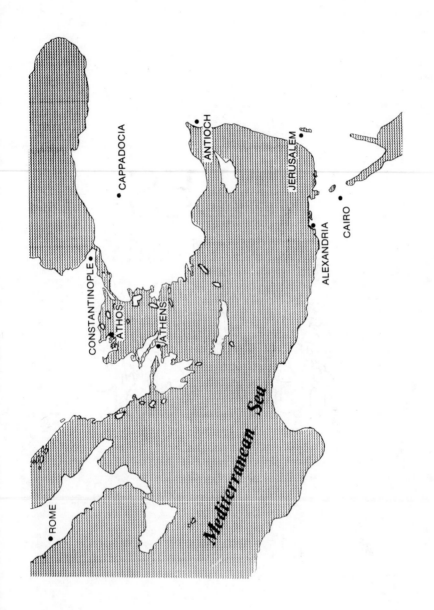

ROME

CONSTANTINOPLE

ATHOS

ATHENS

CAPPADOCIA

ANTIOCH

JERUSALEM

ALEXANDRIA

CAIRO

Mediterranean Sea

AN ORIENTAL TALE

Cairo

Visions of crowded buses and trains in the pilgrimage ahead had prevailed in my packing. On the floor leaning against my chair in the Rome airport sat but a folding suitbag and a day-pack whose pocket was still largely empty. Let the thieves come; they wouldn't get much.

My mind, usually engaged in a steady crawl-stroke, was enjoying rolling over on its back and floating in the unexpected delay. My flight from Geneva was to have arrived in Cairo at 3:00 P.M. A simple change of planes in Rome was quickly complicated by a mechanics' strike, and it was now 11:00 P.M.

The call came to board the plane. Our now-estimated-arrival-time in Cairo was one o'clock in the morning. The person who was going to meet me there was surely already home in bed. With nothing but an address in my hand, my unfamiliarity with the city of Cairo and ignorance of Arabic began to evoke feelings of both insecurity and adventure.

The DC-10 touched down with enough jolt to rouse those who were still dozing. Grateful for my carry-ons, I passed immediately through the swing doors and strode down the hallway toward the baggage check gate. Plan "A": see if there was still an airport bus running; plan "B": hail a cab. As I passed through the gate, a young woman in her thirties dressed in faded powder-blue jeans and jacket stepped forward from the right and lightly touched my arm: "Are you Thomas Ryan?"

My expression must have registered somewhere between surprise, delight, and relief. Her name was Marie. She insisted that she hadn't minded waiting, and dismissed the hours with "I love to read." A wonderfully gracious response, I thought, and resolved to remember it.

In the taxi I made two guesses, both of which she confirmed: from her accent that she was Belgian, and from the book in her hand that she was devoted to Egyptology. She, too, like myself, was a guest of Fr. Xavier Eid, the pastor of the Greek Catholic parish in downtown Cairo, while she did some research work in Egypt. Fr. Xavier, who is behind or involved in most of what happens ecumenically in Cairo, had asked Marie to meet his new, incoming guest at the airport. She had been faithful beyond the call of duty. The taxi sped by giant and gaudily colored billboards whose black arabic script was highlighted by a bright yellow border.

Reports of an exciting renewal among Christians in Egypt—specifically, the Coptic Orthodox Church—had brought me to Cairo. The word "Copt" derives from a Greek word *aigyptos* used by Greeks to designate the inhabitants of Egypt. Thus, "Copt" simply means Egyptian.

The Coptic Orthodox Church was known through the first quarter of its existence as the Church of Alexandria, allegedly founded by St. Mark the Evangelist in 42 A.D. when he came there to preach the good news of Jesus Christ. According to tradition, St. Mark returned to Alexandria a second time in the year 61 to find a flourishing Christian community and three churches. Seven years later, he sealed his evangelizing work with his blood and died a martyr.

Since the native population of Egypt was Christian at the time of the Arab conquest of Egypt (641), the names Copt and Christian came to be synonymous in the Arab mind. Henceforth, from the seventh century, the Church of Alexandria is the Coptic Church. The Copts call themselves the truest of Egyptians, because their ancestors tolerated little genetic inter-mixing right from the time of the pharaohs. They are a people with one of the longest of recorded histories, proud descendants of that race to which the civilization and culture of the ancient world were so largely due.

Marie was telling me of the days she had just spent in Alexandria in the museums. Every time she mentioned "Alexandria" she pushed various memory buttons from my courses in early Church history.

The theological school of Alexandria was the first university and the first library of the Christian world. It played a determining role in the history of Christianity through the early centuries and attained its peak toward the middle of the second century. Among its most illustrious professors were Athenagoras, Clement of Alexandria, Dennis the Great, Didymus, Heracleas and Pantaemus who, as principal of the school, established the Coptic alphabet by using the Greek characters and adding seven characters from the Egyptian which correspond to sounds that do not exist in Greek. He thus recorded phonetically the vernacular of Egypt, a development with direct links to the ancient Egyptian language spoken since the early days of the pharaohs but originally written in picture-forms called hieroglyphics.

All branches of learning flourished at the school of Alexandria, and it soon became a stronghold for the expression of Christian doctrine over against the non-Christian philosophers who had held undisputed sway until that time. The first systematic attempt to harmonize the tradition of faith with the free conclusions of human intellect was made neither at Rome nor at Athens, but in Egypt. Alexandria counted among its star pupils Basil the Great, Gregory the Wonderworker, John Chrysostom, Gregory of Nazianzus, Jerome and the historian Rufinus.

The continued flourishing of the Coptic Church from St. Mark's martyrdom onward, despite centuries of persecution and torture, is one of the more remarkable chapters in Christian history. Under the reigns of the Roman emperor Trajan (98–117), Septimus Severus (202) and Decius (250), persecution raged. So dramatic were the repercussions under Diocletian that the Coptic Church dates its liturgical calendar, filled with the feast days of martyrs, from 284, the year Diocletian acceded to the throne (the year 1983 corresponds to the year 1699 A.M.—the year of the martyrs—in the Coptic calendar).

There is no particular surprise in finding a vitalized missionary movement beginning very early from Egypt. Where the Church is most persecuted it gives the purest and most generous witness. The initiative originated in Upper Egypt at Aswan, moved outward in north Africa, reached Palestine and Syria and spread from there to Asia Minor. The missionary and evangelical tradition practiced by the Copts exercised an influence that even penetrated deep into Europe. John Cassian, after visiting monasteries in the Egyptian desert, built two establishments for monks at Marseilles, France. St. Athanasius put up a church in Belgium. The village of Saint-Moritz in Switzerland owes its name to Maurice, commander of the Theban legion who assisted the Roman army in defeating the Gauls in 287. After the victory, the emperor Maximian gave the order for the entire army to present offerings to the gods. Under the commands of Maurice, the Theban legion pulled back and refused, for they were all Coptic Christians. The abbey and town of Saint-Moritz today mark the site of their massacre. Similarly, the Swiss city of Zurich honors three Coptic missionaries as its patrons and bears their effigy upon the official city seal: three beheaded evangelists carrying their heads in their hands. Egyptian monks were pioneers of the faith as far west as Ireland.

But this descendant of Ireland was now as far east as Egypt and getting an object lesson in Middle Eastern cab driving. The centrifugal force of a turn pushed me hard against the door. I would sleep but briefly this first night in the land of pharaohs. Marie handed me an envelope containing the program of meetings and visits that had been prepared for my stay in Egypt. The following morning featured an orientation tour of Old Cairo, including a visit to the cave in the crypt of Abu Sargah Church where tradition holds that the Holy Family stayed during their flight into Egypt. When one grows up in the New World, such historical places seem located in a never-never land far away. That it was far away there was no denying, but never-never was now.

Amid the sensory bombardment and disorientation of my first Cairo morning came the blessing of a familiar face—Yousriya Sawris, a delegate of the Coptic Church to various World

Council of Churches meetings, whom I had met in Geneva on a couple of occasions where we had done some advance planning toward this visit. She arrived two hours late and took me on a tour of the Old City. In the mayhem of traffic she was cut off from a desired exit and found herself going in the wrong direction. A string of police barricades separated our lane from the oncoming lane. Much to the chagrin of the line-up of cars behind us, she stopped to politely petition a policeman to open up the barricade, stop the oncoming flow of traffic, and let us make a U-turn in the middle of the road. As they discussed, the policeman's expression went from "adamantly-against" to "wavering." Unperturbed by the storm of horns and impatient voices that rained down upon us, she continued to negotiate as though what she was asking was well within his power to give. Suddenly, his dark face broke into a broad smile and within seconds we had reversed our direction. "You just have to be nice to them," she said in a matter-of-fact tone.

Old Cairo seemed to be literally falling down. We made our way in the narrow streets amid the dogs and the chickens and the robed children at play, visiting a half dozen of the oldest Christian churches in the world. In the same neighborhood of Kasr El-Cham'e stands the Coptic Museum, one of the four principal museums of Egypt, containing antiquities of every kind as well as displays of Coptic Christian art in icons, vestments, sculptures and vessels. Toward the end of the fourth century, when Christianity became the recognized religion of the Roman Empire, the Christians of Egypt speedily transformed the temples into churches. Crosses were sculptured on columns and on door lintels, the ancient bas-reliefs were hidden under a coating of whitewash or plaster on which pictures of saints and martyrs were painted, and the Egyptian "ankh," sign of the breath of life, became the Coptic cross with three-ended points symbolizing the Holy Trinity. Examples of these artistic and cultural transitions abound in the Coptic Museum and serve as a review of great moments in Coptic annals.

The fourth and fifth centuries were a glorious epoch for the Church of Egypt. St. Athanasius (295–373), the twentieth patriarch of Alexandria, whom the Church calls "equal to the apostles," was the champion of the definition of the faith according to which the Son is of the same substance as the Father. He established the teaching of the Trinity as a symbol of the faith while struggling against the heresies which ravaged the Church all around the Mediterranean basin—most notably that of Arius who said that the Word is not eternal, but is rather a creature, begotten by God and mediating between God and the world. The teaching of Athanasius prevailed at the First Ecumenical Council held in 325 at Nicea, and the Son was declared to be of one substance with the Father.

St. Theophilus, the patriarch of Alexandria, was an important pillar of the faith at the Second Ecumenical Council in 381 at Constantinople. With the other Council fathers he underlined the teaching that in God absolute unity is inseparable from a diversity of persons; the Father is the source of divinity with his Son and the Holy Spirit.

St. Cyril, the twenty-fourth patriarch of Alexandria, consecrated in 412, was the president of the Third Ecumenical Council at Ephesus in 431 which defined a perfect unity between the divinity and the humanity of Christ, combating the heresy of Nestorius (who divided the human and divine natures) and affirming that Mary is the Mother of God. For having defended the divine maternity of the Virgin, who henceforth would be honored in the East under the title of Theotokos (God-Bearer), St. Cyril received the title of "Pope" at this third council.

Against this storied backdrop, a schism is about to disfigure the doctrinal unity of the universal Church, and the Church of Alexandria is at the middle of the fray. For reasons that were as much political as theological, the Church of Alexandria became separated from Byzantium and Rome at the Fourth Council of Chalcedon in 451. With it were the Armenian, the Syrian, the Ethiopian and the Indian Churches—all of whom have since been identified by various titles: pre-Chalcedonian, non-Chalcedonian, the Churches of the Three Councils, or the Oriental Churches. From the time of Chalcedon, the Churches of Rome and Byzantium who were alone as adherents to Chalcedon's teachings were called "Orthodox."

From the time of the schism between Byzantium and Rome (eleventh century) the Byzantines continued to apply this title to themselves. Today, "Orthodox" strictly speaking refers to the Byzantine Churches who follow the decisions of the first seven, as opposed to the first three, councils. The terminology is confusing because the Oriental or pre-Chalcedonian Churches also call themselves "Orthodox." They will be referred to here as "Oriental" Churches so as to maintain their historical and doctrinal distinctiveness.

Even though from our perspective today the rift seemed to result more from a quarrel of words than a disagreement of meaning, the issue was an important one: the two natures in Christ. The Coptic Church confessed the doctrine taught by St. Cyril of Alexandria: the divinity and humanity of Christ are united in him in one perfect unity forming *one* nature, one indissoluble existence. An image used was that of fire and iron which, though different in nature, become inseparably one through their union. The theologians of the Oriental Churches felt that the definition of Chalcedon understood the two natures in Christ as *separate* entities, not really united. To their mind, this contradicted the profession of faith of the Council of Ephesus which had declared one perfect union of the divinity and humanity of Christ, against the Nestorian heresy which attempted to separate them.

The Oriental Churches have never formulated their Christology in these terms: God + Man = Jesus Christ. It has always preferred to express its conception with a tighter unity: God-Incarnate = God-Man = Jesus Christ. As a Coptic monk later remarked: "We don't like the number 'two'; we much prefer the number 'one.'" Because of their stress on the unity in Christ in *one* nature (Greek: *mono-physis*), these Churches are also oftentimes referred to as "monophysite."

One of the important results of the visits between leaders of Oriental Churches and Rome begun in the wake of Vatican II (1962–65) has been an increasingly deeper mutual understanding through discussion of doctrinal problems. The fundamental disagreement which was at the basis of the separation in the fifth century has been clarified through these discussions. The Chalcedonian definitions were not accepted by the Oriental Churches primarily because of a problem of terminology. The Orientals understood the terms "person" and "nature" in another sense than understood by the definitions of the Council of Chalcedon. They possessed, therefore, the correct doctrine on the incarnation, but they expressed it with other terms and formulas.

In May 1973, the Coptic Patriarch, Shenouda III, visited Pope Paul VI in Rome. They signed together a profession of faith which contains the doctrine of incarnation. In formulating it, the contested terms were avoided and the doctrine was not expressed with the terms "person" and "nature." After fifteen centuries of misunderstanding, the two leaders recognized the identity of their faith in the mystery of the Incarnate Word, expressed in the terms of the Council of Nicea rather than that of Chalcedon.

Fr. Pierre Duprey, under-secretary for the Secretariat for Christian Unity in Rome, told an ecumenical conference in Lourdes, France, in 1978: "One can say that after fifteen centuries, in the declarations of Pope Paul VI and of Syrian Patriarch Mar Ignatius Jacob III, and of Pope Paul VI with Coptic Pope Shenouda III, the Christological difference has been resolved. The Pope and the Patriarch recognized the identity of their faith in the mystery of the Incarnate Word. . . . They solemnly affirmed that they were professing the same faith in the mystery of the Incarnate Word, even if, during the centuries, they were not agreed on a given expression of that faith. This fact is important because it liquidates a contentious issue of fifteen hundred years."

One can legitimately ask whether it is still appropriate to include the Coptic and Syrian Churches among the non-Chalcedonian group of Churches. The teaching of Chalcedon has been clarified through use of other terms and the Coptic and Syrian Churches have accepted it. The neglect of practical follow-up on the implications of this agreement remains a curious hiatus in the ecumenical movement.

After reliving the history of the Coptic Church through cool rooms filled with antiquities, we sat for a while in the museum's courtyard and sucked a fruit drink from small plastic bags with straws. I was surprised to learn that the museum is staffed by volunteers.

On our way out of the Coptic Museum, I broke off a piece of the round loaf of bread I was carrying and gave it to two young boys in the street. They spontaneously touched it to their forehead, their lips and their heart. "Whatever their religious affiliation is," Yousriya said, "bread is sacred." There were both Christians and Moslems living in the neighborhood. After the Arab conquest in 641 A.D. the Copts benefited from the general policy of Islam which allows those who refuse to accept the teaching of Mohammad to continue their own worship and to administer their local affairs without interference as long as they paid the necessary taxes to the successive Arab dynasties which ruled them.

That evening, Fr. Eid, my host in Cairo, Coptic Bishop Samuel and I broke bread together at Yousriya's house for supper. We learned from Bishop Samuel that despite the professed policy of religious tolerance for dissenters from Islam, the Church has to guard its rights with militance or find the island on which it lives eroding beneath its feet. At first Copts welcomed the arrival of Islam because they had been oppressed under the Byzantine Empire. But in recent decades some Copts have complained of being second-class citizens and of being discriminated against in obtaining government jobs. Copts are prominent in Egypt in small businesses and the professions, primarily law and medicine. Today, out of forty-three million inhabitants in Egypt, about eight million are Coptic Orthodox, with another half million spread out among the membership of several other Christian Churches. The following evening I witnessed a display of Coptic solidarity wherein the sense of ethnic pride and religious fervor were like two fountains that mutually filled each other.

It was the anniversary of the first apparition of Mary over the Church of the Virgin Mary located at Touman Bay Street in a quarter of Cairo called Zeitun. The appearances are said to have taken place intermittently since the evening of April 2, 1968. They have been witnessed by Muslims as well as Chris-

tians. Attempts to verify the authenticity of the appearances
have resulted in various interviews of witnesses and those who
link healings and cures to the event. Whatever conclusions one
draws about the apparitions from the reports, there is no questioning the positive benefits that the claimed event has gener-
ated among the Coptic Christian community.

Fr. Eid and I arrived about 6:30 P.M. An area of several
blocks had been roped off, the streets had been cleared, and
some sixteen thousand chairs had been set up. They were all
full, and there was no telling how many were standing. It was
early April, but it felt like Christmas. Thousands of decorative
lights and a continuous border of colorful bunting traced the
outline of the square. A representative of the church met us
and led us through the crowd down a long corridor maintained
by the clasped hands of young black-cassocked seminarians
and red-robed altar boys. We had not yet reached our seats on
the erected platform stage when behind us the sense of anticipation I had experienced moving through the crowd turned to
something close to frenzy. Three black sedans came to a flying
halt at the edge of the throng, doors flew open, and all bodies
turned in the direction of a sturdy, bearded figure with the
tranquil, piercing countenance of an icon. Shenouda III, revered as the 117th successor of St. Mark as Patriarch of Alexandria, emerged from the back seat of the lead car. The crowd's
enthusiasm seemed strangely fueled by his stoic detachment.
Protected by a ring of attendants, he made his way around to
the back of the stage where bazaar-type booths had been
erected for the sale of church-guild crafts. He stopped and visited with the workers in each booth. They kissed his hand and
tried to contain their pleasure. Though his manner seemed distinctly other-worldly, he seemed close to the concerns of his
people. Then he mounted the stage and greeted each of us in-
dividually before taking his seat in the center behind a small
table which he used to make some last minute notes for his address. Children and students came forth with songs and poems.
It was too big for the metaphor of family, and yet it possessed
that kind of informality; it was too expressly religious for the
label of nationalism, and yet it had that kind of intensity. An

extraordinary sense of solidarity filled the night air. He then spoke for an hour in Arabic about the role of Mary in Christian life, and the crowd hung upon his words with the same fixity as the thousands on New Year's Eve in Times Square watching the clock approach midnight.

The days to follow brought visits to mosques, a Caritas International meeting, and a get-together with the apostolic nuncio. But Marie, the Belgian devotee of Egyptology who had rescued me at the airport, didn't feel I was making the right connections. "To understand the Copts," she said, "you have to understand something about the ancient Egyptians." She set up a rendezvous with Fr. Gérard Viaud, a French expert on Coptic history. It was a fascinating encounter. The tradition of ancient Egypt, the hieroglyphs on papyrus and the engravings and paintings in the royal tombs are reflected in the lives and customs of the contemporary native Egyptians, he contended. As a point of departure, he chose the Book of the Dead, a book of incantations pronounced over the body of the deceased to help him surmount all difficulties in his passage from this life to the next. A guidebook for the voyage toward "life after life," it was then placed in the sarcophagus with the corpse. The monuments and tombs, paintings and engravings express an entire Egyptian eschatology, a theology accommodated to Christianity and lived by the modern Copts.

It is no coincidence, Gérard Viaud stated, that the underworld of the ancient Egyptians was peopled with evil spirits and frightful creatures, and in the Christian liturgy of baptism the priest pronounces a blessing over the water to chase away the demons and clear the way before the child who will be plunged into these waters in a ritual of passage toward fullness of life. It is no coincidence that the dead of the ancient Egyptians were believed to pass through twelve journey stages corresponding to the twelve nocturnal hours, encountering serpents and dragons along the way, and that the priest prays in the Coptic funeral rite: "Lord, receive the soul of the dead and guide him along the safe path so he will not fall into shadowy precipices. Let him crush the head of the serpent and lay low the dragon. Lead him safely into the presence of the Divine Judge, who sits before the twelve portals of Heaven." It is no coincidence that the ancient Egyptians made supplications to Ra and Osiris to hear the prayers of those who had already entered into the Kingdom of Light, or supplications to send other divinities to meet the soul on the way and serve as guardians, while the Coptic liturgy for the dead invokes the communion of saints or implores God to send the Archangels Michael or Gabriel, the Virgin or St. George to guide and protect the soul in passage.

The richness of the Coptic funeral rites did indeed seem pharaonic in archetype and imagery. The Coptic genius was to integrate and accommodate the traditions of their ancestors to the doctrines of Christianity. Among the pharaohs, death was not an end but simply a doorway symbolized by the false doors engraved in the tomb chambers through which one passed to a life of rest and fulfillment. The Coptic funeral prayer speaks of the bosom of Abraham, Isaac, and Jacob as a place of light, refreshment, and peace. And the food offerings brought to and left in the tombs by the ancients find a clear parallel in the Coptic practice of bringing special cakes and breads, placing them on the grave, and subsequently distributing them to the poor. In the dynasties of Egypt, when the soul of the dead arrives into the Kingdom of Light and Peace, it is crowned; to ritualize this hope, a crown is placed on the head of the deceased. This practice finds its echo among modern Egyptians on the day of baptism when one dies and is reborn in the new life of Christ. A crown is placed on the head of the child with the prayer: "Bring this crown of glory and justice, love and sanctity, into the Kingdom of Light."

Upon learning that the soul of the dead was believed to remain on earth three days after death, and only then was sent off on the journey of forty days to arrive at the gate of the Kingdom of Light, I wanted to pursue the obvious Christian parallels which posit identical time-lapses in the burial, resurrection and ascension sequence, but we had run out of time.

Early the next morning Marie and I set out for Memphis, Sakara, and Giza to make the "right connections."

By mid-morning we were standing amid the ruins of the

ancient city of Memphis which seemed to appear in the history of Egypt by virtue of some quantum leap from an unrecorded to a very high level of civilization. Represented today by the ramshackle village of Mitrahina, Memphis perplexed me. Recalling the poor huts we had passed along the Nile, looking at the poverty of Mitrahina, and trying to reconstruct in my mind the remains of the once great temple of Ptah in which we stood, I wondered aloud about what had happened to this great people and their civilization. But Marie's response indicated that she beheld the same scene from an entirely different perspective. "Just stand here quietly," she said, "and feel the sacred energy that still hangs in the air. This place was once a revered contact point between the Divine and the people who inhabited this land. The Energy-Source that inspired among them such creative and lasting works of the human spirit is still available, can still be tapped into. What is needed for a new rich merging is a window of entry through which that eternal and creative Force can electrify this people in this time. All the essential ingredients are still there. With the right combination of vision, faith and leadership, what happened can burst forth again—if not here, somewhere else on our planet. This temple, even in this state of ruin, is a sign of the potential available to us." I looked at Marie reflectively and felt like a neophyte in the presence of a mystic.

The saggara pyramids were so much embellishment to her theme. The walls of the interior passages and chambers are covered with the oldest written religious literature so far known: hymns, prayers, magic spells, and legends of great beauty.

We rode a camel to the Serapeum, the underground burial chambers of the Apis bull, the sacred animal of the God Ptah. At Memphis we had seen the huge alabaster embalming tables on which the bodies of the holy animals were prepared for immortality. The sides of the tables were carved to represent elongated lions, and their upper surfaces sloped downward so that the animals' blood and the water used for purification would drain off into an alabaster basin, carved in one piece with the table. The Apis bull was black in color, with a white triangular mark on the forehead and another white mark like a spread-eagle on the back. It was said to have been born of a virgin cow who had conceived him by a flash of lightning.

We approached the underground burial place through an avenue of sphinxes and descended into a maze of passages and chambers cut into the living rock. The main passage, shorter than most of the others, was six hundred and sixty feet long, sixteen feet high, and ten feet wide. On either side of it opened burial chambers with a great sarcophagus in each one for a bull. We had a flashlight, but Marie vetoed its use immediately: "Just walk down to the end of the main passage," she suggested, "and let yourself feel the place in the dark. The first burials were made here in the sixth century B.C." I earned my merit badge for Passage Through Haunted Dwellings and rewarded myself at the end of the corridor with a calming beam of light from my flashlight. The beam fell upon an enormous black granite sarcophagus with a glass-like polish and beautiful engraving.

Late that afternoon, by the time I had emerged from the entrance tunnel of the Great Pyramid of Khufu at Giza I felt lightheaded and intoxicated from having inhaled the air of ancient Egypt the duration of the day. Emerging from this 4,700-year-old royal tomb whose pointed top soared 451 feet high in a symbolic merging of earth with heaven, my dream-state only intensified with the vision of Cairo's minarets shimmering on the horizon. The desert heat-haze induced the illusion that we had slipped into a zone of timelessness.

Later that night we sat on the roof terrace under a clear star-spangled sky eating pretzels and drinking juice. Marie spoke of reincarnation, a subject for which I normally have little patience. Yet given all I had seen that day, it somehow seemed no longer outside the realm of possibility. Egypt, I decided, does that to one.

The following Friday night I made my way toward the new Coptic Cathedral of St. Mark, in Anba-Ruweis, Cairo, to attend one of the renowned weekly question and answer sessions with Pope Shenouda. A former hermit, Shenouda had led a completely solitary life in the Western desert for six years, devoting his time to prayer, meditation, and fasting, before being called to the responsibilities first of arch-priest and then bishop, a post open in the Orthodox and ancient Oriental Churches only to monks, as priests marry. Since his consecration as Patriarch of the See of St. Mark in 1971, he has ordained nineteen new bishops and eighty new priests and added over sixty new churches in Egypt. His commitment to Christian unity is well known. He is the first Alexandrian patriarch to visit the Vatican since the differences at Chalcedon in 451, and he had exchanged visits with the Orthodox patriarchs in Constantinople, Moscow, Romania, Bulgaria and Antioch, as well as with the Catholic patriarchs in the Middle Eastern countries. Under his leadership, the Coptic Church has become a member of the Middle East Council of Churches (it already exercised active membership in the World Council of Churches) and has taken steps toward effecting reconciliation with the Anglican and the Protestant Churches of Egypt and with the Roman Catholic Church at large. His humility and asceticism have made him a charismatic personality of powerful spiritual influence with an inspiring ability to lead his people.

By the number of people still milling about outside, I surmised that it would be some time yet before the start. Unable to find the place where I was to rendezvous with my interpreter Sonya, I entered the cathedral by a side door. As fortune had it, it was most likely the only door through which I could have gained passage. The huge church was packed with eight thousand people, mostly young, and I suddenly realized why there were so many still outside: there was no more room within.

As I had entered through a transept door, I found myself at the front of the church. Recognizing that I was a visitor and not Egyptian, several in the front row spontaneously moved to offer their seat. While everyone was waiting for Shenouda to enter, three young people came up of their own initiative to inquire what language I spoke and to see if I needed an interpreter. The man on my right wanted to know if the people in North America go to Communion each week and if they fast. Sonya, whom Bishop Samuel had appointed as my interpreter, found me and squeezed herself into a half-space.

Then Pope Shenouda entered, surrounded by his coterie, all in black, and strode briskly to his table and chair at the top of the sanctuary steps. With one movement the whole crowd rose to its feet and shook the walls with a thundering sung doxology. My mind flashed on Marie's words as we had stood amid the ruins of the Temple of Ptah at Memphis: "The Divine Energy-Source that inspired the ancients is still available . . . with the right combination of vision, faith and leadership, a tremendous flowering of the human spirit can burst forth again." Goose bumps stood out on my arms.

When everyone finally sat down, several assistants collected little pieces of paper throughout the congregation, on which were written various questions pertaining to the spiritual life which the contributors wished to pose to their leader, Shenouda. He spread them all out on the table before him. As there were many more than he could respond to in one evening, he selected two or three, made some notes to guide his thoughts, and for the next hour responded. Then he gathered the pieces of paper together and placed them off to the side. He would devote the second hour to a topic of his own choosing: the importance of integrating all the virtues and, in particular, living with the wisdom and alertness of serpents but with the guilelessness and simplicity of doves—a message well-tailored to the reality of Coptic life as a militant Christian minority among a Muslim majority.

On his way out, he saw me sitting in the front row and, recognizing me from our brief encounter at Zeitun, stopped. My gesture was entirely spontaneous and natural: it felt right to kiss a holy man's hand.

Afterward, when the church emptied, the scene in the parking lot was like the aftermath of a football bowl game. Sonya, who had provided non-stop translation for two hours, flagged down a car and asked the occupants if they could give me a lift home. They waved me inside. On the way I learned from them that they came every Friday night. "We wouldn't miss it," the driver affirmed. There is a similar event every Sunday in Alexandria, they said.

Five months later, Egypt's Coptic pope, Shenouda III, would be deposed by President Anwar Sadat. Shenouda's removal would come as part of a crackdown on the Moslem Brotherhood and other Islamic extremists. Fifteen hundred people would be swept up in the dragnet, one hundred and fifty of them Copts.

Sadat and Shenouda had been feuding for almost a decade over issues ranging from the construction of Christian churches to noisy demonstrations. Acts of violence directed against the Copts were on the increase. On January 6, 1980, two bombs went off in Alexandria, killing one and injuring several others. At Minia on the same evening, police had to intervene to allow Christians to hold a worship service that Moslem militants wanted to prevent. In Assuit a caroler was stabbed on the same night. On January 31, 1980, a movie theater showing a film on Jesus Christ was burned down. Inflammatory literature began to appear in Cairo during February. According to Bishop Samuel, the inflammatory literature was more dangerous than the bombs.

Accusations of bloody anti-Christian persecutions were leveled at Sadat by American and Canadian Copts during Sadat's visit to Washington and New York in April 1980. Sadat angrily blamed Shenouda for instigating the embarrassing demonstrations. Shenouda deplored the incidents and the Church denied Sadat's allegation.

Around the same time, Shenouda cancelled customary Easter festivities and the Coptic Church boycotted Sadat's ceremony of festival greetings to the Christians of Egypt to protest the mistreatment of Copts by Moslem extremists. Coptic officials cited instances of church burnings, attacks on Christian university students, and the abduction of Christian girls. The Coptic pope, with his bishops, retired to the desert monasteries northwest of Cairo.

The cancellations were another embarrassment for Sadat, who was generally a defender of the Coptic minority, doing his best to defuse religious tensions.

In July 1981, the worst battle in decades occurred between members of the country's Muslim majority and its Coptic or Christian minority. At least eighteen people were killed.

Against this background, Sadat would dissolve thirteen Muslim and Christian societies that he said mixed politics and religion and threatened Egypt's national unity.

Although he would not welcome the Sadat move, Shenouda would be reported by associates to have agreed to it for the good of the Church. Stripped of administrative power but not of his ecclesiastical functions, Shenouda would remain the Coptic pope for life. Bishop Samuel would say that the measures taken by Mr. Sadat were very important for the unity and security of Egypt: "Yes, it was a drastic measure, but we are explaining to the people that we will be the first to benefit from them." Bishop Samuel would theorize that Sadat moved against the pope as a symbolic gesture to mollify Egypt's Moslems, who may have been upset by the harsh crackdown on the Moslem Brotherhood and other Islamic groups whose militant fundamentalism has been blamed for recent Christian–Moslem clashes: "The government wanted to have a balance and not be seen to be attacking one side and not the other."

Shenouda, once a desert hermit, would be sequestered at the Bishoy monastery in the Wadi Natroun desert. Bishop Samuel and President Sadat would both be killed on October 7, 1981 in the attack by Moslem extremists on the reviewing stand where they were seated.

For centuries, the Egyptian desert, where the sun is born and where it dies each day, was a barren griddle to be avoided as much as possible. With the dawn of the Christian era it attracted vast numbers who sought to realize after their own manner the message of the Gospel.

One can only try to imagine the scenario. Suddenly, in the first century, to this people saturated with divinities but as yet unilluminated with the identity of the Divinity, a religion of love and peace is taught where there is only a single God, of whom the Son became flesh and dwelt among the men and women of a tiny neighboring country (he even sojourned for a time in the land of Egypt!) and, most important, he came to save each one of us.

Imagine the difficulty of grasping—the shock even, for this people so profoundly imbued with a sense of religious mystery—that even the least among them was sacred in the eyes of the Single Divinity (something which was hitherto unheard of), and that their ancient gods were but empty vanities before this God.

They believed with enthusiasm. Christianity offered everyone, even the poor and illiterate, the means of salvation. It was not until the middle of the third century, however, that the desert would become part of Christian life.

Anthony, born of a Christian family, became an orphan. One day as he entered a church he heard the words of the Gospel, "If you wish to be perfect, then go, sell what you have and give it to the poor. Then, come and follow me" (Mt 19:21). On another occasion shortly thereafter, he was struck in a particular way by the words: "Do not become anxious for tomorrow" (Mt 6:34). He gave away all that he had and devoted himself to prayer, fasting, and good works in his village. After a certain time, he withdrew from his village. Never had anyone before him dared to act like this. From time to time, certainly, there were those who distanced themselves from public life and took up their residence in a small hut at the edge of town, dedicating their time to prayer. But what Anthony was doing, departing for the veritable desert where his life would be a journey inward to an interior desert, was a radical break with past forms of Christian life. His action would prove to be decisive for universal Christianity.

To live in the desert was to relive the great moments of the Bible in a milieu storied with the lives of those who sought and encountered God. Others wasted little time in imitating Anthony. The hermit and the monk came seeking, in this land of election which inclines so naturally to contemplation, to live the Gospel without compromise and thus leave behind all that is vain and superficial. One did not have to be highly lettered or intellectually gifted. All that was required was to love God, to obey one's spiritual father, and to wish to be saved. That essentially explains the rapid growth of hermits and monks in the desert.

Monasticism developed in Egypt under the eremetical form, a solitary life without an official rule, with St. Paul of Thebes (234–347); under the anchorite form (an extreme form of solitary asceticism involving exposure to hardship such as inadequate clothing or shelter) with St. Anthony (251–356); and under the community life form with St. Pachomius (292–346). The life-spans of these three founders of desert monasticism, when looked at in the light of their simple and ordered existence, offers much food for thought for us moderns. St. Pachomius instituted a monastic rule which, translated by St. Jerome, served as a working base for St. Benedict, the father of Western monasticism. The monasteries of St. Anthony and St. Paul lie in the desert to the east of Cairo. In the Western desert, called the Wadi-Natroun, there are four other ancient monasteries. It was to one of these, St. Macarius, situated just ninety-two kilometers from Cairo on the road to Alexandria, that I was to go.

Night had already fallen by the time I arrived. The sign on the high wall, next to the huge iron doors, said in Arabic and English: "Closed until Easter." Bishop Samuel and Yousriya had arranged for an exception to be made in my case to the usual monastic rule of no visitors during Lent. The big doors swung open. I was received by Fr. Jeremiah, the monk who oversees hospitality. In a short time Fr. Kyrillos, a wizened monk with a long white beard and childlike smile, entered and sat down (I later learned he was the second-in-charge of the monastery, after the Spiritual Father). He told me about the venerable history of St. Macarius.

The monastery was founded in 360 by Macarius who tutored more than four thousand monks of different nationalities. In 1969, with the arrival of twelve monks who had spent ten years in scattered caves, the monastery embarked upon an era of spiritual growth and architectural construction. The

twelve, called by Kyrillos VI, the late Coptic patriarch, to reno-
vate the monastery and fill the surrounding hills with monks
once again, came from their secluded and austere environment where they had studied the precepts of spiritual life
practiced by the founders of monasticism. Their leader was
Fr. Matta El Meskeen who is now the Spiritual Father of St.
Macarius. When they arrived only six monks lived there, and
almost all of the monastery's historical buildings were crumbling. There are now ninety monks, most of them possessing
university degrees in fields as diverse as medicine, agriculture,
engineering, and pharmacology. All of them have had previous
job experience. The single rule which the Spiritual Father has
prescribed for the acceptance of a postulant is "to have felt
within his heart even once the feeling of love toward God."
"We have no other law," Fr. Kyrillos said, "other than submission to the will of God through loving him."

It was late by monastery time. Fr. Jeremiah led me to my
cell. At the door he gave me a candle and some matches. "The
generator which provides our electricity will be shut off at any
moment now. At three in the morning the waking bell will call
the monks to pray for an hour in their cells. At four you will
hear a second bell calling everyone to hymn-chanting in the
chapel." After inquiring whether there was anything I needed,
he bade me good-night and was gone.

I got up at the second bell, dressed quickly, and stepped
out into the desert night air. I couldn't decide which was more
remarkable: the stars or the silence. I suddenly realized that I
didn't know where the chapel was and started to explore the
courtyard for architectural clues. As I rounded the corner of
one centrally located structure, I discerned the muffled sound
of chanting within and saw a host of sandals outside the door.

Inside, the thin burning tapers revealed black-robed,
cowled figures sitting on the floor or against the walls. The
chanting was the only thing in my entire Egyptian visit that recalled for me that the country is on the African continent.
Coptic chant is the kind of music that evolved well before any
written musical lines; the monks seemed to "feel" the melody
and ride it instinctively like a surfer moving on his board with

the shifting stress of the water underneath. I tried to imagine myself learning it, and decided it was an inherited, osmosis-thing.

The Coptic Church acknowledges seven sacraments, administering baptism (by immersion), confirmation and Communion together even for infants, as is the tradition with the Oriental and Orthodox Churches in general. The Eucharist is celebrated only on Sundays, except in the monasteries where celebration of one of the three different Coptic liturgies is daily. The liturgy of St. Basil, an abbreviation of the Byzantine liturgy of the same name, is used on ordinary occasions; that of St. Gregory of Nazianzus, during Christmas, Epiphany and Easter; and that of St. Cyril only once, during Lent. The latter is said to have been transmitted by St. Mark and finally recorded by Cyril in the third century; it is regarded as the oldest and the most complete Mass text in existence. Confession must precede Communion, and it is not uncommon to see a priest in a parish setting confess a communicant right at the distribution station at Communion time, or to hear the priest asking those who approach for Communion who their confessor is.

For the Copts, fasting is practically an eighth sacrament. They fast one hundred and eighty days a year. During Lent, they eat just one meal a day. Their abstinence is from anything that issues from animal life. They see the demise of fasting in the West as decadence and loss of spiritual values. A Roman Catholic priest from Michigan making a month-long retreat in the monastery remarked: "The Copts have an ability to fast and to memorize which stupefies me! Each day the monks recite all one hundred and fifty psalms—by heart!"

We emerged from the chapel about 6 A.M. The monks went off to the various duties assigned to them by the Spiritual Father—jobs which, for the most part, take advantage of their pre-monastic education and developed skills. There is a general feeling of pride among the Copts today that so many university graduates are entering the monasteries; few, however, have had the benefit of any theological education. Pope Shenouda and the Spiritual Fathers of the monasteries are trying to train teachers and provide educational materials. The monasteries have only recently begun to take advantage of study grants offered, for example, through the World Council of Churches enabling their monks to study in Europe. Since few Western scholars learn Coptic, Arabic or Greek, the mastery of one or more European languages is a necessary first step. In any educational undertaking, whether theological or linguistic, the failure of the mail system to deliver many books that have been ordered is a constant frustration.

One Western priest-scholar who spent some time in St. Macarius told me of a monk who approached him and said, "I've heard you have done research in the Coptic liturgical tradition. I'd like you to teach me."

"But I came to learn from you, not to teach you!" the guest replied.

"You don't understand," the monk persisted. "Though I've been a Copt all my life and know certain things from experience, I've never had a chance to study our tradition formally, and I want to learn."

In general, there is much less emphasis on formal theological study in Eastern monasticism as compared to the Western form, and a much more charismatic approach to monastic life and even priesthood is taken. More than one monk has received his invitation to holy orders by being tapped on the shoulder by a visiting bishop and told: "Tomorrow we will ordain you." As one monk put it, "We would rather *have* an interior experience of the presence of God than be able, through education, to articulate and *talk* about its meaning." He accepted that there was nothing mutually exclusive about either one and that, theoretically, the goal of theological education was indeed to bring one into closer contact with God.

I decided to take a walk in the desert before the sun became too hot, and strode off across the sand, cassock flapping in the breeze. Cap or hood I did not have, and it is somewhat jarring for Eastern monks to see Western clergy with heads uncovered, but through visitors they have become more accustomed to it and accept without entirely understanding. Along the way I visited an abandoned hermit's cave, filling in slowly with blown, drifting sand. It was quite large, apparently having

had three rooms and a chapel. Only those who have the inclination and who are judged through careful discernment with
the Spiritual Father to be spiritually mature enough are permitted to go off and live in solitude. Even then great care is
taken, for instance, that there not be too much dampness in
the cave lest the monk invite a subsequent rheumatic condition.

When from a distance I turned and looked at St. Macarius,
it seemed to sit like a great ship on a gentle rolling sea. There
was nothing else to draw the eye. It is thus that the desert milieu inclines one more easily to contemplation. A rapid examination of the history of the Church demonstrates that, among
the Oriental and Orthodox Churches in any case, the life and
witness of the monastic communities have forged the worship,
theology, spirituality and pastoral and missionary efforts of the
Churches all along the centuries. Orthodoxy is, in fact, often
called a "monastic religion." If Orthodox Sunday parish liturgy
is longer than that to which Westerners are accustomed, it is
because the liturgy was shaped first in the monastery by
monks who had more time to give to prayer, and only later was
the liturgy brought into parishes.

Each period of renewal of spiritual life among Orthodox
Churches has been marked by a corresponding renewal in the
monastic communities. It has also been the vocation of the
monasteries—particularly in those historical periods when the
Church, situated in the midst of society, was inclined to compromise the principles of the faith because of political and other pressures—to transcend such concerns and cling to the
Gospel in a more disciplined, uncompromising, and radical
fashion.

Back inside the monastery wall there was much creative
activity: new buildings on the rise and old ones being restored,
experimentation with seeds that have yielded the largest peas,
carrots, and onions I've ever seen, and the second-most-mod-
ern printing press in Egypt—a great asset for publishing, in
various translations, the old manuscripts in the library. A large
area of land around the monastery, donated by the government of Egypt, is being worked for agricultural purposes. Out-

side of Lent, visitors are welcome to come for retreats and days of prayer or just to receive the blessing of a venerable holy place. Special fathers are assigned to direct the guests spiritually and to provide guidance and advice.

I was fortunate to have a chance to speak with the Spiritual Father, Matta El Meskeen, during my stay. He shuffled into the room with his cane (he has regretted not taking better care of his body during his solitary years as a hermit) and seated himself slowly. We spoke about some of his writings on Christian unity.

The monk, he said, lives for all people, regardless of difference in faith. Hence the monastery lives for the development of Christian unity, which is ultimately achieved by living in Christ. The Church, with regard to its catholic nature, is greater than man, his concepts, his structure, and his dogmas. For the Church is the new creation, and Christ is the only one who can fill it. His body is a source of life and unification, capable of abolishing all sorts of barriers created by time and place, whether social, cultural, sexual, or religious. The mystical body of Christ in the Church is that source of power which makes it capable of gathering and unifying all within its own unique catholic nature. In other words, the Church, by nature of its catholicity, is against all sorts of division, isolation, and whatever causes them. The fault in the Church's schism lies not in the nature of the Church, but in our inability to conceive and grasp the nature of Christ and the Church. It is only when people renounce their own will that the will of Christ appears; it is only when people earnestly surrender their lives to Christ that the life of Christ which is one and undivided will be manifested in the Church, his body. The "new man" can never live as a separate part in relation to others, or in hostility against other parts. The new man must be whole, for it is out of one nature and one Father that he emerges. How, he asked, is it going to be proved to the world that God is one but through the oneness of those born from him?

I returned inspired and refreshed to the crowds, the heat, the noise, and the dirt of Cairo. Three urban planners from France, asked to study the Cairo congestion and make constructive recommendations, suggested razing half the city and starting over. Built for three million people it now claims ten million. One sees contraceptive information distributed on shopping bags, serving trays, and the inside of rice bowls—in pictographs, for seventy percent of the women are illiterate.

Marie and I had planned a rendezvous to debrief our respective experiences—her latest trip to Alexandria and mine to the monastery—but transportation from Alexandria to Cairo had been snarled by a sandstorm, and she had been forced to remain in Alexandria.

I elected to use my last afternoon to visit the pastor of the Anglican Cathedral of Cairo to get a perspective from someone outside the Coptic community. Rev. Derek Eaton was all in favor of the amazing renewal among the Coptic Orthodox.

"It both challenges and enriches me," he said. "Beyond that my congregation has tripled in size in the last two years, mostly with people arriving from the West. They're literally assaulted by belief. They're evangelized in the streets, if not by Muslims, then by Copts—not 'evangelized' in the sense of being approached on the corner by someone with a Bible or a Koran, but evangelized by the whole ambience: the dress, the muezzin calling people to prayer five times a day from the mosque towers, etc. Belief in God here is not a question, but a given, a presupposition for all life. The secularized Westerner arrives and is thrown back upon himself or herself with the question 'What do I believe?'

"I've seen a lot of people come from the West—people who had given up on Christianity—who, after several months here, have been reconverted and joined the Church anew. For the first time they experienced Christianity being lived by a people who experience faith in their hearts.

"I've been personally enriched by my contact with historical Christianity and with a believing people who have a sense of geographical relatedness to and continuity with the biblical events—the exodus, the sojourn of the Holy Family, the first monasteries, and the Fathers of the Church, many of whom, though called 'Greek' by virtue of the language they spoke, were Egyptian. There is a great sense of community, of identity-in-togetherness among the Copts; one derives little or no sense of a spirituality founded on a Jesus-and-me approach. This is a family-in-faith."

He had no way of knowing the dramatic upheaval that lay ahead. Five months (September 5, 1981) after Derek Eaton's enthusiastic portrayal of the revival in the Coptic Church, the Egyptian government put Pope Shenouda under house arrest in the monastery of St. Bishoy and arrested eight bishops, sixteen priests and many Coptic leaders. The Egyptian newspapers accused the Church leaders of fanaticism and attacked Shenouda's weekly meeting in St. Mark's Cathedral as a "meeting to stir up the youth."

Sadat appointed a five-member committee of bishops chaired by Bishop Samuel to run the Church in Shenouda's stead, thus laying a menacing precedent for the interference of the state in the affairs of the Coptic Church. Sadat's deposition of Shenouda III left the Church in a state of confusion and division. Many of the Copts reject the deposition of their leader and Sadat's appointed committee as well. Coptic clergy serving their churches in North America issued statements denouncing the moves.

The division created within the Coptic Church hierarchy, with its resulting dissension on all levels, seemed to encourage Sadat's successor, President Mubarak, to follow Sadat's suit in dealing with the Coptic issue. Instead of releasing Shenouda or any of the imprisoned bishops and laymen, he appointed a new bishop (Athanasius) to take the place of Bishop Samuel. This move seemed to clearly indicate that the government intends to run a divided Church through a loyal, subservient committee.

The Christian population is increasingly losing its legal protection in that the Napoleonic Code which has heretofore been the law of Egypt is steadily being replaced by Muslim law. Practically speaking there is an urgent need for Muslim-Christian study and encounter which will aid a deeper and sounder understanding of present day social, legal and religious problems. Very little progress has been made in this area thus far.

The problem of the civil and national coexistence of Christians and Moslems in the Middle East can be summarized as follows. Both groups are indigenous and, in this case, Egyptian, the Christians pre-dating the Moslems. They clash over their divergent concepts of the relationship between religion and civil society.

For Christians, influenced by the Gospel and Western history, civil equality can take no account of religious affiliation. Although the Church and state must be separated, the state must not be anti-religious but be respectful of religion. In its quest for the common good, the state must strive to guarantee to its citizens the freedom to practice their religions. For Moslems, there is only one true faith, and the state must be organized according to the directives of the Koran. Non-Moslem citizens need not be forced to convert or to leave; their presence may be tolerated as long as they do not rock the boat. The Christians in Egypt, however, like the Christians in Lebanon, are fiercely proud of their historic roots and refuse to be relegated to the status of second-class citizens. The present struggle centers around the question of whether it is possible for a non-Moslem citizen to play a political or key economic role in his own country.

Pope Shenouda made outspoken demands for the rights of the Church in Egyptian society, as well as for equal employment opportunities and equal educational rights. Since Anwar Sadat's death the Mubarak government has placed a moratorium on this debate and indicated that it is a subject that will not be reopened before the fall of 1982. Coptic communities in Britain, Europe, and North America, where young professionals are seeking positions denied them in their own land, have not been silenced; they continue to demand Shenouda's freedom and Church rights.

To commemorate the first anniversary of the imprisonment of the Coptic Pope, American Copts held a National Conference in Jersey City, September 9, 1982. A large number of Copts came from parishes scattered across the United States, fifteen hundred people signing the attendance roll representing congregations from Chicago, Palm Beach, California and many centers in the eastern states. There are over one hundred thousand active Copts in the United States.

American Copts remain loyal to Pope Shenouda as God's chosen and anointed leader and therefore declare the government Committee of Five Bishops as heretic and excommunicated from the body of Coptic Orthodoxy (because in accepting and working with the situation as it is, the Committee of Bishops is seen to accept the breaking of a Coptic canon law that permits of no government intervention in the affairs of the Church). The Conference declared a Year of Coptic Orthodox Struggle. American Copts will regard as apostate any Coptic priest who cooperates with the Cairo Committee. Resolutions to these effects were communicated to the five bishops of the Cairo Committee in a document which described them as traitors.

At the same time as the Conference, United States Congressman Steve Solarz was in Egypt to make a personal appeal to President Mubarak for the release of the Coptic Patriarch together with many bishops and priests who remain under house arrest. A further petition signed by thirty-two Coptic bishops in Egypt was submitted to the President. And the chairman of the U.S. Committee on Human Rights, Don Bonker, addressed the Egyptian President on behalf of the House of Representatives, recalling that in response to representations made to Mr. Mubarak when he was visiting the United States an assurance had been given to the Foreign Affairs Committee that Pope Shenouda and the other members of the Coptic community would be released "in the near future."

Meanwhile, in Egypt, the only two Christian newspapers have closed, some Church property has been confiscated, and arbitrary regulations have been established that hinder the building and renovation of churches. The Egyptian People's Assembly approved changes in the Egyptian constitution which make the Koran the source of laws.

The Copts see and fear the continuing process of Islamizing Egypt. In the full theocratic state sought by the Muslim fundamentalists, a non-Muslim cannot hold a position over a Muslim, own land, testify against a Muslim in court, or inherit goods from Muslim relatives. As for any Muslim who converts to Christianity, the death penalty is prescribed.

Christianity was born in Egypt under the yoke of Roman persecutions, only to pass from there to domination by the Greeks, and, finally, it endured the Arab conquest in 641. The banishing and imprisonment of their patriarch is a blow to the Coptic Christians without parallel since Amr Ibn al-As conquered their land. Whether Shenouda III will be allowed to come out of the monastery to once again actively lead his people remains to be seen.

The flower of the Coptic revival is being severely threatened, and the Christians of Egypt have been plunged into a new period of trial.

Jerusalem

A more classical Lenten journey there could not be: out of Egypt, across the Sinai desert, into the promised land for the celebration of Passover in Jerusalem. I went up to Jerusalem for two Holy Weeks: the Western and the Eastern. Easter Day, on which all the movable feasts and holy days depend, is the first Sunday after the full moon which happens on or after the twenty-first of March. This is the same rule used in the Western Church, but there are two reasons why the celebration of Easter does not always coincide. First, the Oriental and Orthodox Churches still observe the rule laid down by the Council of Nicaea (A.D. 325), and now disregarded by the West, that the Christian Easter shall never either precede or coincide with the Jewish Passover, but must always follow it (thereby indicating, presumably, a fuller development of revelation). Second, most Eastern Churches still use the Julian Calendar, which, since March 1, 1901, has been thirteen days behind the Gregorian Calendar used in the West. The celebration of two Good Fridays and two Easter Sundays (which is the case in most years) is a source of embarrassment and derision for the Christians living among Islamic or Jewish populations, and though on the popular level there seems to be great sentiment for a common celebration, it will take a Pan-Orthodox Council to effect it. This year the Western Holy Week coincided with the Jewish feast of Passover, and the Orthodox Holy Week would follow it. The situation, regrettable as it was, permitted me to give my full attention to the richness of first one and then the other.

I walked from Jerusalem to Bethpage to take part in the Palm Sunday procession. Among processions, it must be unique in all the world. For forty-five minutes I stood by the gate to the courtyard of the fourth century church built to the memory of Jesus' meeting with Martha and Mary when he came to raise Lazarus from the dead, and I just watched the palm-carrying pilgrims come through the gate three or four abreast like the unraveling of some great ball of string that would never end—people from every nation in the world, of all ages and sizes and colors, singing Hosanna along the narrow picturesque road that once carried the Savior, seated upon an ass, into the Holy City. At a point which I thought must be near the end, I joined in, only to discover from the top of the next hill that I was in the middle and that the thousands of marchers would easily span in one unbroken song the mile between Jerusalem and Bethpage. The image of that procession will unquestionably fill my memory in all my Palm Sundays to come.

My room in the old city at the Armenian Catholic Patriarchate was right on the Via Dolorosa above the third station of the cross. All week I thrilled to the sights and sounds and smells of the ancient streets: the heavily laden burros stepping surely along the cobblestones through the narrow arcades; the Orthodox Jews with their knee-length black coats and long sideburns striding briskly to the synagogue or the wailing wall; the piercing cry of the muezzin (prayer-announcer) calling the Moslems to prayer ("Lā ilāha illā Allāh! There is no God but Allah!") five times a day from the mosque minaret; the shopkeepers hawking their wares to the Christian tourists passing by. Jerusalem!

On Holy Thursday evening I joined the community of scholars and students at Tantur for liturgy and a devotional walk. Tantur is an ecumenical research center located midway between Bethlehem and Jerusalem, founded by Pope Paul VI at the close of Vatican II. Equipped with our Bibles and flashlights, we began with the Cenacle (site of the Last Supper), walked down the road to the Church of St. Savior where stood the house of Caiaphas where Jesus was judged, and made a visit to the Church of St. Peter in Gallicantu (cock-crow), built in memory of the repentance of Peter over a cave to which the apostle was said to have fled to weep. From there we went to a lookout over Haceldama, the Potter's Field, bought with the thirty pieces of silver Judas received (but returned) for his betrayal. We then crossed the Kedron Valley of the Garden of Gethsemane where some of the group stayed the night. At each of the places, we read the appropriate Scripture passages and spent some time in quiet prayer. Early Friday morning, I joined an English-language group for the Stations of the Cross along the Via Dolorosa. It was easy to recreate the scene of that first Good Friday when Jesus stumbled up and along the ascending passageway. Then, as now, the shopkeepers must have looked up momentarily: "Who is it this time?" And then, when the crowd had passed, there was a return to business as usual.

On Holy Saturday, before the Easter Vigil service, I called some acquaintances on the medical team at the French hospital in Nazareth and said that I wanted to keep pace with the Scriptures on Easter Day which said: "He goes before you into Galilee—there you shall see him." I would hence be coming up into Galilee the next day. They had a better idea: they would drive down and meet me early Easter morning at Damascus Gate, we would all go to Abu Gosh (one of the claimed sites for the Emmaus story), and after "recognizing him in the breaking of the bread" we would all go into Galilee together.

The liturgy of the Resurrection of the Lord at the Benedictine Monastery at Abu Gosh was sublime. The air was cool and fresh, with the flowers reaching for the rising sun as the monks and nuns led us through the garden in a simple procession into the church. After the density and richness of the Vigil service hours before, I could not have coped with another high-voltage experience. But this was perfect: the mixed choir voices of the monks and sisters filled the old crusaders' church with soft, pure Gregorian alleluias that bathed the spirit. The paschal candle shone clearly through the sweet-smelling wisps of incense that drifted lightly upward.

We dined long and leisurely in true Near Eastern fashion

under the palm trees of Jericho. It was, after all, Easter Sunday.

An Arab woman on the medical team in Nazareth obtained a bicycle for me from her brother and for the next three days I coasted, pedaled and puffed through the hills of Galilee: Cana, Magdala, Tabgha, Capharnaum, the Mount of Beatitudes, the Lake, and Mount Tabor. The Bible will never be the same to me. My favorite place was a quiet little bay on the north end of the Sea of Galilee where Jesus, according to tradition, preached to the multitude from the bow of a fishing boat. The hill forms a natural amphitheater as it slopes down to the water. Unlike the holy places in the cities and towns, there is nothing built over the site here, and one can easily reconstruct the original event. There, as I sat reading Matthew 13, I could hear his voice ring out, and I found him there in a way that did not happen even in Jerusalem or Nazareth.

Two of my friends on the medical team arranged their days off so as to be able to return to Jerusalem with me to live Holy Week with the Orthodox. It was something they had wanted to do for several years, they said, but had never gotten around to doing. And Jerusalem is the best place in the world for it because all the various liturgical traditions are represented there. Each tradition ultimately traces its history back to Jerusalem.

From the fourth century onward there have been various "liturgical families" in Christianity. In the East, these are the liturgies of Antioch and of Alexandria. In the West, there was a variety of liturgies (Ambrosian, Gallican, Monastic, Mozarabic and Roman), all of which have become virtually extinct, except the Roman. Each liturgical family propagated itself in the measure of the missionary outreach and hierarchical influence of the mother-Church from which it was born. The first mother-Churches were Antioch, Alexandria and Rome, but all the liturgies ultimately trace their origins to the "grandmother Church," as it were, of Jerusalem.

Church organization came to follow the model of civil government of the Roman Empire, and bishops of more im-

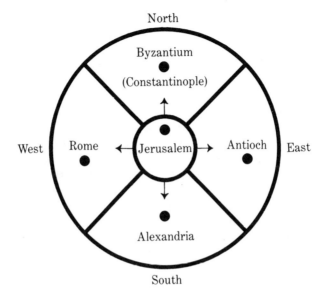

With Jerusalem as the point of origin, Christianity spread east to Antioch, south to Alexandria, west to Rome, and north to Byzantium, soon to become Constantinople.

portant areas became metropolitans as they assumed control over a group of dioceses. Certain of these metropolitans asserted authority over other metropolitans. The first to gain superior recognition were those mentioned above, but to them were added Constantinople and Jerusalem. By the fifth century these stood at the head of the most important ecclesiastical provinces, and from the eighth or ninth century "patriarch" was the official title of the "metropolitan-in-chief" of that ecclesiastical province (patriarchate). The way of celebrating the liturgy which characterizes a particular province has in the past been called "the rite," e.g. the Alexandrian (or Coptic) rite, the Antiochian rite, the Roman (or Latin) rite. (The word "rite" when speaking about a particular Church is being used less and less today because it tends to stress only the external, e.g., liturgical, aspects of the Eastern traditions without conveying that the Eastern Churches have distinctive lifestyles. "Church" or "tradition" is preferable usage because it is more comprehensive.)

The Copts, who trace the oldest form of their liturgy to St. Mark, also use a liturgy by St. Basil and one by St. Gregory of Nazianzus. The liturgy of Antioch is represented by a liturgy attributed to St. James, apostle and first bishop of Jerusalem. From this tradition there have been several derivations: the Maronite, the Chaldean, the Armenian, and, most notably, the Byzantine, because it was from Antioch that the evangelizing effort went forth that resulted in the Churches of Asia Minor. As the political and religious importance developed of Constantinople as the "new Rome" and center of the Byzantine Empire, its tradition evolved independently from the Antiochian Church which had given birth to it. The Byzantine Church uses principally two different liturgies, that of St. John Chrysostom (349–407), priest of Antioch and later bishop of Constantinople, and that of St. Basil (329–379), archbishop of Caesarea in Cappadocia (Turkey). The two orders of service differ only slightly from each other, the latter being a little longer and used during Lent; their general plan is the same. Somewhat in a separate category is the liturgy of the pre-sanctified (bread and wine), which is not a eucharistic sacrifice, but the office of vespers followed by a solemn communion. It is celebrated on the Wednesdays and Fridays of Lent, and on the first three days of Holy Week.

As is readily apparent, no one particular liturgical practice was imposed by the apostles or their immediate successors. Full liberty was left to the one presiding over the assembly in the earliest times. Little by little, however, in the key Christian centers, a certain uniformity of celebration began to take hold and have sway throughout the province. The rites of the Church, therefore, have not gone from unity to diversity, but from diversity to a certain unity. There never was a primitive liturgical rite that was common to the whole Church and observed with uniformity in all the ecclesiastical provinces. This is not to say, however, that there was not a certain similarity between the various ways of celebrating observed in the different provincial Churches. The rare liturgical documents of the second and third centuries show, by their allusions, a certain uniformity of cult in the different centers—which uniformity, nonetheless, allowed for differences and liberty.

It is in the fourth century that the documents become more numerous and explicit, revealing the existence of a few main liturgical families. From the fifth century and the establishing of the five great patriarchates of Rome, Antioch, Alexandria, Constantinople and Jerusalem, the liturgical formats used in these centers will result in the progressive disappearance of other practices used in these five centers' provincial jurisdictions. And, according to the missionary resources and hierarchical influence of a given patriarchate, a particular liturgical tradition will spread or lose ascendancy. Hence, between the eighth and eleventh centuries, the Byzantine tradition will become official in Cyprus, Bulgaria, Rumania, Russia and the Ukraine, and become the most representative tradition of Orthodoxy vis-à-vis the West. Given the different peoples who use it and the numerous languages in which it is employed, the Byzantine liturgy has come to be considered as supranational and universal.

The Greek word "Orthodox" is given various meanings: "right teaching," "right praise," "right worship." Before the fifth century there was predominantly only one apostolic Church made up of various nationalities each possessing its own language and liturgical expression of the essential unity of doctrine, sacraments, and hierarchical magisterium (teaching authority). In 431 Nestorius was condemned and Nestorianism removed the East Syrian Church from the unity of the whole Church. Twenty years later, at the Council of Chalcedon, monophysitism was condemned and the Churches of Armenia, Syria, Egypt (Coptic), Ethiopia and India moved into a sphere separate from those that accepted the doctrinal teachings of Chalcedon. The Churches of Constantinople (Byzantine tradi-

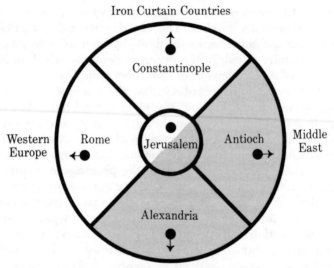

The four major centers of Christianity became the launching sites for the evangelization of neighboring regions, eventually reaching beyond the confines of the Roman Empire.

Those bishops, priests, and members of the laity of the Antiochene patriarchate who had chosen in 431 to accept the teaching of Nestorius after it had been condemned at the Council of Ephesus were outside the community of orthodox believers.

Similarly, as a result of the condemnation of monophysitism at the Council of Chalcedon in 451, the patriarchate of Alexandria in Egypt became separated.

tion) and Rome (Latin tradition) remained faithful to the teachings of the Councils of Ephesus and Chalcedon and hence called themselves "the Orthodox," i.e., those holding the true, correct teaching of the early Christian Church as promulgated in these two councils.

In the ninth century, the estrangement which had begun even earlier became more apparent. In the course of the next three centuries, it culminated in a division between the Eastern Churches that employed the Byzantine tradition and the Church of the West that followed the Latin tradition and acknowledged the primacy of the Roman Pontiff. The Eastern Churches in this sense included the Greek and Rumanian and much of the Slavic-speaking world. They continued to call themselves Orthodox, insisting on their fidelity to the "right teachings" of the first seven ecumenical councils. In its conventional historical sense, "Orthodox" designates those Churches that had accepted and have maintained the teachings of the Council of Chalcedon but became estranged from Rome, refusing to recognize the jurisdictional primacy of the Pope. These Churches preserve an essential unity in doctrine under an apostolic hierarchical magisterium that existed among them before the eleventh century. They form a loose confederation, bound together not by any centralized authority, but by loyalty to a common faith. The ecumenical patriarch of Constantinople enjoys no special prerogative of jurisdiction, but is accorded primacy of honor among them. Outside of the decisions of the seven ecumenical councils, the self-governing (autocephalous) Churches have the authority to define the non-dogmatic teachings for themselves. They are, as a matter of fact, fairly uniform, though it need not necessarily be so.

Orthodoxy is largely shaped by a Byzantine theology and spirituality to a certain Byzantine way of thinking. Its approach to monasticism, asceticism, contemplation, popular piety, iconography, and liturgical symbolism all bear the Byzantine stamp. Yet, while there are permanent and universal characteristics to the Church's identity (apostolicity, conciliarity, and faithfulness to the patristic tradition), it has taken on many different historical accents through the cultural and institutional styles of local churches. Thus Orthodoxy cannot be limited or circumscribed by a certain Byzantine theological and spiritual "treasure chest."

It cannot be reduced, for example, to a Church of a particular region ("the Eastern Church"), nor to a doctrinal mold that suggests lack of growth and evolution ("Church of the first seven councils"), nor to a self-contained theological system (Byzantine theology). Orthodoxy has always had to be aware of its universality, a universality forged from theological confrontation in the councils which at that time included both East and West. It was in this universal context that the symbols of the faith (the creeds) were formed which continue to be the Orthodox Church's criterion for discerning between the tradition of the Church and historical traditions of various Churches. To avoid an idealized caricature, an unreal image of the Orthodox Church, it is necessary to situate the orthodox tradition in the framework of the history of the universal Church and to see it as forming a part of that Church.

After the patriarchates of Constantinople, Alexandria, Antioch and Jerusalem, four other patriarchates have been formed in the course of history: the Bulgarian (formed in 917), Serbian/Yugoslavian (1346), Russian (1589), and Rumanian (1925).

The liturgical rites used in all these Churches—Orthodox and Ancient Eastern—can be found in the city of Jerusalem. As my companions and I approached the fortress walls of the old city from a distance, we read together from Luke's Gospel of the triumphal entry of Jesus into Jerusalem, and began to try to roll ourselves back psychologically to live through the events of Holy Week again. Serge Bulgakoff has written that "the resurrection of Christ is the festival of the whole Christian world. But nowhere is its luminosity celebrated as in Orthodoxy." We were to put this claim to the test.

I went to the Christian Information Center, obtained a master schedule of all the services for Orthodox Holy Week, and my friends and I put together a plan whereby we would spend every morning, afternoon and evening in a different Di-

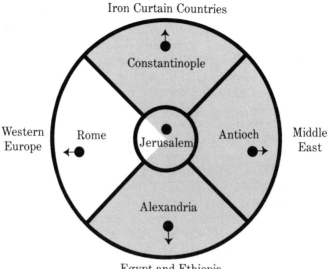

Here is illustrated the Christian world after the eleventh century from the Roman point of view. From the point of view of Constantinople and the Orthodox, one should black out the Roman quadrant, rather than that of Constantinople, which would indicate Rome's separation from the Church at Constantinople and from the community of Orthodox believers.

vine Liturgy. For the next three days we would literally live in church!

After having briefly checked into Ecce Homo hostel on the Via Dolorosa to make sure that rooms had indeed been held for us, we left our bags at the reception desk and set off through the labyrinthine streets to catch the Syrian Orthodox procession that had already begun from the house of Caiaphas. By the time we arrived, the procession was in its final stages. We turned our steps toward St. James' Armenian Orthodox Cathedral, where a mourning service was scheduled to begin shortly. When we entered the cathedral, gliding black-robed figures were moving about lighting candles, their veils, attached to their pointed Armenian hats, flowing gently behind them. Though the twelve Gospel readings, sung in ancient Armenian, were incomprehensible to us, the shadowy, melancholic ambience moved us forward into a Passion Week frame of mind. When we emerged, it was dark.

We retraced the devotional walk I had made a week earlier with the Tantur group. I was irked to find the churches which are built on the venerated places, and in Latin hands, closed. The week before they had all been opened to accommodate the Western pilgrims. If these churches all mark the sites they claim to, one would think that some Eastern pilgrims might be interested in visiting them in a similar manner, too, even if they are Roman rite churches.

We ended up sitting on the steps of the Grotto of Gethsemane, a cave in which Jesus and his disciples are believed to have often spent the night on the Mount of Olives. Tradition holds that here the disciples slept while Jesus prayed a stone's throw away (which location is now marked by the Basilica of the Agony), and it was because of this grotto that "Judas knew the place, because Jesus had often gone there together with his disciples." As we sat and prayed together, a large cloud passed in front of the moon, leaving all in darkness. It was eerie.

I was struck by how all the events of Holy Thursday are summarized and contained in the prayer Jesus taught us: "Our Father, who art in heaven, hallowed be thy name" . . . in John's Gospel, before entering into the garden, Jesus prayed, "Father, the hour has come. I have glorified thee on earth; I have accomplished the work thou hast given me to do."

"Thy kingdom come, thy will be done" . . . Jesus' prayer in the garden: "Let this cup pass from me; yet not my will but thine be done."

"And forgive us our trespasses" . . . three times Jesus pardoned the disciples for sleeping when he needed their support, and he forgave Peter for denying that he even knew him.

"And lead us not into temptation" . . . Jesus' words to his disciples: "Rise and pray, that you may not enter into tempta-

GENEALOGY of the CHRISTIAN CHURCHES/NATIONALITIES/LITURGIES

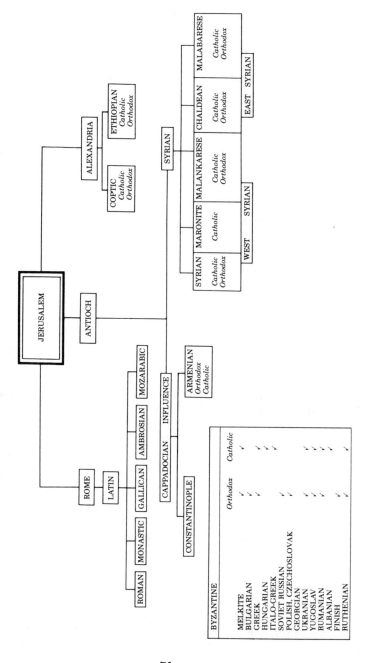

51

tion." (How seldom I pray this prayer—to not be tempted—outside of the Our Father!)

"But deliver us from evil" . . . as Judas approaches with the soldiers, "Now is the hour of the evil one."

There they were, the events Christians commemorate on this night, reflected in the phrases of that one prayer.

It was near midnight and we walked back to Ecce Homo through the deserted streets of Jerusalem. It was clear why the chief priests who were afraid to take him during the day for fear of the crowds were able to execute their desire at night once they had found out where to arrest him. There was no one in these streets to raise a protest. The narrow passageways belonged to the cats.

We sat for a while on the hostel's roof terrace. It was in just such a city as this that the drama of the impromptu trial took place—a sleeping city. Then that nightly occurrence in Jerusalem split the air: a cock crew.

"Jerusalem! Jerusalem! How often would I have gathered your children together, as a hen gathers her young under her wings, but you would not." Jerusalem. Jerusalem. One understands the stories of the Gospel better for having spent some time within her walls.

The next morning, "Great Friday" among the Orthodox, I patiently threaded my way among the army of black-clad, cane-wielding pilgrims from Greece and Cyprus. With a folding seat in one hand and a bundle of candle tapers tied together in the other, they moved like a slow, steady tide toward the Basilica of the Holy Sepulchre. Last week these streets had been filled with camera-carrying pilgrims intent on bartering in the shops between services. But the sun-baked, deep-lined earnest faces all around me now suggested that these peasant folk had been saving all their lives to come to Jerusalem for but one thing: to celebrate the banishing of that ancient terror which beset the life of humankind. This it is which has won and kept the allegiance of the masses: "By his death he has trodden death under his feet."

The Orthodox Church is often criticized among Western observers for being too heavily clerical in its liturgy. But the people clearly do not feel that the Church belongs to the priests and not to them. They are utterly at home in their church, moving about, lighting candles, kissing icons, touching everything. Between services in the Holy Sepulchre (the Greeks, Armenians and Copts all hold services in the same church—sometimes simultaneously!) I stood by the anointing stone which lies midway between Calvary and the tomb. It is a marble slab in memory of the anointing of Christ's body before burial.

From a short distance away, I watched these faithful people kneel before the stone and anoint it with water and aromatic balms, rub their hands over the slab and then rub their own face and neck and hair with the transferred ointment, place their cheeks to the stone with great tenderness and closed eyes, soak up the sacred balm with scarves and any available cloth, take out lengths of cord and lay it lengthwise on the stone, soak it with the ointment, and reroll it so as to take it back home to be worn around the waist by those family or friends who could not make this pilgrimage. Some might deride these simple expressions of faith and love, seeing in them elements of superstition. But I was inspired, touched.

Yet it was not "me" to do that. We Western and Eastern Christians are like John and Peter, I thought. Both raced to the tomb, and John, upon arriving, only stuck his head in and looked. He stood somewhat aback (just as I was doing at that very moment). He looked; he saw; he believed. But the Orthodox Christians are more like Peter, who did not hesitate to go right in and touch and see from up close. It was the same way in Jesus' resurrection appearance on the shore of the lake. At the cry of "It is the Lord!" Peter jumps in the water and starts swimming for shore. He follows his heart and moves impetuously and spontaneously to express that movement of the heart. But John stays in the boat as if to say, "Well, let's take one thing at a time here. Get the fish in the boat, and then we'll sail to shore." A more rational approach, one might say. We can have the netful of fish and talk to the Lord, too. Just don't get excited.

What is important is that the Lord loved them both. Between the two responses is a lovely balance between reflection and action, a faith contemplated and a faith lived. Here lies the richness that East and West have to give one another.

The people at the anointing stone gave me much within the half-hour that I stood there. Their actions spoke to me of my need to live a more incarnated faith, to be less stiff and rational, more free and comfortable with physical gestures that express realities of the heart—in a word, to put my head in my heart and live from there. The image of the two lobes of the brain is useful for us Westerners. Religion tends to be a very left-lobe affair, which sees the world more in terms of rational thought, logic, and philosophy. But the Christian East corresponds more to our right lobe which perceives the world in a more poetic, creative and intuitive way.

To many in the West, as Fr. Kallistos Ware has noted, the Orthodox Church seems chiefly remarkable for its air of antiquity and conservatism; the message of the Orthodox to their Western brethren seems to be, "We are your past." But for Orthodox themselves, loyalty to tradition means not primarily the acceptance of formulas or customs from past generations, but rather the ever-new, personal and direct experience of the Holy Spirit *in the present*, here and now. That requires creative, intuitive living.

After the Greek Orthodox procession to the Holy Sepulchre, I participated for a while in the Coptic burial service. In Orthodox liturgies there is a constant coming and going of people. Given the length of the liturgies, the practice of taking a short break and then returning is not unusual. When I returned in the afternoon for the Greek Orthodox service, however, space was at a premium and no people were leaving their square foot of standing room. The traditional absence of pews in Orthodox churches was designed to permit movement and activity during Divine Liturgy. The people are accustomed to move about freely, reverencing icons, making standing or kneeling bows called "metanias" with the sign of the cross—in short, to worship with their bodies as well as their minds.

The realism of the Orthodox rites is replete with dramatic

power, and there is a good deal more symbolism than that to which Protestants, Anglicans, and Roman Catholics are accustomed.

On the morning of Holy Friday, the service of the Royal Hours is held, consisting of Old Testament prophecies relating to the passion and crucifixion of Christ and their fulfillment in the New Testament. The Vespers for Great and Holy Friday are celebrated in the afternoon. During this service the final events of the life of Christ are recalled: the trial, the sentencing, the scourging, the mocking, the crucifixion, the death, the descent from the cross and the burial. As the Gospel account is read, the priest, representing Joseph of Arimathea, removes the body of Christ from the cross, wraps it in a shroud and carries it to the altar, representing the tomb. Toward the end of this service the priest lifts a richly embroidered shroud-length cloth on which is represented an image of Christ lying in the tomb. One priest leads the procession with the book of the Gospels while other celebrants lift the cloth and carry it above their heads in the manner of a funeral cortege. But it is not only a funeral procession. It is also the Son of God, the Immortal One, proceeding through the darkness of Hades where he preached his Gospel, announcing the joy of the resurrection to all those who had died before his coming. Finally, the icon-cloth is brought into the center of the church, among the people where it is laid in a specially prepared tomb with the book of the Gospels upon it. The symbolic tomb, in some churches, is beautifully decorated with flowers and venerated in various ways by the faithful.

It is necessary to dispel any illusions about the manner in which these liturgical dynamics proceed. The interactions involve masses of hot, tired, hungry and thirsty people, many of whom have been fasting and standing on a marble floor all day long. Occasionally a small row would break out here and there and necessitate a stage-voiced "Shhhhhh!" or threatening wag of the finger from the patriarch himself.

My companions and I sought refuge from the packed conditions of the Holy Sepulchre Basilica's main chapel. After some fresh air, we elected to go to the late afternoon service at the Armenian Cathedral. A fundamental distinction has been noted between the architecture of the temples of ancient Greece (upon which Byzantine Church architecture is based) and that of the Western, Gothic tradition. The Gothic Church and all the styles dependent upon it, such as the New England colonial churches with their single spire, give the impression of upward seeking and movement. Humanity stands with its feet firmly planted on the earth, the architecture says, and stretches its hands upward, searching after God, straining to reach him. Gothic architecture with its multitude of upreaching spires symbolizes the Western world's active searching for God.

The Greek temple is quite different. It is complete in itself. It is not "going anywhere" and it is not "struggling" for anything. It has found its completion, its balance. The Byzantine and Ancient Eastern Churches are the same. Instead of spires, they have domes. Liturgical architects see the whole universe symbolized within the floor, ceiling, and walls of the church building. The dome, whose circular shape has no beginning and no end, is heaven; the floor, where we stand looking up, is earth, whose finiteness is indicated by right-angles in each corner of the walls. The narthex (roughly equivalent to the vestibule in Western architecture) represents the non-believers, for it was here that the catechumens attended the Divine Liturgy. The nave, or main part, of the church represents the faithful. And the apse or sanctuary, nearly always showing an icon of the Mother of God holding the Christ Child, is a symbol of the way which heaven (the dome) and earth (the Christians) are joined together: through the incarnation. Entering an Orthodox church with its spherical dome, its walls covered with painted icons of the saints, and the soft luminescence of many hanging candle-lamps is meant to be an experience of entering another reality. That has never been more literally true for me than when we entered St. James' Cathedral the afternoon of Great Friday.

A film of incense swayed gracefully upward, for the service had already begun. In the front, surrounding a large monstrance on an elegantly draped table, stood some fifty tall white candles, interspaced with long-stemmed red roses. To each side was a floor-standing fan candelabra, all aglow. From the ceiling hung an immense chandelier which refracted the light of the late afternoon sun in all directions. A constellation of hanging sanctuary lamps encircled the entire nave creating a celestial space of light. The saints gazed out upon us from the side and back walls.

We joined the worshipers, not nearly so crowded here, sometimes sitting, sometimes standing on the Oriental carpets. It was one of the most exquisite liturgical experiences of my life. The effectively proclaimed Word, the magnificent (and non-stop) singing, the uniformity of attractive vestments, the rhythmic incensing by the two deacons, the prayerful involvement and decorum of the people, the dignified and unified movement of the bearded priests in their pale green capes and black hoods, the interior environment—all worked together harmoniously into something truly beautiful for God. We had arrived around 4:30 P.M. and had planned to leave at 6:30 to return to the hostel for supper. At 6:30 we just looked at each other and with one movement shook our heads sideways: we weren't going anywhere!

Needless to say, the liturgical "language" was very different from the stark and stripped-down approach to the Good Friday service that characterizes Western Churches. But what is revealed is a truth about the Orthodox approach to mysteries of the passion, death and resurrection celebrated in Holy Week. On Good Friday they are talking about the resurrection, and on Easter Sunday they are talking about the passion and death. It's all one mystery. There is no effort to take the various "stages" of the one mystery and compartmentalize them. There is no effort to try to make Good Friday all one way, e.g., sadness and mourning, or Easter Sunday all one way, e.g., gladness and joy. There are elements of the whole in each celebration, and the whole mystery of the passion, death and resurrection is lived in each celebration of Holy Week. Even death is filled with God. This service had not mourned a tattered victim, dispossessed of all majesty, but the death of one who even in the tomb did not cease to be the Son of God. If the Orthodox services of Great Friday are already penetrated with reminders of the resurrection, they thereby manifest fidelity to the Gospels, for each time Jesus announces his passion, he also announces his resurrection on the third day.

We emerged from St. James' Cathedral refreshed and uplifted. We could not ourselves believe that we still had the energy or the "appetite" for yet another experience, but we did. We got home from the Greek service in the Holy Sepulchre about midnight. The next day proved to be even more of a liturgical marathon.

When as a schoolboy I would dilly-dally along the way to church and arrive late, my proffered excuse was that "I got held up on the way." This time, however, it was true. If the truth be told, we got stuck in a parade. For a while, I was concerned that we would miss the lighting of the Easter fire, which was to take place shortly after noon on Saturday. Trying to get around the bands, the scout troops and the pilgrims in these narrow streets was like water trying to bypass a clog of leaves in a rain spout. Then when I asked for a translation of what the young men who were riding on one another's shoulders were chanting in unison, I realized that we were all going to the Basilica of the Holy Sepulchre, and I relaxed. "We've lived the season of Lent, and now we arrive at the House of God, our House" was the rough translation I received. The parade, including the elevated young chanters, went right on into the Basilica.

Of the Easter liturgy all other rites are but reflections or figures. Several hundred people had camped inside the church the night before to hold their place near the tomb from which the sacred fire would shortly be passed. And every other cubic inch had progressively been claimed since the opening of the doors at 5 A.M. Even the huge courtyard outside was filling up. After several minutes of attempted penetration into the crowd in the direction of the tomb and after one near suffocation in which we were forced against the wall in an uncontrollable crush to make room for yet more people inside, we half-crawled and pulled one another into the saving glory of light and air.

We spotted a rooftop opposite the Basilica door on which people were starting to collect and were soon looking down on the courtyard and into the church as far as the angle permitted. As the moment for the lighting of the fire drew near, the black army below folded their seats, righted themselves for the moment, and started moving toward the doors as if pulled by some invisible magnet. A bundle of thin tapers tied together was held aloft in every hand and strained as far as the arm could take it toward the door, toward the inside, toward the tomb. I had seen a gesture like that before, on the movie advertisement for *Exodus:* the outstretched arms, the open hands, the straining fingers—straining for liberation, straining for freedom. "By his death he has trodden death under his feet": the sung Easter hymn that is repeated a thousand times in tones ever more triumphant, repeated to the point of ecstasy and of overflowing mystic joy, was about to break forth.

The roar came suddenly, like breakers crashing in quick succession upon the beach. Thirty seconds could not have elapsed between the time the fire was passed through the tiny window in the atrium of the tomb until the time it reached the courtyard, so quickly did the fire skip and dance across the tapers inside the church. People were crying out with joy and singing below. They passed their hands through the flame of their candles and rubbed its warmth upon their faces. It gave them life. They wanted to be as close as possible to the Easter reality. They wanted to experience the warmth, the liveliness of the risen Christ. Did not Christ in his third resurrection appearance prepare bread and fish for his disciples because he knew they had a need to experience him as real and not as a phantom, an idea? Does not faith come through the senses?

An elderly woman in the yard below was about to give me one of the most poignant images of the whole week. She had received the flame from another and gotten it into her little glass-enclosed candle-lantern. She held it high above her head, with an ecstatic serene smile upon her face. She walked—no, floated—in and out among the people, showing this fire to all around her, as if it were the most precious treasure in all the world, and it was hers!

In her whole being was written the comprehension that the resurrection is not the liberation *from* the body, but the glorification *of* the body by God. In the risen Christ, the "dust" of the body of which the Old Testament speaks will no longer return to the dust of the earth to lose itself there, but, ever living, mounts to heaven, to the intimacy of the life of the Trinity, dwelling there for eternity as the living body of God the Son. Indeed, this pilgrim below, illuminated with fire, *held* the most precious thing in all the world. For eternal life is not life *after* death; it is life with God. And that life begins in baptism where, mystically, we are grafted into the life of Christ crucified and risen. The Holy Spirit, who enables us to participate in this life, insures through the life of the Church that the cross and resurrection do not remain just past events, but living realities in the lives of all of us who *are* the body of Christ. The woman below, with her lantern raised high, sang the Orthodox Easter morning refrain with every fiber of her being: "Yesterday I was buried with you, O Christ / Today I awake with you, the Risen One / I was crucified with you yesterday / Glorify me with you, O Savior, in your kingdom."

Yet the culminating celebration was still to come later this night. Did the people below and those who filled the Basilica know that? Did they know that Easter was not "officially" here yet—not until the Vigil Service? I'm sure they wouldn't have understood the question. Their Church does not separate the cross and the resurrection either in its theology or in its spirituality. The power of God's love is as present on Great Friday as on Easter Sunday. The power of the resurrection is already contained in the total and voluntary gift of love on the cross. And the spiritual configuration of the cross rests eternally inscribed in the wounds of the risen Christ. So tightly are these realities woven together in Orthodoxy that even during Lent the Alleluia, a joyous Easter refrain, is sung. If the Orthodox spirituality is not pessimistic in tone about human nature or idealistic or sentimental in its joy, it is because Orthodoxy never dissociates the mystery of the cross from that of the resurrection. These people had been celebrating the one Mystery all week long, all Lent long, all their lives long.

The Israeli soldiers watched in dispassionate duty. A little less than two thousand years ago they had been the guarded ones. Fearing an outbreak, a religious riot among the Jews gathering at the temple for the feast of Passover, the Romans had doubled their guard. This time it was the Jews who, in the minds of the Arab Christians, were the occupying force; this time it was they who lined the courtyard and stationed their soldiers on the rooftops. This time it was they who feared a terrorist attempt not unlike the one mounted by Barabbas and the zealots, they who feared a riot amid all those gathering in the holy city for the religious festival of Passover. I wondered if this historical irony was playing upon their minds too.

We climbed down from the roof and walked in silence to the Anglican Christ Church which is just down the street from the Armenian Cathedral where we wanted to be in an hour's time. Christ Church was cool and quiet. Our overloaded senses needed a break. We went in and sat down and closed our eyes.

Later we returned to St. James' Armenian Cathedral, partly out of curiosity to see whether yesterday's worship had been exceptionally good, partly out of hope that we would find that it hadn't been, and partly kind of "daring them" to touch us as deeply as they had the day before.

They did. I never would have believed that I could be so held, so nourished, so transported right out of myself by a three-hour liturgy in which I didn't understand a word. One of my former profs used to say that "if your symbols and your non-verbals are clear and expressive, you don't *have* to say a lot." The time between 4 and 7 P.M. simply collapsed. All we knew when we came out was that we had been filled up.

We reflected on the richness of the Oriental rites. They are an ornament for the whole Church, a spiritual richness which one could no more wish to sacrifice than to let go of the early Fathers of the Church. Desirable for their own sake, they constitute a principal element of the apostolic tradition. They are a proof of the unity of the faith in the Church, for there is no schismatic or heretical liturgy: all the Oriental liturgical rites pre-date the schisms which divided Christianity. They testify to an admirable unity-in-diversity within the one undivided Church and are a meeting place where all the Churches today can rediscover their apostolicity. As such they are a foundation-layer for the different Churches of our time.

In their diversity, the Oriental rites are a mark of the catholicity of the Church—a catholicity that would be lost if there were ever just one uniform, obligatory and exclusive rite for all Christians. For a true catholicity must embrace, beyond a diversity of races and civilizations, a similar diversity of liturgy and art.

It is a consolation to pray—to learn how to pray—in union with Christian brothers and sisters from whom we are in some way separated. As we wait and work and pray for the reunion of Christians, these rites and our familiarity with them are like so many bridges that have not been destroyed.

In the Roman Catholic Church there has been a growing criticism that the post-Vatican II liturgical renewal purged too many of the "smells and bells." One of the functions of liturgy is to transport us out of ourselves and put us in contact with a reality beyond ourselves, to alter or transform our state of consciousness. Some report that they are no longer transported nor is their consciousness altered.

Yet the liturgical renewal in Catholicism performed a valuable service in putting Catholics back in touch with the early Christian traditions and trimming the Mass of some dispensable medieval barnacles. What can be safely said for all Western Christians is that there is much for us to learn from the richness of the Orthodox liturgical traditions which can help us achieve a fine balance between simplicity and economy on the one hand and richness and ceremony on the other.

One of the reasons why the Orthodox faithful themselves habitually come late or not at all is because the service is long. Fashioned by monks, the formats also need to consider the family and working types. Also, there is the question of giving the people more of an active role in the Divine Liturgy. One gets the impression at times that there is a prevalent attitude of "watching" the liturgy. While the cantor or choir sings; the congregation remains silent and unresponsive, expecting to be "acted upon," or being left little choice in the matter. And although Orthodox liturgy theory is that frequent and regular Communion is vital and that participation in the Divine Liturgy is not full and complete if one does not receive Holy Communion each time one attends, the number who do not receive is surprising. Up until recently, Orthodox liturgists would not be inclined to receive sympathetically such reflections, their tendency being to see Byzantine liturgy as the greatest of all possible developments in every aspect. Today, however, some Orthodox liturgists (see, for example, Stanley Harakas' book *Living the Liturgy*) are manifesting a healthy sense of self-criticism and saying these things about themselves.

The ways in which our liturgical traditions have developed offer a great deal for our mutual benefit. And this, surely, is the main argument for conceiving of theology and theological study in ecumenical terms. Each of the confessional families in Christianity needs the corrective and balancing of the traditions that lie to its right and left. I offer one example at the expense of my own tradition.

The week previous I was assisting in offering the Mass with a group of pilgrims on Calvary in the Basilica of the Holy Sepulchre. Out came another priest who, all by himself, began to celebrate the Eucharist on a little altar a scant two feet from our own. Among the Orthodox, liturgical discipline and Byzantine canon law have avoided this unfortunate development and protect the unifying and catholic character of the Eucharist. They require that on each altar no more than one eucharist be celebrated each day. Similarly, a priest or bishop is not allowed to celebrate twice on the same day. Whatever the practical inconveniences, these rules aim at preserving the Eucharist at least nominally as the gathering of "all together at the same place" (Acts 2:1) to reflect that there is only one Christ, one Church and one Eucharist. These rules place the ecclesiological reality of the one Church, realized in the one Eucharist, above all practical considerations. As in the early Church, the Eucharist is never the action just of a particular group of faith, nor does it serve solely any partial (for a deceased person) or accidental (for favorable weather) purpose.

It is always offered on behalf of all and for all by the entire Church. Hence, in the Byzantine rubrics, there are no "private Masses" because the whole Church conducts the sacraments. "Liturgy" literally means, in Greek, "work of the people." From pre-Christian times the word has meant a service to, for, and by the people. This idea that the Eucharist is a sacrament uniting the whole Church prevented in the East the multiplication of "Masses of intention" which influenced the development of "private Masses." To be sure, correctives have been applied since Vatican II in Roman practice, but there are still some attitudinal shifts to be made: Eastern monks continue to be scandalized by visiting Western priests who say Mass in their rooms; Protestant and Orthodox pilgrims to Rome continue to shake their heads when they enter St. Peter's and see Masses being offered simultaneously at different altars; and a traveling priest still finds himself asked at many convents and rectories where he stays: "Father, when would you like to say *your* Mass?" (emphasis mine)

My friends and I had been saving the Russian Church of St. Mary Magdala on the Mount of Olives for the Easter Vigil. It did not begin until 11 P.M., however, so we still had the evening in front of us. We decided in favor of the Ethiopian celebration at Dier el Sutan, on the roof of the Holy Sepulchre Basilica where their dwellings are built. The Ethiopians (who follow the Coptic rite) emerged festively dressed. They carried drums, candles, and highly decorated colorful canopies over the heads of their hierarchs. Due to the number of the people, there was not a great deal of space for them to dance. They did the best they could, circling the dome on the rooftop three times, one for each of the days the Lord had spent in the tomb below.

When it was over we went into the Basilica. There seemed to be a rare hiatus between services there with everyone waiting or resting for the great celebration that would last the whole night. It seemed like the right moment to visit the tomb. Filled with the incredible resonances and experiences of the past two weeks, I could have stayed within the tomb a long time just looking at that empty slab and reflecting on what it has meant for the world. But as there was only room for two or three of us in the burial chamber and others outside were waiting to bend down and come in the low, tiny entrance, I kissed the stone where the Savior lay and left. It had been wonderfully anointed throughout the day and smelled like lilies.

The golden, onion-domes of the Russian church were gloriously illuminated over the tops of the trees of the Mount of Olives. As the Russian nuns moved unhurriedly about arranging and lighting candles, I extracted a personal truism from the week's services: they will not begin on time, and they will be long, but they are so good that at the end of them I will not care that they did not begin on time or that they were long.

The night before at the hostel, I had joined four Roman Catholic priests from Australia (where there is the largest conglomeration of Greek Orthodox outside of Greece) at table for supper. We shared notes on the day and what we were doing. I had spoken enthusiastically of the Armenian service and remarked to them that since they were in Jerusalem for the Orthodox celebration of Holy Week they shouldn't miss joining in on an Easter liturgy. "Oh, the Orthodox Church—that's pretty severe, isn't it!" one of them retorted with disinterest. "The priest just comes out from behind the wall every now and then, says something to the people, and goes back in." I felt so depressed at what that remark represented that I nearly put my face down in my mashed potatoes and cried.

The celebration of the resurrection of the Lord had begun, and the brilliantly vested celebrant, all in white, was coming through the royal doors of the iconostasis and pronouncing in a thundering voice: "Christ is risen!" And, in an even louder clap, came the return from all the people: "He is *truly* risen!" Yes, I thought to myself wryly as the priest toured the whole congregation sprinkling everyone with baptismal water, "he just comes out from behind that wall every now and then and says something to the people. . . ."

But what a message!

The liturgy had started at 11:20 P.M. and by 2 A.M. had

just reached the proclamation of the Gospel in various languages. We took the good news and exited. We were saturated with liturgy. We had spent twelve hours in church that day among the various services and needed some sleep.

Our timing was superb. When we stepped out onto the portico that looks out over the city of Jerusalem across the valley, the great bell of the Holy Sepulchre began to ring out the Easter message. In the liturgy taking place there they must have reached the proclamation of the Gospel at the same time we did. At the sound of the bell pealing, one of the Russian sisters came out of the church and set the carillon bell-chimes of St. Mary Magdala singing back in reply. There we stood under a nearly full moon and starry sky, in the place where Christ had sweat drops of blood in agony at his impending death, listening to the carillon respond in joy to the great bell which proclaimed over the place where he had been crucified and buried: *"Christ is risen!"*

The next morning, before my friends returned to Nazareth, I shared with them a dream-image.

My dream is of a great house of but one level. All the rooms are situated around a common dining room with but one great table. Each room is decorated differently, but there is a common motif that runs through them all, essentially uniting them. The doors to all the rooms are open, and people go back and forth between them freely, though everyone has a preference for a particular room in which he or she is most comfortable and which most expresses his or her style or taste. And as for meals, there is a common table, open to all the inhabitants of the house.

The different rooms with their individual style and decor represent all the different Christian Churches of East and West with their particular liturgical rites, traditions and disciplines. The motif that unites all the rooms in the house is a common creed and appreciation for how the Lord is present to us through word and sacrament. And the common table is, of course, the Eucharist.

I want to be able to be comfortable in all these rooms, to appreciate the distinctness of each, and to feel enriched by their diversity in unity.

I want to be able to say, as a Christian, that the whole house is mine, and that I live there, with my brothers and sisters.

Constantinople

Turkey was a revelation. As a biblical Holy Land it defers only to Israel. The missionary journeys of Paul traversed Asia Minor; the Seven Churches referred to in the first three chapters of the Book of Revelation are locations relatively close to one another in Western Turkey; and in Central Turkey, called Anatolia, is a 3,000-foot-high plateau called Cappadocia.

The Christians of Anatolia settled there around 200 A.D. fleeing from persecution. What drew them to this particular area was the terrain. Thousands of years ago, eruptions from Mount Argaeus covered the area with lava which solidified into a soft porous tufa. Constant wind and water erosion have fashioned a moonscape of towering cones, pyramids, monoliths, and valleys. The cone shaped peaks are called "fairy chimneys" by the Anatolian Turks.

In these cones and their hidden vales, the Christians found an ideal refuge. They created elaborate homes and churches by carving out the soft tufa rock of the fairy chimneys.

Pilgrims I met along the way had repeatedly insisted that if I was anywhere within striking distance of Cappadocia, it was a "must." I arranged my train route accordingly and, with two others, hired a local guide to show us everything that two days could hold. Sinan, a Muslim (as were all the local guides), knew and loved the area, but his knowledge of its Christian past was rudimentary at best. When he heard me speaking to my two companions about the Christian history that had trans-

pired here, he said: "I will show you twice what is normal to
see in the time we have if you will tell me things like this that I
can pass on to other tourists to make it more interesting for
them."

He had a deal.

Sinan roused us at sunrise and we visited one area after another until sundown. The incredible troglodyte churches (of
which there are hundreds in the area) are decorated with remarkable biblical frescoes and iconography. The underground
cities of Kaymakli and Derinkuya, early Christian centers that
housed thousands of people in the eighth and ninth centuries,
extended downward into the earth for eight "floors" in a maze
of tunnels and rooms.

In the seventh century, the Byzantine provinces in Anatolia were threated by the Arabs. Christians in Caesarea, then
the most important center of religious activity in Anatolia,
gradually migrated to the Cappadocia region where they bur-
rowed into the earth and established colonies.

As a "special," Sinan took us to the Ihlara Valley. It would
be more aptly called a canyon. A river with an abundant flow
of water winds its way between tall cliffs that reach to five
hundred feet. Dug into the cliff faces at regular intervals are
numerous churches which permit the visitor to trace the development from pre-iconoclastic to post-iconoclastic decoration. From a distance, there is nothing to indicate that the
churches are there. When one draws near, one only sees a
cave-like opening about four feet high in the cliff wall. But
within awaits an experience completely incongruous with the
outer environment and with what the tiny entrance has prepared one to find. A large space opens up with nave and transept. False columns and vaulting are carved out to recall for
the residents their associations with the symbolism of the cross
and the heavenly dome. Although the soft rock was suitable to
a more plastic form, the design reflects the architects' familiarity with and slavish dependence upon the conventional Byzantine style. Today, in some of the churches, the ravages of time
have deteriorated pillar bases and caused an occasional wall to
crumble, leaving columns that hang from the ceiling and arch-

es that end in mid-air. The colorful frescoes on the walls heighten the sense of the fantastic, even though Muslim peasants, for whom a human visage in a temple of prayer is outlawed by the Koran, have scratched out many of the faces.

From the Ihlara Valley we drove to the modern-day city of Kayseri, which is none other than the famous Caesarea of ancient times, capitol of Cappadocia and homeland of the three Fathers of the Church called "The Cappadocians": Basil of Caesarea and Gregory of Nyssa, who were brothers, and their friend Gregory of Nazianzus. Their personalities and their work, like the region of their birth, have been the subject of a renewed and lively interest in the past few decades.

Their corner of history is the fourth century—all three were born around 330—in the peace brought to the Church by the conversion of Constantine in 310. In a hitherto backward region of the Roman Empire, these three flames started to burn. The Christian faith in their families was only two generations old. Their grandparents told stories of a time when one had everything to lose and nothing to gain by professing oneself Christian.

When Basil's studies were completed in Athens, he returned to Cappadocia and organized monastic communities, giving them a written rule by which to live. After a time he became a priest (to be distinguished from being a monk—the two do not necessarily go together) and then bishop of Caesarea. He installed his brother Gregory as bishop of Nyssa and tried to convince his friend, Gregory of Nazianzus, to accept a bishopric, too. But his friend's heart was in the solitude of the monastery and he was loath to leave it for the exigencies of episcopal life.

The written work of these three Cappadocians is abundant. Great preachers all, their sermons serve as a mirror both for the issues of their epoch and for their personalities. They addressed the human vices and, as an aid in the struggle against the tyranny of the senses, they insisted on a Lenten fast of eight weeks. Baptism surfaces often in their preaching. In the fourth century, it was usually put off by the people until their deathbed, partly out of a respect for baptism, partly out of a reluctance to change their lives, and partly out of their fear that sins committed after baptism would not be forgiven. The sermons of the Cappadocians solemnly invite them to the water.

But the career-long preoccupation of all three was the defense of the Trinity. They championed the teachings of the Council of Nicea (325) by preaching and by pen. At the second ecumenical council in Constantinople (381), they promulgated again the Nicene Creed concerning the consubstantiality of the Son with the Father, completing it with the expression of the faith concerning the Holy Spirit.

Intellectuals from aristocratic families, these pastors and Doctors of the Church were, above all, contemplatives. This is an assertion one knows the truth of intuitively upon seeing the Cappadocian landscape—surely one of the most astonishing in the world.

The Franciscan community at St. Anthony's Church welcomed me to Instanbul.

How good it felt just to sit at table with a group of brother-priests and talk and laugh. All five Franciscans were Italian, and the conversation jumped crazily from Italian to English to

French depending on who was speaking and who was being addressed. The pasta linked us all. After supper Padre Lucio took me to the library, a small, two-room collection of books. "This is one of the few Christian libraries in Turkey. While Turkey is a secular state, about ninety-eight percent of the people are Muslims, though most of them do not practice. There is nothing anyone can give to us that is more valuable than books. So many of the students at the university come here asking for something to read on Christianity and the Church and we have practically nothing to give them. Books in English are fine. If you can send us any books, it would be a great help to us." I asked him to give me a list of the kind of books that would be most useful.

The next morning, after a restorative night's sleep, Fr. Arcangelo took me on an extensive walking tour complete with historical commentary.

Istanbul is the only city in the world which stands upon two continents. The main part of the city, which is located at the southeastern tip of Europe, is separated from its suburbs in Asia by the storied Bosphorus. The Golden Horn then divides the European city into two parts. At the apex of the promontory, the Bosphorus and the Golden Horn flow together into the Marmara Sea, a confluence of striking beauty. A poet writing fourteen centuries ago described this city as being surrounded by a garland of waters. So it must have appeared to Jason and the argonauts when they sailed across them three thousand years ago in search of the Golden Fleece. And so it still appears today to the traveler arriving by boat.

According to tradition, the original settlement from which the city grew was established on the acropolis above Saray Point, the promontory, in the seventh century B.C. The legendary founder of the town of Byzantium was Byzas the Megarian who established a colony in 667 B.C. Situated at the mouth of the Bosphorus it was in a position to control all shipping from the Black Sea, through to the Propontus and the Aegean, while its position on the boundary of Europe and Asia eventually attracted to it the great land routes of both continents. Moreover, surrounded as it is on three sides by water, its short landward exposure defended by strong walls, it could be made impregnable to attack. As the French writer Gyllius concluded four centuries ago: "It seems to me that while other cities may be mortal, this one will remain as long as there are men on earth."

Shortly before the time of Christ, Byzantium became a client state of Rome and thereafter enjoyed nearly three centuries of quiet prosperity under the mantle of the *Pax Romana.* But eventually, in the closing years of the second century A.D., Byzantium found itself on the losing side in a civil war and was besieged by the emperor Septimius Severus. After finally taking Byzantium in the year 196 A.D. the emperor tore down the city walls, massacred the soldiers and officials who had opposed him and left the town a smoldering ruin. A few years afterward, however, Septimius realized the imprudence of leaving so strategic a site undefended and then rebuilt the city and its walls. The new enclosed area was more than double that of the ancient town.

At the beginning of the fourth century Byzantium was profoundly affected by the climactic events then taking place in the Roman Empire. After the retirement of the emperor Diocletian in the year 305, his successors in the tetrarchy, the two emperors, fought bitterly with one another for the control of the Empire. This struggle was eventually won by Constantine, emperor of the West, who in the year 324 finally defeated Licinius, emperor of the East. The last battle took place on the hills just across the Bosphorus from Byzantium, and on the following day in 324 the city surrendered and opened its gates to Constantine, now sole ruler of the Roman Empire.

During the first two years after his victory Constantine conceived the great scheme that would affect world history for the next millennium—the re-establishment of the Roman Empire with Byzantium as its capital. After he made his decision Constantine set out to rebuild and enlarge and adorn the old town to suit its imperial role. In less than four years, the new capital was completed. On May 11 in the year 330 A.D., in a ceremony in the Hippodrome, Constantine dedicated the city of New Rome, soon after to be called Constantinople.

The great dream of Byzantine civilization was a universal Christian society administered by the emperor and spiritually guided by the Church. This idea obviously combined Roman and Christian universalisms in one single socio-political program. It was also based upon the theological presuppositions that have come to characterize Byzantine theology: that man, created in the image of God, is called to achieve a "divine similitude"; his relationship to God is both a gift and a task, an immediate experience and an expectation of even greater vision to be accomplished in a free effort of love. Man, by nature, is God-centered in *all* aspects of his life, and he is responsible for the fate of the *entire* creation.

As long as Christianity was persecuted, this biblical assertion seemed little more than an article of faith, to be realized at the end of history and anticipated in the sacraments. With the conversion of Constantine, however, it suddenly appeared as a concrete and reachable goal. The original enthusiasm with which the Christian Church accepted imperial protection was never corrected by any systematic reflection on the nature and role of the state or of secular societies in the life of *fallen* humanity. Therein lies the tragedy, says John Meyendorff, a contemporary Orthodox theologian, of the Byzantine system: it assumed that the state, as such, could become intrinsically Christian. The fundamental mistake of this approach was to assume that the ideal humanity which was manifested through the Incarnation in the person of Jesus Christ could also find an adequate manifestation in the Roman Empire. Byzantine theocratic thought was, in fact, based upon the notion that the kingdom of God had already appeared in power and that the empire was the manifestation of this power in the world and in history. This strong emphasis on an already-realized end-state explains why Byzantine Christianity lacks a sense of direct responsibility for history as such. The Christian faith is understood to lead to the transfiguration and "deification" of the entire person which is accessible as a living experience *even now* and not merely in a future kingdom.

Byzantine Christian thought, of course, recognized the reality of evil, both personal and social, but it presumed, at least in the official philosophy of imperial legislation, that such evil could be adequately controlled by subduing the whole inhabited earth to the power of the one emperor and to the spiritual authority of the one Orthodox priesthood. "It is not possible for Christians to have the Church and not to have the Empire; for Church and Empire form a great unity and community; it is not possible for them to be separated from one another," said Patriarch Anthony IV as late as 1397, showing that the Byzantine still understood the universal empire as the necessary support of Christian universalism.

The idea of the Christian and universal empire presupposed that the emperor had obligations, both as guardian of the faith and as witness of God's mercy for man. The system was an authentic attempt to view human life in Christ as a whole: it did not admit any dichotomy between the spiritual and the material, the sacred and the secular, the individual and the social, or the doctrinal and the ethical. Church and State cooperated in preserving the faith and in building a society based on charity and humaneness.

Great changes took place in the Roman Empire in the two centuries following the reign of Constantine the Great. After the death of Theodosius I in 395, the Empire was divided between his two sons, with Honorius ruling the West from Rome, and Arcadius the East, with his capital at Constantinople. The western part of the Empire was overrun by Germanic peoples during the following century, and in the year 476 the last emperor of the West was deposed, leaving the emperor in Constantinople sole ruler of what was left of the Empire. This soon bro ght about a profound change in the character of the Empire, for it was now centered in lands populated largely by Greek-speaking Christians. And so, although Latin remained the official language of the court up until the beginning of the sixth century, the Empire was becoming more and more Greek and Christian in character, and it began to sever its connections with the classical traditions of Athens and Rome. As the great churchman Gennadius was to write in later times: "Though I am a Hellene by speech, yet I would never say that I was a Hellene, for I do not believe as Hellenes believed. I should like to take my name from my faith, and if anyone asks me what I am, I answer, 'a Christian.' Though my father dwelt in Thessaly I do not call myself a Thessalian, but a Byzantine, for I am of Byzantium."

Especially after the disappearance of the ancient Christian centers in Egypt, Palestine, and Syria, Constantinople became the unquestionable center of Eastern Christianity. Its bishop assumed the title of "Ecumenical Patriarch" (ecumenical from *oikomenos*, Greek for "the whole inhabited world"). In the Balkans, in the great Eastern European plain, in the Caucasus, its missionaries converted immense territories to the Christian faith. In fact, New Rome became the cradle of civilization for the Middle East and Eastern Europe, just as the "old Rome" had been for the Latin West.

That night at table, Fr. Arcangelo proposed a toast to both the new and the old Rome. We had just gotten up from supper when the doorbell rang. It was Sr. Arlene, from the community of Sisters of Sion in Istanbul. She had heard that "there was someone from Canada in town" and had come to receive first-hand news about her country. Undaunted in hearing that I had been away for almost a year and had little news to give, she nonetheless put her day off on the morrow at my disposal. She refused to recognize as an obstacle the talk I was supposed to give a day hence to the ecumenical association. She would help me transcribe it into French. A visit to Hagia Sophia, the Church of St. Irenaeus, the Blue Mosque, and the Sultan's Palace was what she suggested for the first half of the day—then a two hour boat trip up the Bosphorus, crossing back and forth from Europe to Asia, descent by mini-bus, an evening liturgy and supper with the Sisters of Sion.

Who was I to argue?

Hagia Sophia was Justinian's jewel. "Glory be to God, who hath deemed me worthy to accomplish such a work! Oh Solomon, I have surpassed thee!" cried Justinian. Solomon's temple is only a memory, but St. Sophia continues to awe architect, Church historian, and casual tourist alike.

A new epoch in the city's history began during the reign of Justinian the Great who succeeded to the throne in the year

527 and who set out to rebuild the city on an even grander scale than before. When he had finished, the city of Constantinople was the greatest and most magnificent metropolis on earth, an imperial capital beginning the first of its golden ages. The crowning glory of Justinian's new city was the Church of Hagia Sophia, still a symbol of the ancient city of which it was so long the heart.

"The church presents a most glorious spectacle, extraordinary to those who behold it and altogether incredible to those who are told of it. In height it tops the neighboring houses like a ship anchored among them, appearing above the city which it adorns and forms a part of. . . . It is distinguished by indescribable beauty, excelling both in its size and the harmonies of its measures. . . ." So wrote the chronicler Procopius fourteen centuries ago, describing Hagia Sophia, the Church of the Divine Wisdom, as it appeared during the reign of its founder, Justinian. Dedicated in 537, for nearly a thousand years thereafter Hagia Sophia served as the cathedral of Constantinople and was the center of religious life of the Byzantine Empire. For almost five centuries after the Turkish conquest (1453) it ranked first among the imperial mosques of Istanbul under the name of Aya Sofya Camii. Hagia Sophia continued to serve as a mosque during the early years of the Turkish Republic, until it was finally converted into a museum in 1935. It is emptied now of the congregations which once worshiped there, but it remains one of the truly great buildings in the world and still adorns the skyline of Istanbul.

In the year 1071 the Byzantine army suffered a catastrophic defeat by the Selcuk Turks at the battle of Manzikert and much of Eastern Asia Minor was permanently lost to the Empire. In the same year the Normans' military forces brought an end to Byzantine rule in Italy. The forces were now gathering that would eventually destroy the Empire. In the next century it was subjected to increasing pressure by the Latins of Western Europe whose armies first passed through Asia Minor in the year 1097 during the First Crusade.

As time went on, it became increasingly apparent that the Latins were less interested in freeing the Holy Land from the

Saracens than they were in seizing land and wealth for themselves. And the prize which attracted them most was the rich and magnificent city of Constantinople. In 1203 the Latin armies of the Fourth Crusade made their first assault upon Constantinople. Although they were not able to take the city at that time, they did so in a second attack the following year. In April 1204 the Crusaders breached the sea-walls along the Golden Horn and took the city by storm. They then proceeded to ruin and sack Constantinople, stripping it of its wealth, its art treasures, and its sacred relics, most of which were shipped off to Western Europe. The French knight Villehardouin, describing the sack of the city by the Crusaders, later wrote: "Of holy relics I need only say that it contained more than all Christendom combined; there is no estimating the quantity of gold, silver, rich stuffs and other valuable things—the production of all the climates of the world. It is my belief that the plunder of this city exceeded all that had been witnessed since the creation of the world."

Set into the pavement of Hagia Sophia, just opposite to the Deesis (a mosaic of Christ and the Virgin possessing great power and beauty) is the tomb of the man who was responsible for the ruin of Byzantium. Carved in Latin letters on the broken lid of a sarcophagus there one sees the name "Henricus Dandalo." Dandalo, doge of Venice, was one of the leaders of the Fourth Crusade and was the one chiefly responsible for persuading the Latins to attack Constantinople. After its final capture, Baldwin of Flanders was crowned in Hagia Sophia as emperor of Rumania, as the Latins called the portion of the Byzantine Empire which they had conquered. But the Latin emperor did not reign supreme even in his capital city, for three-eighths of it, including the Church of Hagia Sophia, was awarded to the Venetians and ruled by Dandalo. However, the proud doge had little time to lord it over his fractional kingdom, for he died the following year and was buried in the gallery of Hagia Sophia. After the Turkish conquest, according to tradition, Dandalo's tomb was broken into by the natives and his bones thrown to the dogs.

By the beginning of the fifteenth century the Byzantine

Empire consisted of little more than Constantinople and its immediate suburbs, with the old city decaying within the great walls which had protected it for so long. Though the Byzantines hung on for another half-century, it was increasingly obvious that time was running out, for the city was then completely surrounded by the Ottoman Empire.

Toward the very end before the conquest, travelers reported that the church was showing signs of grievous neglect and had been all but deserted by its congregation who stayed away in protest over the emperor's attempted union with the Church of Rome. The people of the city began returning to their church only in the last days before Constantinople fell to the Turks, when doctrinal differences no longer seemed important even to a Byzantine.

On the night of May 28, 1453, the prayers continued in Hagia Sophia throughout the night and the church filled with crowds of refugees as the sound of the Ottoman artillery grew more intense. Shortly after dawn word came that the defense walls had been breached and that the city had fallen. Then the doors of the church were barred and the congregation huddled inside, praying for a miraculous deliverance which never came. Soon afterward the vanguard of the Turkish soldiery forced its way into Hagia Sophia, bringing to an end the last tragic hour of Byzantium.

Sultan Mehmet the Conqueror entered the city late in the afternoon of May 29 and rode slowly through the streets to Hagia Sophia. He dismounted at the door of the church and bent down to take a handful of earth, which he then sprinkled over his turban as an act of humility before God. Evliya Celebi's account of the historic occasion reads thus: "Sultan Mehmet II, on surveying more closely the Church of Aya Sofya, was astonished at the solidity of its construction, the strength of its foundations, the height of its cupola, and the skill of its builder. He caused the ancient building to be purified of its idolatrous objects and purified from the blood of the slain . . . and converted it that very hour into a mosque."

During the century after the conquest the Turkish armies swept victoriously through the Balkans and the Near East and its buccaneering navies dominated the Mediterranean. By the middle of the sixteenth century the Ottoman Empire stretched from Baghdad in the east to Algiers in the west, and from lower Egypt to the southern borders of Russia, rivaling in extent the Byzantine Empire in the days of Justinian. The Empire reached the peak of power during the reign of Suleyman the Magnificent who ruled from 1520 until 1566. Even during later periods when the fortunes of the Empire declined, it was vast and prosperous and some of its institutions remained basically sound so that it held together for centuries after it had passed its prime.

World War I was its definitive undoing. The victorious Allies proceeded to divide up the remnants of the Ottoman Empire among themselves. Turkey was only saved by an extraordinary rallying effort on the part of its people, who fought to preserve their homeland when it was invaded by the Greeks in 1919.

At the time of the establishment of the Turkish Republic in 1923, the city of Ankara was chosen as the capital and the seat of Parliament. Soon afterward the embassies of the great European powers packed up and moved to new quarters in Ankara. And so, for the first time in sixteen centuries Istanbul was no longer the capital of an empire. Now, half a century later, history would seem to have passed Istanbul by, and no longer do the wealthy and powerful adorn her with splendid buildings. But the glory of emperors and sultans is not all that has faded; the glory of the Christian Byzantine Empire and its patriarchate have faded, too.

He bears ancient and august titles: Ecumenical Patriarch and Archbishop of the "New Rome" in Constantinople, the mother Church of Eastern Orthodoxy since the fourth century. He is the symbolic leader of the world's eighty-five million Orthodox Christians. Yet when His Holiness Demetrios I presides over the Sunday Eucharist at the Patriarchal Church of St. George in Istanbul, the giant chandeliers cast their feeble light across ranks of empty pews. Like almost all post-conquest churches in the city, it is a small basilica. This form was adopt-

ed partly because of its simplicity, but largely because the
Christians were forbidden to build churches with domes or
masonry roofs, so that the basilica with its timbered roof, a traditional Christian edifice, was the obvious solution. On the
right side of the aisle is the patriarchal throne, but the one who
sits there looks out on a congregation that numbers only a doz-
en or so worshipers, most of them elderly. The historic see,
once the center of half the Christian world, is struggling gal-
lantly to survive.

The ecumenical patriarchate has had great difficulty oper-
ating as an international Orthodox center. The government of
Turkey shut down the patriarchate's press and its once renowned seminary. The regime has tightly controlled overseas
travels of the patriarchate staff. When a new patriarch had to
be chosen in 1972, the government exercised undue influence.
The 62-year-old Demetrios was selected, though he was the ju-
nior archbishop. He thereby assumed jurisdiction over millions
of Orthodox in the West and became heir to an historic recognition as "first among equals" of the Orthodox patriarchs.

There is no comparing a visit to the present Phanar with,
say, a visit to Lambeth Palace, home of the head of the Anglican Communion. The neighborhood is humble, even run-
down, the patriarchate having moved around for a number of
years after leaving its celebrated site at the Pammakaristos in
1586. One could mistake the four-story, square, stone structure
for a family mansion with an aristocratic past. Two men
laughed at me in the street as I took a picture of it. The main
gate is permanently welded shut and painted black. It is the
famous Central Gate from which Gregory V, Patriarch of Constantinople, was hanged for treason on April 22, 1821 during
the war in which Greece won its independence from Turkey.
It has become almost a symbol of Greek-Turkish intransigence.
Across the courtyard from the palace is the Church of St.
George. It is hard to believe that this modest complex of buildings is a revered center of the entire Orthodox Church, or that
in its great days the Ecumenical Patriarch of Constantinople
exerted great influence on the religious affairs of the entire
Eastern Christian world. Today, although Demetrios I is still

the spiritual leader of Orthodox Christianity, his temporal powers are extremely limited and his actual flock consists of only the few thousand Greeks still resident in Istanbul and the rest of Turkey.

I entered the palace and was met in the hallway by Demetrios' secretary. He showed me to a small waiting room where I put on for my audience with the Patriarch the cassock that was in my hand-satchel. No religious garb is permitted in public in Turkey. Then he led me down the corridor and into the Patriarch's office. There was no waiting, no bureaucracy, no tiny rituals of protocol. It was really quite refreshing. Within moments after my arrival at the Phanar we were seated and conversing through the medium of his secretary who interpreted his Greek for me and my French for him. Demetrios impressed me as a quiet, shy person. He speaks softly both in church and in his office, and left the initiative in the conversation to me, seeming quite content to limit his own role to responding. I felt welcomed as a fellow Christian and worker for the unity of the Church; I recorded no impressions that being a Latin priest was a strike against me. The moment at which his face showed most feeling was when I told him quite simply that in that part of the sacred liturgy where Roman Catholics pray for the Church's leaders, it has become my practice to add his name after that of the Holy Father and the local bishop. As the interpreter relayed this to him, his eyes opened wide as he gazed at me in appreciation with his gentle, vulnerable expression: "I am very grateful," he said. "I rely upon these prayers, and the knowledge that they are there gives me strength."

One day there may be no more youths entering the priesthood for the Church in Turkey, or no more community to serve. And if it becomes necessary for the Patriarch of Constantinople to leave his see of "New Rome," there is no guarantee that the ancient patriarchates of Alexandria and Antioch, or Constantinople's historic rival, the huge Orthodox Church of Russia, will continue to recognize him as the Ecumenical Patriarch. But one thing is sure: the contribution of Byzantium to the history of humankind in the field of religious thought is permanent and very much alive. Whether one deals with Trinitarian or Christological dogma, or whether one examines ecclesiology and sacramental doctrine, the main stream of Byzantine theology uncovers the same vision of the human person: called to *know* God, to *participate* in his life, to be saved, not simply through an extrinsic action of God's, or through rational acceptance of propositional truths, but by *becoming* God.

As a culture and a civilization, Byzantium faded long ago. Yet the continuous attraction of Byzantine art and the remarkable survival of Eastern Christianity throughout the most dramatic of social changes are the best available signs that Byzantium did indeed discover something fundamentally true about human nature and its relationship to God.

Today, when we hear spoken of a Byzantine Church, we immediately think "Greek Orthodox." There are several historical reasons why the Byzantine Empire and Church, in spite of encompassing many peoples and traditions, took on a Greek identity. The cultural framework of Byzantine theology after the Council of Chalcedon (451) was increasingly limited to the Greek-speaking world. The wealth of the various non-Greek traditions of early Christianity—particularly the Syrian and Latin—was less and less taken into account by the theologians of the imperial capital. Until the emergence of the twelfth century revival of theology in the West, Constantinople remained the unquestioned intellectual center of Christendom and hence developed a sense of increasing self-sufficiency.

The Byzantine tendency to culturally turn away from its Roman past was made even more definite through its confrontation with Islam. The Roman Popes, deprived of protection from the Byzantine emperors with whom they were in doctrinal conflict on the authority issue, turned to the Franks and associated themselves with the newly emerging Latin Middle Ages.

In the aftermath of the Turkish conquest (1453), the Ottoman Empire divided up its vast holdings into various religious sectors so as to better control each one. All leaders were either appointed by or served under the reigning authority in Istan-

bul. For example, the ecclesiastical provinces within the Ottoman Empire received their patriarchs by appointment and
approval of the patriarch residing in Istanbul and the Sultan.
Hence, the following nomenclature: the Greek Orthodox Patriarchate of Antioch; the Greek Orthodox Patriarchate of Jerusalem; the Greek Orthodox Patriarchate of Alexandria. All
the Orthodox of the Middle East were under the authority of
the Greek Patriarchate of Constantinople (Istanbul).

In the late nineteenth century the Patriarchate of Antioch
revolted against this system. Its constituency was Arab Christian and they wanted an Arab to govern their Church. Patriarch Meletios Doumani was the first Arab to be elected
patriarch of Antioch in 1896 after many centuries of Greek
hierarchs. Today, Orthodox Patriarchates of Alexandria and Jerusalem are still headed by Greeks over the protests of their
Arab constituencies.

Yet another reason explaining the identity of the Byzantine Church as "Greek" in the popular mind is to be found in
the rise of Slavic Orthodox nationalism. The Greek response to
this threat to its own position of dominance was to impress the
Greek stamp more firmly upon what was being imparted. Language, because of the way it embodies a whole culture, is perhaps the best example.

Although Byzantine Christianity kept its universalist missionary vision, which expressed itself in a successful evangelization of the Slavs and other Eastern nations, its theological
development took place in an exclusively Greek setting. The
resumption of the veneration of icons, for example, after the
iconoclast crisis (a movement which covered the eighth and
ninth centuries and was hostile to the veneration of images)
was a victory of *Greek* traditions. Still bearing the title of
"Great Church of Constantinople—New Rome," it became
known to both its Latin competitors and its Slavic disciples as
the "Greek" Church—so Greek, culturally and intellectually,
in fact, that the Emperor Michael III in a letter to Pope Nicholas I designated Latin as a "barbarian" tongue. These developments and attitudes obviously had a great impact on the future
of theology and of the relations between East and West.

The controversies of the fifth century over how to describe the divinity and humanity in Christ provoked the initial major break in Christendom, separating the ancient spiritual families of the East (Syrian, Egyptian, and Armenian) from the Greeks and Latins, who alone remained in their common faithfulness to Chalcedon as the two main cultural expressions of Christianity inside the Roman world.

One of the most striking facts about the schism between the Greeks and Latins is that it cannot be dated or identified with any particular event. The year 1054 is often cited as the date of the split. In this year anathemas were leveled against Patriarch Michael Cerularius and two other persons by the personal legates of Pope Leo IX under Cardinal Humbertus. These legates then became the object of a similar sentence pronounced by the Patriarch and the Synod of Constantinople. These sentences, however, were directed at particular persons and not at the Churches, and were not aiming at breaking ecclesial communion between the sees of Rome and Constantinople. Besides, Humbertus' bull of excommunication exceeded his powers as legate and was apparently null and void in the first place. In 1054, high school history texts notwithstanding, no schism occurred between the Churches as such.

Political opposition between Byzantium and the Frankish Empire, gradual estrangement in thought and practice, divergent developments in both theology and one's vision of the Church and how it structures itself—all played their respective parts in the process. Historians admit today that East and West parted their ways through a progressive estrangement which coincided with the equally progressive growth of papal authority. The difficulties created by history could have been resolved if there had been a common theological criterion to settle the issues keeping the West and East apart. But the medieval development of the primacy of the Patriarch of the West, the Bishop of Rome, as the ultimate reference in doctrinal matters stood in obvious contrast with the more synodal concept of the Church prevailing in the East. There could be no agreement on the manner of solving the issue as long as there was divergence on the notion of authority in the Church. Still, in spite of all this, in the Middle Ages it was generally presumed that Greek priests, when traveling in the West, would receive the sacrament from the hands of the Latins, and vice versa. Even in the seventeenth century there are records showing that local priests in the Greek islands were inviting Dominicans in to preach missions.

One Sunday toward the end of my stay in Constantinople, I participated in the Divine Liturgy, presided at by the Ecumenical Patriarch, at the monastery of Zoodochos Pighi in Balikli. Afterward, all in attendance went outside to the tomb of Athenagoras I which has become a pilgrimage site for Christian visitors to Istanbul. On the tombstone is engraved "Ecumenical Patriarch Athenagoras who came from America, 1 November 1948—7 July 1972." Next to the epitaph is the patriarchal emblem. Athenagoras was patriarch from 1948 until his death in 1972. He was responsible for the re-emergence in our own day of the prestige of the Patriarchate of Constantinople and for the Orthodox Church's move toward conciliarity. Amazingly, as a Church dedicated to the synodal principle, it has operated for centuries without a major council. Wars, persecutions, national crises, lack of leadership—all have contributed to this anomalous situation. It was Athenagoras who organized the first Pan-Orthodox Conference held at Rhodes in 1961—the most representative Orthodox assembly since the eighth century. Out of this conference came plans for greater inter-Orthodox cooperation, three additional conferences, and the idea for a Great and Holy Pan-Orthodox Council, which is now in planning.

It was in January 1963 when Pope Paul VI and Athenagoras embraced in Jerusalem, the cradle of Christianity, that a new impetus for dialogue was given between their two Churches. A second action that had widespread ramifications was effected simultaneously in Rome and Istanbul on December 7, 1965 by the mutual lifting of the anathemas of 1054. The removal of the anathemas was clearly intended to have a symbolic more than a canonical effect since the excommunications did not address the two Churches as such. When in July 1967

Pope Paul visited Athenagoras in Istanbul, the public image of a Pope appearing in Istanbul as a *brother* (and therefore an equal) of another bishop could not be reduced to mere diplomacy or protocol. The well-known definitions of papal supremacy were in no way denounced, of course, but neither were they publicly expressed in any way. Facing the Orthodox, the Pope presented himself in a way perfectly compatible with the function of "first among equals," which the Orthodox have always granted to him. This attitude of Paul VI reversed a thousand-year-old tradition which required that the authority of the Supreme Pontiff be scrupulously preserved under any circumstances, and particularly in his relations with the East, where the existence of a center of opposition to Roman centralism was a well-known fact.

Granted, these events were largely symbolic in nature, but they changed the overall atmosphere. "It is now the task of theologians," as Meyendorff has noted, "to discover how these events can be interpreted and used, not for the narrow purpose of ecclesiastical diplomacy, or even the progress of Orthodox-Catholic relations (which is only one aspect of our responsibility for a united Christian witness), but for the solution of the problem of authority in the Church, without which no real Christian unity is possible." In other words, the symbols need to be given a substantial content.

The year 1920 was a decisive date in the general relations between the Eastern Churches and the West. The entry of the Orthodox Churches into ecumenical relationships was preceded by a letter addressed in January 1920 "unto all the Churches of Christ wheresoever they may be" and signed by the Ecumenical Patriarch and eleven Metropolitans. This epistle invited the Churches to renounce proselytism and to form a league of the Churches for mutual assistance. It suggested various practical ways of promoting good will, and declared that doctrinal disagreements should not stand in the way of joint action. This letter signified a departure from the usual cautious attitude of the Orthodox toward the West, and showed the desire of some at least among their hierarchs to take the lead in the movement toward closer friendship. In August 1920, a large Orthodox delegation came to Geneva to the preparatory Conferences of the Faith and Order and Life and Work movements. For many of the Orthodox delegates, this was the first occasion of meeting with representatives of non-Orthodox Churches. The coming of the Orthodox to Geneva brought their Churches into the ecumenical movement. From that year, to their participation in the founding of the World Council of Churches in 1946, Orthodox delegations were present at every one of the international councils and meetings. The first Pan-Orthodox Congress of Theologians, held in Athens in 1936, passed the following resolution:

> The first Orthodox Congress of Theology, regarding the ecumenical movement for the union of the Church as a happy manifestation of the present general renewal of interest in the Church and in theology, welcomes this movement and is prepared to collaborate with it in an Orthodox spirit.

When in 1975 the Orthodox Churches were of the opinion that the times were ripe to offer the Vatican a serious theological dialogue with Orthodoxy as a whole, the offer was communicated and accepted in a memorable liturgy in the Sistine Chapel at the end of which Pope Paul knelt down and kissed the feet of the head of the delegation of the Ecumenical Patriarch. By some accounts, the gesture was expressive of Pope Paul's joy at the news of the opening of the official international Orthodox-Roman Catholic dialogue. By other accounts, it was a sign that he conceived the primacy simply as humble service.

Catholics and Orthodox have both long hesitated before assenting to this dialogue because both are very aware that, once begun, it must, within a reasonable period of time, realize its fulfillment in the re-establishing of full communion between the two Churches. "The dawn of the century that is approaching," Pope John Paul II said to the Roman Curia in June 1980, "must find us united in full communion. . . . It will be necessary to learn again to breathe fully with both lungs, the Western and the Eastern." If Catholics and Orthodox are not capable of re-establishing full communion between themselves, the entire ecumenical movement stands to lose its credibility. It is a dialogue which both parties realized could not be entered into without a genuine will to arrive at a decisive result within a reasonable amount of time between the two Churches.

"The theological dialogue which has been opened officially on the island of Patmos is an important event, and in the relations between Catholics and Orthodox it is the major event not only of this year, but for centuries," said John Paul II just days after his address to the Roman Curia. "We are entering a new phase of our relations, for the theological dialogue constitutes an essential aspect of the wider dialogue between our Churches. The Catholic Church and the Orthodox Church as a whole are engaged in this dialogue."

A month later, in a letter to Patriarch Demetrios I, John Paul wrote:

> I have asked all the Catholics in the world to take part in this dialogue by their prayers. It is a decisive moment in the relationships between our Churches. It is a matter of eliminating the remains of age-old misunderstandings, of overcoming a lack of understanding inherited from the past, of definitively resolving the questions in controversy between our two Churches. This is indispensable for the attainment of a stable unity in which, in full communion, we shall be united with one voice in the praise of God and in the bearing of a common witness to him before the world.

The "wider dialogue" the Pope referred to, and the participation of the two Churches "as a whole," are more important than one might think. Indeed, this wider dialogue is, in the minds of many surveyors of the scene, more important than the *official* dialogue between the theologians. For more divisive than the doctrinal differences is the trench that we have succeeded in digging around ourselves for centuries. We seem to be two different civilizations. The self-isolation that the two Churches have built up over the centuries has resulted in a reluctance to pray together, a reluctance to worship together, a reluctance to interact together. While doctrinal differences seem to be diminishing, other factors are growing in importance. The "Westernization" or "Latinization" of the Eastern rite Churches that have entered into communion with Rome is one such factor. Anti-reunion propagandists point to the absence of icon screens and the presence of confessionals and of stations of the cross in many Eastern rite Catholic Churches as evidence of the slow but inevitable process of Westernization that takes place when one enters into union with Rome. Though the Popes have insisted perseveringly that the Eastern rites be preserved in their purity, effective assurance must be given that full union will not require the Orthodox to remove their icon screens, don Western vestments, ban their married clergy, or change their method of receiving the Eucharist. Their liturgical language and their liturgical calendar will remain as they are. In like manner, the Catholic Church will not be forced to adopt any or all of the Eastern rite customs. Certain concessions will be made without a doubt, but voluntarily rather than under duress or as a prerequisite for reunion. Once trust is restored through this "wider dialogue" a spontaneous sharing in each other's riches will inevitably occur because they will be recognized for what they are: riches.

The mostly likely places for this cross-denominational sharing are countries like France, Germany, England, the United States and Canada. Sizable populations of Eastern Christians have emigrated to these countries. In their efforts to integrate themselves into pluralist societies, good and open relations with neighboring Christian congregations have developed. This diaspora situation represents the best hope for significant advance in the wider dialogue that relates to a sharing of faith and practice among the members of Eastern and Western Christian Churches.

I had planned to stay in Istanbul a few days longer before departing for Mount Athos, but itineraries charted from afar off never have benefit of the unexpected on-the-spot developments which keep the adventure even in programmed travel. As we stood around outside after the prayers at Athenagoras' tomb, I was introduced to Orthodox Bishop Ezekiel of Derry,

Australia. He was leaving the next morning for Athens and then going to Mount Athos with two laymen from his diocese, Kostas and Stephanos, who were traveling with him. Upon hearing that I was also going to Athos, he invited me to join them. The opportunity to arrive at Mount Athos in the company of three members of the Orthodox Church, all of whom spoke Greek as well as English and one of whom was a bishop, was worth throwing my script for the next few days to the winds. Metropolitan Bartolomeos, whom I had met and talked with at the Phanar and who had introduced me to Bishop Ezekiel, was standing next to me.

"Take it," he said simply. "It's a rare opportunity for you."

We left the next morning for Athens.

Mount Athos

After four days in Athens, we crammed ourselves into a rented Damatzu and drove seven hours to Thessalonika. The bishop and Kostas harmonized on hymns from the Orthodox liturgy most of the way. Wild flowers lined the highway like long brush strokes of yellow and white. The occasional field of poppies contributed splotches of red. Mount Olympus hid its crown in a conference of clouds. In Thessalonika we found rooms in a thin, three-story hotel squeezed between a hardware store and a dress shop.

At 5:30 the next morning, we were on the road for Ouranoupolis to catch the boat leaving for Athos at 10 A.M. The scenery was reminiscent of the Irish coast: rugged promontories and surf crashing against sheer cliffs.

When the thirty-foot converted fishing trawler pulled away from the dock, there were no women on board. An ancient and revered Athos legend reveals why. According to one tradition, the Virgin Mary, accompanied by St. John the Evangelist, was on her way to visit Lazarus in Cyprus, when a sudden storm arose and her ship was carried by a violent wind to Athos. They are said to have come ashore where the Virgin rested for a while. Overwhelmed by the beauty of the place, she asked her Son to give her the Mountain. In response, a voice was heard saying, "Let this place be your inheritance and your garden, a paradise and a haven of salvation for those seeking to be saved." Thus the Holy Mountain was consecrated as her inheritance and garden. An imperial edict with the golden seal of Emperor Alexios I forbade entry to the mountain to any female human or animal. The monks of Athos have chosen to honor in perpetuity both the spirit and the letter of the legend. The Holy Mountain's absolute ban on women has achieved a notoriety out of all proportion and is often the only thing that many people know about Athos. The monks want to keep this tradition intact not out of misogyny but because it greatly reduces the flow of visitors and is thus conducive to greater silence and solitude. A certain ground rule among the monks—that whoever leaves the Mountain and goes into "the world" for a time is not, upon his return, to receive Communion for two weeks—would seem to indicate further that the absence of women would be considered a positive support to the monks in their effort to live celibate chastity.

Athos is the easternmost of the three promontories of Chalkidiki, a Greek peninsula that stretches into the Aegean Sea between the Thermaic and Strimonic Gulfs. Some forty miles in length, Athos varies in width from five to nine miles, covering an area of approximately two hundred and twenty-five square miles in an isolated mountainous and forested region of northern Greece. As the hillocks of the landward end extend seaward, clusters of peaks swell higher and higher to end finally in the bare slopes of Mount Athos, whose pyramid-shaped summit rises sheer from the sea to more than six thousand feet. The name Athos was that of a Thracian giant who hurled the whole stony mass at Poseidon in a clash between gods and giants. By another version, Poseidon was victorious, burying the rebellious giant Athos under the great rock.

Athos was an area eminently suited to those wishing to practice the rigors of an ascetic life, and from the earliest years of the Byzantine period it attracted men from all parts of the Empire. The earliest historical data indicate that contemplatives had already begun to frequent the mountain in the seventh century. Founded later than the desert monasteries of Egypt, Athos claims to be the only monastic center with a continuous and unbroken history. Lavish support from both the Byzantine emperors and foreign royalty raised it to a peak of one hundred and eighty monasteries and dependencies sheltering no less than forty thousand monks at the end of the eleventh century. Though today the number of monasteries and monks is much diminished, this autonomous monastic community is the cradle of Orthodoxy and the bastion of Eastern Christianity. By the middle Byzantine period the whole peninsula was commonly known as the Holy Mountain.

The Crusades, and particularly the attack on Constantinople which occured in 1204, are frequently seen by historians as the real beginning of the schism between East and West. Constantinople, one of the five great patriarchal sees, was the undisputed home of the Greek patriarch. Rome's establishment of a parallel hierarchy and its appointment of a Latin patriarch in Constantinople put the schism in clear evidence. During this period of the Latin occupation (1204–61) the Mountain suffered with the rest of the Byzantine Empire from the Frankish raids. It was placed under the jurisdiction of the Latin kingdom of Salonika, and the monks were subjected to much pressure to accept the union of the two Churches. The efforts to "Latinize" the monks resulted in the despoliation of the monasteries, destruction of the churches, and the torture and execution of a number of monks. Once life on the Mountain resumed its normal course, the monks became noted for their fanatical resistance to any suggestion of a union of the East with the Western half of Christendom. An attitude of contempt for the Western Christian Churches, seen as heretical and corrupt, persists today.

At an Extraordinary Joint Conference in 1980 of all the representatives and superiors of the twenty ruling monasteries of Athos, it was formally stated that "the 'churches' and 'confessions' of the West, having in many ways perverted the faith of the Gospel, the apostles and the fathers, are deprived of sanctifying grace, of real mysteries and apostolic succession."

In the hour and a half boat ride from Ouranoupolis to Daphne, the point of entry onto the Holy Mountain, we passed six monasteries all of which had been constructed as near the water as the landscape permitted. The constitutional charter of Athos has fixed the number of monasteries at twenty, and it is no longer possible to found more. If the number of monks

increases beyond the capacity of the monasteries, then monks are to be sent to live in monastic settlements called dependencies which are sometimes as large as the mother-monastery. Each of the monasteries is self-governing. Their obedience is primarily to the ecclesiastical authorities on the mountain. Even the jurisdiction of the ecumenical patriarchate over Athos is limited to issues which concern the spiritual life of the Athonite community. Each of the twenty monasteries contributes one member to a legislative authority called the Holy Assembly and one member to an administrative authority called the Holy Community.

The question inevitably arises as one passes by and regards these daring buildings, marvels of monastic architecture perched on cliffs like eagles' nests high above the sea: Why do monks come to spend their lives here? The answer is in the ideal of primitive monasticism, which remains in force within the Orthodox Church to this day. The physical reality of harsh surroundings is a natural adjunct to the spiritual process of *kenosis* and *plerosis,* the emptying of oneself in the desert and filling-up of oneself with the life of God. In the context of a theology steeped in the early Desert Fathers and of a long-standing eremetical (hermit) tradition in the Orthodox Church, the manner of life of the Athonite monks and hermits is neither surprising nor exceptional. The first duty of a person is to achieve the kingdom of God in his or her own soul, and the best way to attain such an end is to stand face to face with God in silence and retreat. The primeval forms of monasticism have survived more in the East than in the West. And the solitary life, in all its ancient forms, may still be found today on Mount Athos.

On the boat a young monk passed by Bishop Ezekiel who was talking with an old hermit monk. "Shame!" said the young man to the hermit, referring to the bishop. "Tell him he should not have cut his hair." The old hermit was silent, but the bishop said to the hermit, choosing not to give the young monk the benefit of a direct remark (for all three were speaking the same language): "Tell him I'll pray for him." On the mountain, cutting one's hair, shaving one's whiskers, or swimming in the clear waters of the blue Aegean are all regarded as concessions to style, fashion, or pleasures of the flesh and are thus renounced.

We docked at Daphne and mounted a bus that had probably seen both world wars. Slowly it picked its way like an overburdened old mule up the steep gradient. At one comparatively level stretch the driver attempted to move from first to second gear and failed. The bus stalled. Everyone dismounted. We were precariously close to the eroding shoulder which veered off sharply into a deep valley. We pushed and pulled and rocked the old chariot until it started up again. We were eventually delivered to Karyes, the capital of the monastic state, where we had to produce our passports in the office of the civil governor who is responsible to the Office of

Foreign Affairs in Athens for the maintenance of law and order (the Holy Mountain is an autonomous part of the Greek
state). From there we were taken to the office of the Holy
Epistasia, the secretariat of the Holy Community, where, one
by one, we presented our papers, were interviewed, and were
given a certificate of permission to visit the monasteries on the
Mountain.

Getting in to Athos is not an easy task, except for Greeks. I
had gone, as directed, to the Ministry of Foreign Affairs in
Athens armed with letters of commendation from a Greek
archpriest in Montreal, a Greek bishop in Toronto, the representative of the Ecumenical Patriarch at the World Council of
Churches in Geneva, and the Ecumenical Patriarch himself. It
still was not enough. I was sent to my embassy for a letter
which said that I was a citizen in good standing and was not a
refugee from the law.

When I emerged from the interview with certificate of
permission in hand, I felt a certain sense of victory-against-the-
odds. Then came the custom which was to repeat itself in all
the monasteries we would visit: a monk brought out a glass of
water and with it served the traditional ouzo, loukoumi (a can-
dy) and coffee. Since it is not every day that a bishop visits
Athos, the two monks who had been conducting interviews
came out from the office and conversed with us in an adjoining
room.

Somewhere in the conversation Stephanos asked them if
they had heard about the shooting of Pope John Paul two days
previous. The stout but fatherly monk who had interviewed
me immediately regarded me with a long and reflective look:
"We hope he gets better," he said, "but we do not want him to
return to the style of papacy which some Popes have exercised
in the past. You cannot dialogue with somebody who keeps
putting himself above you."

There it was—right on the line. I had not been there fifteen minutes and the crux of the problem had already been
clearly addressed. The Orthodox recognize the changes that
have been taking place in Roman Catholicism, not only in the
way that papal ministry is exercised but also in the visible ef-

forts to relate papal ministry to episcopal collegiality. The Orthodox view the Church as a communion of local churches which find their prototype in the Trinity, where there is a distinction of Persons but unity based on love. In keeping with this view, the bishops, sharing in the ministry of Christ, are equal among themselves as far as episcopal dignity is concerned. They and their churches are bound together by love and not law. The Orthodox do not have problems with the idea of Roman primacy up to a point. If the primacy could be viewed as a pastoral primacy in the service of the unity of the Church, the Petrine office would no longer present a major obstacle to reunion not only among Catholics and Orthodox but among all other Christians.

At Vatican I primacy was described as a primacy of jurisdiction. In practice this jurisdiction was given the widest meaning: full, supreme, and universal power over the Church. The Orthodox are willing to see the bishop of Rome as the "first among equals" of the bishops, but primacy in the expression of Vatican I is reacted to as an exaggerated form of jurisdiction and authority. Anyone exercising this kind of authority can no longer be considered *equal* in dignity with other bishops; he would be *over* them, as a super-bishop. For Orthodox, the unitarian model, one God–one Church–one Pope, must be discarded for the Trinitarian model: unity in multiplicity. The Pope would be the model pastor who protects Christian freedom. As center of unity and communication he would be the one who safeguards the unity of faith but in all other things promotes variety and freedom to meet the particular needs of local churches. This would essentially be, the Orthodox say, a return to the way things were in the period of the seven ecumenical councils—before the Patriarch of the West, the Bishop of Rome, became separated from the other four Patriarchs through the schism and evolved into a monarchy.

Only the way of the ancient Church is acceptable to the Orthodox. The Pope should be understood primarily as Bishop of the local Church of Rome and Patriarch of the West. This would obviously entail a loss of administrative responsibility, but would allow for a qualitative concentration on the essentials of the Petrine service of the unity of the Church: strengthen the brethren in the one faith in Jesus Christ. Since that would result in more freedom for the local Churches to accommodate to their concrete situations, it would manifest that only in the one faith is unity necessary; in all else variety and freedom would reign.

Before we left Kayres, the old monk disappeared into the office of the Holy Epistasia and came out with a guest book. I took the pen he offered me and wrote, in Greek, "In the unity of the Spirit, in the love of Christ," and signed my name. He was pleased and took me back into his office to write down his address for me. "Always have your pockets full of gifts in the East," a monk of Chevetogne had counseled me. I produced one and gave it to him in exchange for his address. We kissed on both cheeks, and when I continued to a third (a custom among the Orthodox), he smiled and said with a wink: "If you could spend a little time with me, I would make you Orthodox. Come again."

"I didn't realize you knew any Greek," Stephanos exclaimed when we had set off walking with our bags to the monastery of Stavronikita. I was not about to reveal that I had used fully half of it in the guest book. We walked for a time in silence. The seascape before our eyes reduced language to poverty. The beauty of Athos is unrivaled. The government of Greece is well aware that a person wanting a holiday environment of mountains, sea, and unfailing sun could do no better than this peninsula. It would dearly love to displace the monks and transform Athos into an alluring vacationland. But the monastic community is accustomed to adversity; indeed, it has made struggle a way of life.

A movement was mounted to internationalize the Mountain in the past century when a marked influx of non-Greeks came to Athos. But the Athos monks resisted, keeping it a protectorate of Greece and a mostly Greek-born community. A Salonika University report shows that the number of monks has risen to 1,400 from a low of 1,146 in 1972. Most are Greek, although twenty percent are of Russian, Bulgarian, Rumanian or Serbian origin, and there is a sprinkling of West Europeans and Americans. The average age is forty-nine, down from sixty-one a decade ago. In one monastery of fifty monks that we visited, the average age was thirty-five. Greek is still the chief language, as it has always been, notwithstanding the presence of monks of other nationalities. Mount Athos represents for the Greeks the cradle of the national tradition and that part of Greece where for more than a thousand years the Greek-Christian heritage, Greek letters, and the true Byzantine style of worship have been preserved. The whole of the living tradition on the mountain is like a sacred repository for the understanding of theology, philosophy, history, Byzantine and post-Byzantine art and Eastern mysticism. It is also like a living museum richly stocked with artistic treasures of the Orthodox past.

Stavronikita, named after two monks Stavros and Nikitas who, according to one legend, lived in separate cells and united to build a monastery, is built on a level headland above the sea about an hour and a half walk from Karyes. When we were shown to our rooms, we stood mute and wide-eyed at the windows. All that separated us from the sea below us was one hundred and fifty feet of clear Aegean air and a pane of glass. The scenic promontories stretched out in both directions like the half-submerged backs of whales floating in a row. It had taken us a full day of travel by car, boat, bus and foot to arrive. If this moment of visual splendor had been the sole object of the day's journey, it would have been worth it.

Meals are eaten twice a day—once a day on fast days, which comprise roughly half the year. On fast days, numerous restrictions with regard to cooking oils and dairy products apply. With the exception of one monastery, meat is not eaten at all. One does not go to Athos to eat. Indeed, some Greeks who make regular visits bring their own food with them. The monastery food is monotonous and on the whole badly prepared, though it can vary greatly from one monastery to another. Washing and toilet facilities are in general rather elementary if not primitive. Water is unheated.

When we had finished our supper of a salad, potato, egg, bread, and cheese, Stephanos reported that the bishop was going to ordain a deacon in the morning and we would have the good fortune of witnessing an ordination in the monastery.

Customarily, all the monks unite in common worship. The most common services are Vespers, Compline, Matins and the Divine Liturgy, as the Eucharist or Mass is called among the Orthodox. Almost all services are held at night when the rest of the world is either carousing or sleeping. Stephanos' words "in the morning" meant 3:30 A.M.

At 2:30 A.M. I heard the semantron. This instrument, unique to Byzantine monasteries, looks like a wooden propeller about eight feet long. It is gripped in the middle by a monk who walks up and down the courtyard banging out a fascinating cadence upon it with a hammer. From what I already surmised, it called the community to prayer and to meals. A look out the window at the darkness eliminated the latter.

A monk in good health literally never experiences an unbroken night's sleep, as the principal liturgy begins in the small hours of the morning. Numerous feasts are frequently the occasions for all night vigils. I dressed and went down to chapel. It was the anniversary of my ordination and the day on which some friends back home were being ordained. I wanted a good seat to celebrate it all.

I was one of the first to arrive and slipped into a choir stall in the nave. Despite almost two months of constant participation in Eastern rite liturgies, I would still forget to head for the icon of the Christ and the Theotokos upon entering. There are no genuflections in the Byzantine rite; instead there are icons and metanias. In making a metania, the worshiper lowers his hand with palm turned up either to his knee or all the way to the floor with a deep bow, as if humbly offering his whole being to God in a gesture of surrender and adoration. The act is an expression of humility and penitence, a recognition of our unworthiness in the presence of God. Then one kisses the icon of the Christ and/or the Virgin and Child while making the sign of the cross. The sign of the cross is made in such a way as to express faith in the three basic dogmas and to consecrate oneself to God in all one's human activities: thoughts, actions, and affections. The thumb, index and the middle finger of the right hand are joined together while the third finger and little finger are bent so that they touch the palm of the hand. The three fingers together express faith in the Trinity: one God in three Persons. The two fingers together signify the two natures but one person in Christ. Western Christians who use this sign to evoke their faith in the redemption, Christ's suffering and death on the cross to save us, do so by going from left shoulder to right. The Orthodox follow the reverse: by touching the forehead with the fingers so joined, one consecrates one's thoughts; by touching the breast, one's feelings and sentiments; by touching the right shoulder, one's good actions (since, in Scripture, the right side always represents good); and by touching one's left shoulder, forgiveness of one's sins.

The liturgy and rite of ordination finally got underway. In Orthodox Churches the Book of the Gospels always lies on the middle of the altar. While no mark of worship is paid to the reserved eucharistic elements (when, as is not necessarily the case, they are reserved), each priest approaching the holy table kisses the Gospel first, for the Scriptures are the substance of the dogmas and the liturgies. Just before the first reading, the book was brought forward in the nave for all to venerate. I lined up behind Kostas and Stephanos, but as I drew near to the book, a monk stepped from his choir stall, touched my arm, and motioned me back to my place. The signal was clear: I was not to kiss the book of the Gospels. I left the line and went back to my seat.

After the reading of the Gospel, the same monk came over to me and led me by the arm from my place in the nave into the narthex (the rear portion of the church) where he said to me, indicating a seat against the back wall, "If you wish to watch the ceremony, you may do so from there." The narthex was that portion of the church traditionally reserved for the catechumens, the candidates for the faith who could watch from a distance but not participate.

By that time I felt better in the shadows anyway. Just before Communion in the monasteries, the curtain is drawn over the royal doors of the iconostasis and the monks circulate around the church venerating the icons and making metanias to one another. A monk standing in the doorway between the nave and the narthex turned around and motioned me to come forward and participate in the veneration of the icons. I felt on the horns of a dilemma: I was quite sure I had been sent to the rear with the intent that I stay there. What then was this monk doing signaling me to come forward? He turned and gesticulated a second time, more insistent. Charity, I thought, rules all. I don't want to offend this monk by giving him the impression I don't *want* to enter in. So forward I went and followed suit. No sooner had I finished than my friend of the gentle touch was at my side again, serving me as escort to the rear.

When the service was over, one of the monks walked around distributing the *antidoron,* bread which is blessed at the beginning of the liturgy (but not consecrated during the liturgy) and passed out at the end to all present. Since intercommunion is officially strictly forbidden in the Orthodox Church and even unofficially is not practiced except in the rarest of circumstances, the *antidoron* (which means "in place of the gift") is the way non-Orthodox Christians are made to feel, at least to some extent, in union with the Orthodox worshipers and with the faith expressed in the liturgy. I had received the blessed bread at every Orthodox Divine Liturgy I had ever attended and had just, the Sunday before, received it dressed in my Latin vestment at the liturgy presided at by the Ecumenical Patriarch. The monk who was passing out the bread was now on his second tour, trying to empty the plate. When he passed me by a second time without permitting his eyes to look in my direction, I gave him the benefit of the doubt. I was, after all, in the shadows. By now everyone had left the church save the distributor, who set the plate down on a ledge, and one or two others. It was now 9:30 in the morning. I had persevered for the duration of seven hours, and decided I *deserved* one of those remaining pieces of bread left on the plate. After all it was the anniversary of my ordination.

But he saw me coming. The wag of the finger. The shake of the head. There would be no blessed bread for me today.

The next day the bishop and Kostas set off in one direction and Stephanos and I in another. We walked along a narrow hilly trail which sometimes took us down to the sea and then routed us back up to the bluffs. Our destination was the monastery of Iviron, about an hour and a half walk from Stavronikita. There are no vehicles that travel between the monasteries. All travel is by foot, by mule or by boat. The trails that link the monasteries are like back-packing trails, patterned with rocks and roots and an occasional serpent. Stephanos wanted to talk about our experiences at Stavronikita. He had been well aware of the "special treatment" I received during the ordination liturgy and didn't understand why. "I was talking with three or four monks of the monastery," he offered, "and I asked them why you were treated like that. They said they didn't like you 'acting like an Orthodox.' They believe it creates an illusion of a unity which is not there. They said there are some other monasteries on the Mountain which would have thrown you out."

I thought about that in silence for a while. There was a strange irony to it all. Though the monks of Mount Athos would be displeased to hear it, they have something in common with most Roman Catholics: neither realizes that the Byzantine rite also "belongs" to the Catholic Church. It is truly a universal rite, supranational and confessional. About five percent of the Christian faithful who use the Byzantine rite are in union with Rome. A similar point could be made with the other ancient rites: fifty-eight percent of those who use the Syrian rite, eighty-nine percent of those who use the Chaldean rite, five percent of those who use the Armenian rite, and two percent of those who use the Coptic rite are in union with Rome. When a member of the Roman Catholic Church, therefore, celebrates according to the Byzantine rite, he or she is totally within his or her own "rites" (and hence, "rights"). It's like someone living in "English" Canada deciding to learn French. There may not be many people who are doing it, but it's still one of the official languages of Canada and, strictly speaking, it wouldn't be correct for someone to say: "What are you speaking that foreign language for—that's not yours!" But that's how the monks had seen it. The Byzantine rite was "theirs" and by praying that rite as it should be prayed I was "trying to act like an Orthodox." The fact of the matter was that for the past few months I had been praying according to the Byzantine rite in Chevetogne, in Cairo, and in Jerusalem, most of the time with a congregation who were members of my own Church. From the point of view of many Orthodox (and especially the Athonite community), that is precisely the point: the rite may be the same, but the Church is not. Catholics who celebrate the Byzantine rite tend to be viewed as subversives, as wolves in sheep's clothing, if you will, playing as though they are Orthodox while really retaining their heresies relating to the papacy and the *filioque.*

But as the monastery of Iviron came into sight in a picturesque inlet on the northeast side of the peninsula, I came back at Stephanos with a problem of a practical nature. I had brought a cassock to the Mountain because the Orthodox monks expect to see a priest or religious in a habit and are scandalized to see them in civic attire. Just before leaving Stavronikita the bishop suggested that perhaps I should take it off "lest some of the zealots throw stones at you. If you travel as a simple pilgrim," he said, "it might go easier for you and you may avoid having a bad experience."

There are some internal polarizations on the Mountain. The zealots, a hard-core group of about three hundred monks with a slogan of "Orthodoxy or Death," regard the other monks as impure in their Orthodox faith. In the last two years, police have been called in upon occasion to deal with skirmishes between zealots and moderates in their tussle for control of monasteries. Some analysts on the local scene say that the zealots feel threatened by the new recruits, some of whom have more "European" ideas such as advocating practical good-deed functions instead of concentrating on Orthodox mysticism, or who support the Ecumenical Patriarch even though he has entered into various ecumenical contacts.

Stephanos and I pulled up on a turn in the trail that looks down at Iviron, set low and close to the sea. I posed the question to Steve. What was it to be: Should I immediately identify myself for cool treatment by arriving in a cassock, or should I risk scandalizing them if they find out I'm a priest and not wearing it? The decision was largely worked out on empirical grounds. I had worn the cassock in the last monastery and it had not been a very good experience. The only way to know if the other option would make any difference was to try it. We decided in favor of "simple-pilgrim" status.

As soon as we arrived at Iviron, we joined in with a group of Greeks who were being taken on a tour of the treasury, library and church. We were standing at the door of the church when a slender red-bearded monk came out. He looked at us and, seeing me, paused as if trying to remember something. Then he drew near and pointed a finger at me: "Katholikos?"

"Nai" (yes), I answered.

"Hiereus?" (Priest?)

"Nai," I answered again. Then he motioned to his own garb, and then at mine, with a question that I did not understand in Greek, but understood in Human. "Oh, no," I thought; "it's happening." But how did he know?

Just then Stephanos came out of the church where he had been taking pictures. "Steve," I said with utter resignation, "help!" The red-bearded one was now talking with the monk who was leading our group. There was no question about what, for the eyes of all the Greeks in the group were now turned in my direction. Stephanos listened long enough to get the gist of what had transpired and then turned and said to me, "The red-haired monk was at the ordination. He saw you and wants to know why you haven't got your habit on."

Then Stephanos interceded for me and explained that I had been told by the bishop that it would perhaps be better if I took it off. They considered that and, with the group of Greeks as a silent but attentive jury, tried my case.

In spite of all my good intentions, it was the second monastery in a row in which I'd gotten off on the wrong foot. I was in the process of taking "the law" into my own hands and was opening my little satchel to take out and put on the black robe when the judges decided that, no, if the bishop had told me to take it off, I could leave it off.

The following morning we got on the "taxi" boat for Great Lavra, the earliest and biggest establishment on the Mountain. Built on a rocky outcrop where the peninsula ends, it stands where Mount Athos itself shelves gently down to the sea in green hillocks. Its port is guarded by a fortification tower, a throwback to an age when the monasteries were pillaged by frequent pirate raids. It was a good twenty-minute climb from the dock to the monastery gate, over which hung a large icon of the Theotokos. The foundation of this monastery marked the changeover on Athos from individual asceticism to organized monasticism.

Today the monasteries are divided into two categories: coenobitic and idiorrhythmic. The former live a community life, property is held in common and a common rule is followed under obedience to a single abbot, very much as in the Western tradition of Benedictine monasticism and its offshoots. The latter live their monastic lives at their own rhythm, as the name indicates. They are really groups of hermits living together for general convenience but following their individual intuitions without a common rule or submission to a common leadership except in a very general way. They may own small plots of land, money for routine purchases, and personal property in general. No organized form of Western monasticism provides an exact analogue. Of the twenty ruling monasteries fourteen are now coenobitic and the remaining seven idiorrhythmic. The monks of Great Lavra (*Lavra* here means a monastery with a great number of monks) had just a year previous voted to change from an idiorrhythmic to a coenobitic lifestyle. We arrived just in time for noonday prayer. The meager attendance indicated that a good many monks were still struggling to make the shift from an individual to a communal approach.

Though I could not join in on the prayers in Greek, there are always a good many things to look at in an Orthodox church. The iconostasis, a high wall or screen covered with rows of icons which divides the chancel from the nave, was particularly beautiful. At one time in the past, it was just a chancel rail or Communion-type rail as in Western churches.

With the victory over iconoclasm in the ninth century, those who had supported the veneration of images triumphantly placed them in the opening of the chancel rail until it was so full and high that it became an image-screen with three doors in it leading into the sanctuary. The central opening is called the Royal Gate because through it the King of Glory comes to feed his people with the word of the Gospels and the Eucharist.

With time the holy images came to have a standard placement in the screen. The customary arrangement is generally as follows: to the right of the Royal Gate is the image of the Savior, and next to it the image of the patron saint of the church. On the left of the Holy Door is the image of the Theotokos (God-bearer, Mary) and, next to it, St. John the Baptist. On the Royal Doors themselves is depicted the annunciation, since it was through that event that we received the good news, and the four evangelists who, like the Archangel Gabriel, announced to the world the glad tidings of the Savior. Over the central door is the Last Supper, reminding us that those who wish to obtain entrance to the kingdom of heaven (symbolized by the area behind the screen) must be accounted worthy to partake of the Lord's Supper which is prepared within the Holy Door. On the northern and southern doors are depicted angels, the messengers of God, or holy deacons.

In large churches there is a second row above these, images of the feasts of our Lord, and of the Theotokos. Sometimes there is a third row which includes the images of saints. The overall effect is of a wall of carefully ordered images that extends from the floor to near the ceiling, depending on how many rows of icons are placed atop one another.

In Greek, icon literally means "image" or "portrait." When the Christian image was being created in Byzantium, this word was used to mean all representations of Christ, the Virgin, a saint, an angel, or an event from sacred history. Yet it is not just a simple image or decoration. It is something greater. It is an object of worship and an integral part of the liturgy. This explains why some Orthodox object to the placing of icons in museums, where they might receive much artistic appreciation but little reverence, not to mention the now fashionable accumulation of icons for large sums of money as investment items to be parted with a few years later for vast sums of money when the market is right. One does not need to be Orthodox to sense the moral outrage involved in reducing a sacred object to an object of financial speculation and commercial barter.

According to the teaching of the early Fathers, icons correspond to the word of Scripture. "That which the word communicates by sound, the painting shows silently by representation," says St. Basil the Great. And the Fathers of the seventh ecumenical council (787) repeat these words and specify that "through these two mediums which accompany each other . . . we acquire the knowledge of the same realities." The icon is often called "theology in images."

Nowhere did Christ order that his words be written down. Nevertheless, said St. Theodore the Studite, "his image was drawn in writing by the apostles and preserved up to the present. What is, on the one hand, represented with ink and paper is represented on an icon with various colors or other materials." In other words, the visible image is to be venerated in the same way as the verbal image. For the Church therefore the icon is not an art illustrating Holy Scripture, but a language corresponding to the very meaning of Scripture, just as the liturgical texts do. Hence, the icon plays the same role as Scripture in the Church, and both through the liturgy and the icon the Scripture lives in the Church. If the word and the song of the Church sanctify our soul by means of hearing, the image sanctifies by means of sight.

The teaching of the seventh council is that the image is based on the incarnation of the Second Person of the Trinity. The prohibition of the image which appears in Exodus (20:4) and in Deuteronomy (5:12–19) is a provisional measure which concerns only the Old Testament in which, when God forbids the making of his image, he stresses the fact that he is invisible. To be sure, neither the people, nor even Moses, saw any image of him. They only heard his words. Not having seen God's image, they could not represent it. They could only write down his divine word, which is what Moses did. "But," wrote St. John of Damascus, "when the Invisible, having clothed himself in the flesh, becomes visible, then represent the likeness of him who has appeared . . . then paint and make visible to everyone him who desired to become visible." The words of the Lord in the Old Testament mean: "Create no images of God *as long as* you have not seen him." In the New Testament, the non-representable became representable.

Thus, the truth is revealed not only by the word but it is also shown by the image. In fact, Truth has its own image, for it is not an idea or abstract formula, but a concrete, living Person who was "crucified under Pontius Pilatus and on the third day rose from the dead." This is why the Church not only *speaks* of the truth, but also *shows* the truth: the image of Christ. Of course, the honor rendered to an image goes to its prototype, not to the materials of which the image is made. A person who venerates an icon venerates the person represented on it.

I left my seat to look more closely at the icon of St. Athanasios, founder of Great Lavra in 963 and its patron. In iconography a saint is portrayed as a living icon of God. The painted icon is an external expression of this holiness. An icon never transmits the "everyday" face of a person, but his glorious and eternal face. Athanasios' flesh is represented completely different from ordinary corruptible flesh because his icon is the image of a man in whom the grace which consumes passions and which sanctifies everything is truly present. His face transmits peacefulness and is absolutely devoid of all emotional exaltation, communicating a spiritual reality. The icon does not represent him as divine, but as participating in the divine life, as a man who has become a living icon, a true likeness of God. The monks will kiss this image because they believe the grace of God rests upon it and in it. The Holy Spirit which filled the saints during their lives is believed to live on inexhaustibly, even after their death, in their souls, in their mortal remains (hence, veneration of relics), in their writings, and in their holy images—not because of their nature, but as a result of grace and divine action.

As I looked at the other images in the iconostasis, it was

evident that the artists' intention was not to represent these people in their "natural" state, as we see them in life, but to show us a body which perceives what usually escapes our attention: the spiritual world. Their eyes, their whole regard, conveys deafness, impassiveness, detachment from all excitation. Their entire body, their hair and wrinkles, even the garments and all that surrounds them, is unified and restored to a supreme harmony. It is a visible expression of the victory over the inner division and chaos in us and in the world.

In many Orthodox churches, the walls are covered with frescoes. In them everything loses its usual aspect of disorder and acquires a harmonious sense—people, landscape, animals and architecture. Everything that surrounds the saints falls into a rhythmic order. Everything, in short, reflects the divine presence and draws us toward God. From this arises the simplicity, the majesty, the calm of the icon: divine grace, and not the rational categories of the earth or human mortality, reigns in it. What one is looking at is precisely the new order of the new creation. The divine light penetrates everything, and this is why the person and the objects are not illuminated, as are statues, from one side or the other by a source of light. Icons do not project shadows because there is no darkness and light in the kingdom of God. In the frescoes, the saints are very much before us, not somewhere in space. They are rarely portrayed in profile, almost always face-on, so that there can be direct contact, so that we can converse with them. The icon participates in the holiness of the one presented, and through the icon we in turn participate in this holiness in our prayers.

The rules that guide the painters are quite strict. The relationship between the icon and the Holy Scripture, its conformity with the biblical preaching, completely excludes any possibility of painting icons of Christ or of the saints according to the painter's imagination. The decoration of Orthodox churches does not depend on individual conceptions of artists. There are fixed stylistic guides for individual icons or scenes, and the iconographic themes are determined according to the meaning of that part of the church where they will be placed. A careful distinction is made, for example, between an icon and a portrait: the latter representing an ordinary human being, and the former a person united to God. Yet it is essential to abide by an image reproducing, to the greatest degree possible, the physical traits of that historical person as a means of preserving a direct and living link with the man or woman whom the icon represents.

In order to avoid a falsehood and break between the image and its prototype, iconographers use old icons and manuals as models. The ancient iconographers knew the faces of the saints either from memory or by reference to a sketch or portrait, for once a person had acquired a reputation for holiness, an image was made to distribute among the faithful. The artist is expected to limit himself or herself to a few characteristic traits. In the majority of cases the faithfulness to the original is such that a faithful Orthodox can easily recognize the icons of favorite saints, to say nothing of Christ and the Virgin.

What was the original painting or sketch used as a guide for icons of Christ? Some hypothesize that surely St. Luke, who was also reported to be an artist, would have put his hand to a visible image as well as a written record. In Canterbury, England, I saw a display showing the marked similarity between the classical icons of Christ and the image on the Shroud of Turin which would have been available for the veneration of the faithful in the early times, and hence as a model for iconographers.

In any case, the very existence of the icon is based on the incarnation of the Second Person of the Trinity—which incarnation, in turn, is confirmed and proven by image. The icon is a proof that the divine incarnation was not an illusion. This is why, in the eyes of the Orthodox Church, an attack against the icon of Christ is an attack on his incarnation and against the whole economy of salvation for which the incarnation is the central event.

Later that afternoon I met the abbot of Great Lavra monastery, a marvelous man with a wide benevolent face inside a snow-white beard that hung to the middle of his chest. We sat on the steps of an outdoor shrine to the Virgin and talked, with Stephanos facilitating as interpreter.

"Fr. Athanasios," I asked him, "do the monks here pray for unity?"

"What is unity?" he asked rhetorically. "Unity has to be others coming back to us. We are the only ones who have not departed from the truth. That which was established in the first seven councils remains an unbroken tradition in Orthodoxy. The Roman Catholic Church needs to repent of the things it brought in afterward: the universal jurisdiction of the Pope, the Immaculate Conception, and the *filioque*. This is the face of unity."

Orthodoxy, while holding in high honor the role of the Blessed Virgin as Christ's mother, sees no need for any dogma of the Immaculate Conception. In its liturgical worship it addresses Mary as "spotless," "all-holy," and "altogether without stain," but since it does not envisage the fall in Augustinian terms (as a taint of inherited guilt to be washed away), the Latin dogma of the Immaculate Conception seems not so much erroneous as superfluous. Orthodox believe in the assumption of Mary into heaven where she now dwells—with her body as well as her soul—in eternal glory with her Son, but they choose not to define it dogmatically. The Orthodox Church veils and covers what the Latin Church lays open and exhibits. Orthodoxy fears familiarity. Christians of that Church feel reluctant to regulate the approach to the holy mysteries by precise disciplinary canons and to utter too detailed statements on the nature of such and such a mystery. The Orthodox avoid giving officially too many strict definitions, for the simple reason that they want a mystery to remain a mystery.

The *filioque* is the doctrinal formulation expressing the procession of the Holy Spirit from God the Father *and the Son* (in Latin: *filioque*) which the West added to the Nicene Creed. It is now generally admitted even by Roman Catholics that the *filioque* was inserted into the Creed in a way that failed to respect the authority of an ecumenical council and which neglected proper respect for verifying a truly catholic consensus.

But the long-standing debates about the *filioque* between Byzantium and the West could lead to the mistaken notion that in fact the two Churches do not share common views about the Holy Spirit. Actually both Latin- and Greek-speaking Christians shared the same faith, as do East and West today, about the Spirit's inspiration of Holy Scripture, about the Spirit's presence in the sacraments of the Church, and in charisms and graces poured out by the Spirit upon believers. In both Churches the Spirit of God is seen as guiding saints and helping bishops gathered at local synods and ecumenical councils. Reading ancient liturgical texts, one would be hard put, apart from different languages, to identify this liturgy as typically Eastern and that one Western, in regard to its view of the Spirit. Not before the seventh century was there an awareness that liturgical and theological terms used to describe the interior life of the Blessed Trinity, especially in regard to the "procession" of the Holy Spirit, were different.

This divergence between Byzantium and Rome was part of a far broader estrangement of long duration. The tension developed between the Old Rome and the New Rome (Constantinople) or perhaps more accurately between Constantinople and Aachen, symbol of the growing Frankish influence in the Latin church especially after the establishment under Charlemagne of a Holy "Roman" Empire. Constantinople saw this new empire as divisive, thwarting the ancient "Roman" dream of religious and political unity.

The Frankish West, especially at the early local councils that took place in Toledo (A.D. 589, 633), relied on the so-called Athanasian Creed which they, with the rest of the Latin Church through the Middle Ages, mistakenly attributed to the bishop of Alexandria, St. Athanasius (d. 373), the so-called Athanasian Creed. It is only in our day that we know that the Creed was actually written first in Latin about A.D. 500 in southern Gaul. This Creed, which mentioned a procession of the Holy Spirit from the Father and the Son, was congenial to the council fathers at Toledo because it served to present a markedly anti-Arian teaching regarding Christ. For if the Spirit proceeded from both the Father and the Son, then the Son was not in any way inferior to the Father, as the Arian position implied. So when Visigoth King Reccared I entered the Catholic Church from Arianism (A.D. 589) it was useful to have a creedal statement that was unabashedly anti-Arian. The West was not tinkering with the theology of the Holy Spirit; it simply wanted to assert strongly the divinity of Christ.

The cultural-political dimension was that when the Byzantine Church later realized that there was a different Western formula (". . . the Holy Spirit, who proceeds from the Father and the Son" as opposed to just "from the Father"), it saw this as one further example of a Frankish allegation of doubtful value. The insertion of the *filioque* into the sacrosanct Nicene Creed was taken as proof of Roman fears before Frankish rulers and ultimately of Roman capitulation to Frankish demands.

The Churches have long differed on the choice of language to describe the Spirit within the eternal life of the Blessed Trinity, and that eventually contributed a theological dimension to the problem. Both attempted to express in their own way the unity and the diversity of three persons in one God. The West spoke of the principle of unity being a "common divine essence." The Byzantines spoke of the Father as being the source of unity. To their mind "divine essence" is distorted by the West into an abstract idea of divinity and makes of God a philosophical conception rather than a Person. This is the basic Orthodox theological objection. It is seen as an important question because if the basis of the Church's existence is the Holy Trinity, the vision one has of the Church depends on how one approaches the mystery of God. Furthermore, the Western expression of a procession from the Father to the Son to the Holy Spirit emphasizes the hierarchical aspect of the Church one-sidedly. A line of authority is accented and the person of the Holy Spirit is pushed as it were into the background. For the Orthodox, the *filioque* with its attendant notion of a "common divine essence" as the uniting principle of the Trinity is the "symbol" of a distorted view of the Church.

What Byzantine theology has not always appreciated is that the Latins perceived the Father as the special origin within the Trinity, and hence as the uniting source. When the West said that the Spirit proceeds from the Father and the Son, this did not mean that the Father was prevented from being the source—and hence the "uniting principle"—of the whole of divinity. Nor did it mean that the Spirit proceeds from the Son independently of the Father.

The West defended the development of another theological tradition on pastoral grounds. It reasoned that if it was pastorally expedient to add some words that did not distort the faith, indeed words that helped *preserve* the true faith, then this was not innovating but simply continuing a process begun at earlier councils. It must be said however that this reasoning remained at first implicit and became the subject of explicit reflection only after Byzantine objections to the addition of the *filioque*. At the Council of Florence in the fifteenth century the West explained that the *filioque* was "legitimately and reasonably joined to the Creed to declare its truth, since there was an urgent necessity at that time."

In spite of the fact that some continue to find the *filioque* the best way of thinking about the procession of the Holy Spirit in the Trinity, many reason that it has no place in a Creed intended to express not a particular theological opinion but the common faith of East and West. The delicate question is how Western Christianity without acting separately along confessional boundaries could agree to omit the *filioque* addition. Occasionally in a spontaneous or deliberate gesture, Western Church leaders will omit the controversial expression. Even the Bishop of Rome on the occasion of praying the Creed in the presence of Eastern Christians has in recent years publicly omitted the addition. A recent example was Pentecost Sunday 1981. Joint celebrations were taking place in both Constantinople and Rome commemorating the Second Ecumenical Council of 381. Metropolitan Damaskinos preached in St. Peter's Basilica at Vespers on the vigil of the feast, and the following day Pope John Paul II used the Creed agreed upon at the Council of 381 which said that the Spirit "proceeds from the Father."

Whether the decision reached through dialogue and prayer is to drop the *filioque* or to retain it in some Churches, what is important is a deeper comprehension of how the Holy Spirit has worked in different ages and different traditions. Not to

appreciate the truth expressed in other traditions is to be blind
to the saving grace of the Spirit of God.

"I can see you are searching for truth," Fr. Athanasios said
in response to my questions. "You can find it here. Why don't
you stay with us and I will baptize you myself?"

That night, as we were in our room, there came a knock
on the door. Stephanos was already in bed, and I was writing in
my journal. A tall, thin monk entered. His beard was so raven-
black that I could scarcely discern where his long whiskers
ended and the black of his cassock began. His eyes were deep
set and his face gaunt, accentuated by the shadows thrown by
the lantern in whose light I had been writing.

"My name is Fr. Maximos," he offered. "Fr. Athanasios
told me to come by. Since I speak English, he thought we
would be able to talk more freely." I was delighted.

I began by asking him about life on the Mountain. What
was the procedure for becoming a monk? "One to three years
as a novice, and then one becomes a monk—which is always
the goal, not priesthood. That can happen anytime after." And
what about studies? "The education of the monks is quite poor
in general. The West has traditionally been much more concerned than the East with formal study, with defining the
Christian truth in terms which could be more readily understood, with giving man concrete norms for his behavior. But
people can study a lot without ever having their heart
touched. Here, that is what is most important. One's mind
must be in one's heart, and the two must be illuminated by the
energies of God."

The view of humankind prevailing in the Christian East is
based upon the notion of "participation" in God. The human
person has not been created as an autonomous or self-sufficient
being; one's very nature is truly itself only inasmuch as it exists
"in God" or "in grace." This explains why the terms "nature"
and "grace," when used by the Orthodox, have a meaning
quite different from Western usage. The Christian East did not
experience the controversies which raged in the West around
the notions of grace and predestination (Augustinianism, Pelagianism, Semi-Pelagianism, Thomism, Calvinism, Jansenism,

Molinism). The Greek Fathers did not have to deal with the Pelagian heresy which said that a person can find salvation without God's grace. Pelagius believed that all that is needed is the good example of Jesus to follow.

In the Orthodox Church the terms "nature" and "grace" express a dynamic, living, necessary relation between God and humankind. The most important aspect of Greek patristic anthopology is the notion that we only realize our true humanity when we live "in God" and possess divine qualities. The presence in us of divine qualities, of a "grace" which is part of our nature and which makes us fully human, neither destroys our freedom nor limits the necessity for us to realize our full potential by our own efforts. The presence in us of grace secures that cooperation, or "synergy," between the divine will and human choice which makes possible our assimilation to the divine dignity for which we were created. We are called to share in the "deified" humanity of Christ. "God became man," as St. Athanasius put it, "so that man might become God." This is the meaning of the sacramental life and the basis of Christian spirituality. Basil described man as a creature who has received the order to become a god, but it is not through our own activity or "energy" that we can be deified—that would be Pelagianism—but by divine "energy" to which our human activity is obedient. The word "synergy," coined by Clement of Alexandria, expresses the action of these two conjoined energies: grace and human will. Grace, however, is not to be thought of as some "stuff" we received from God, but as God himself.

The term and idea of synergy have remained and represent the doctrine of the Orthodox Church on these matters. For the entire patristic and Byzantine tradition, knowledge of God implies "participation" in God, i.e., not only intellectual knowledge, but a state of the entire human being, transformed by grace and freely cooperating with it by the efforts of both mind and will. "Participation" in God *is* our very nature, not its abolition.

Fr. Maximos' sunken cheeks worked with a great energy

and his words were drawn from a well of certitude: "One doesn't need formal studies in theology to have one's heart touched and one's life purified and illuminated. It is not our way in the East to be too concerned about what we know and how we measure what we know. We are not preoccupied with academic degrees. In the West the monasteries became little universities in the Middle Ages, and the approach to God was through knowledge and the sciences. This is not our way. Our way is apophatic. We reject every image and concept as inadequate to portray the unknowable plenitude of the Trinity. Our way is not knowledge, but rather ascension toward a deifying union, the *experience* of the burning nearness of God. I am afraid that we in the East and you in the West inhabit two entirely different worlds. We worship two different Gods. We are like a lion and a bear."

I wanted to object but knew that if I took that path it would be a long one. We had already talked for two hours and it was past midnight. I had, besides, the sneaking suspicion that his intense, convicted tones were keeping those in the dormitories around us awake. I decided in favor of one last question: "What is the relationship between Mount Athos and the Ecumenical Patriarch?"

"We pray for him in the canon of the liturgy so as to preserve unity, but we are not pleased with the announcement of the beginning of international 'official' dialogues with the Roman Catholic Church, with the goal of eventually resuming full communion. We are wary of compromise. We feel that the Christian West, and, in this particular case, Rome, has blurred the ancient tradition and now wants us to do the same. These theologians who are meeting end their discussions with common prayer. We believe that people cannot even pray together until there is complete agreement on all points of doctrine."

"Cannot even *pray* together?" I asked, wanting to make sure I had heard right and congratulating myself on the level of restraint in my voice.

He affirmed that I had heard him correctly.

All of a sudden I understood the attitude of the monks toward me during the ordination liturgy at the monastery of Stavronikita, why I had been given such a clear message of "you can '*watch*' but you can't participate."

There is a conservatism in the Orthodox Church in Greece—this is especially true of Mount Athos—which most other Orthodox view as exaggerated.

Further, in an age of ecumenism and in particular in the wake of very cordial relations being established between the Patriarch of Constantinople and the Pope of Rome, one might hope to see on Athos an opening toward other Churches, or toward other monastic traditions, or in any case a receptiveness to the interest shown by non-Orthodox visitors in Orthodox belief and practice. To find that the recent papal visit to Constantinople has actually had an adverse effect comes as a shock. The present Ecumenical Patriarch is openly criticized for talking with Rome, in harsh terms that revolve around the concepts of sell-out and betrayal, and at least one monastery has actually gone so far as to omit his commemoration in the liturgy, creating a status little short of schism. No less than six of the twenty ruling houses now refuse to permit non-Orthodox visitors to attend the liturgy at all, an attitude which with the best will in the world is hard to understand.

An official announcement issued in April 1980, from the joint governing body of Athos concerning the dialogue between the Orthodox and Roman Catholics, stated:

> ... Dialogue with the heterodox is not reprehensible from the Orthodox point of view if its goal is to inform them of the Orthodox Faith, and, thus, make it possible for them thereby to return to Orthodoxy when they receive divine enlightenment and their eyes are opened.

> Theological dialogue must not in any way be linked with prayer in common, or by joint participation in any liturgical or worship services whatsoever. ...

> Moreover, the Holy Mountain cannot accept the opinion, expressed in the joint statement of the Patriarch and the Pope, concerning the "cleansing of the historical memory of

our Churches" and the partial opening, by means of a dialogue of love, of the road toward "new movements in theological work and a new attitude to the past which is common to both Churches." Actually, the heretics must cleanse their own historical memory of all their own historically acknowledged deviations in Faith and practice from the true, evangelical Orthodox Faith. . . .

Likewise, the Holy Mountain is disturbed by the great weakness and insufficiency of the Orthodox delegation. . . . The Holy Mountain is . . . not represented, despite the fact that it is the sole monastic center which preserves the Faith and the theology of the Fathers, and which is far removed from the influence of secularism and Scholastic Western theology.

. . . Real help is given only when the Orthodox show (the heterodox) the vastness of their spiritual sickness and the means of its cure by maintaining a consistently Orthodox position.

Fr. Maximos told me of another monk I might want to talk with. "He is from the West," he said, "and he will be able to understand your questions better. When all is said and done, I am still a Greek."

"Where is he from?" I asked.

"From Quebec. He was formerly a Benedictine monk at St. Benoît du Lac Monastery there."

The next morning I set off walking to Prodromos as if to see a fellow patriot.

André Vachon's surprise to be greeted by a Montrealer as he worked in his monastic garden some seven hundred and fifty feet above the sea was surpassed only by his pleasure at being able to speak his native tongue. After lunch I helped him with his kitchen duty so that we could have more time to talk. Fr. Maximos had been right: André did understand better where my questions were coming from. His familiarity with the Western Fathers was truly admirable, and the integration he had made between Western and Eastern theological thought left me envious.

We discussed at length Augustine's impact on the present situation. Augustine had not been in touch with Greek thought because he couldn't read Greek. In fact, it was not until the Middle Ages that theologians in the West began to read in Latin the works of the Eastern Fathers, but by then it was too late. Augustine is a critical turning point because with him Western thought becomes centered on the question: How much can the human person do, how far can he or she go and within what limits, in the struggle for and with the Divine? Even the great Western mystics, like St. John of the Cross, were working within a framework established by Augustine. John, in his "dark night of the soul," speaks of passing by this limit and that limit whereas, in the Greek Fathers, what God is by nature, man is by grace. Your roots are already in heaven. The "seeds of divinization" are given to you in baptism, and all you need to do is let it grow and take over your whole life. The Son was not given to us to be "imitated," as in Thomas a Kempis' *Imitation of Christ,* a Western classic; rather the Spirit was given to us to "flesh out" Jesus Christ *in* our very selves.

In talking about East and West, André raised a question which occupied us for a good part of the five or six hours we discussed. "One of the most frequent criticisms brought to bear upon the Orthodox Church is the lack of a central voice of authority," André said. "The Orthodox have developed into national churches that have in practice become completely autonomous in their relations to one another. Any given Church will react vehemently when a leading outside patriarch tries to interfere in its government. And this is seen as a serious weakness. 'The West has one Pope, but you have fifteen,' it is said.

"The Roman Catholic Church, for example, looks 'more together,' but is it? True, it has organization, universal jurisdiction of the Pope, national and international bishops' synods, but underneath that is there a plurality of theologies that people adhere to? Is there an *à la carte* approach to the doctrine of the Church with people choosing only what they want and leaving the rest? Can adherence to dogma and living the spiritual life go forward quite independently of one another? Take, for example, someone who chooses to disregard birth control or the Immaculate Conception and still considers himself or herself living the spiritual life in union with his or her Church.

"In the East, on the other hand, on the surface what one sees is a lack of organization and unity. But underneath that, there is the same theology—fewer, but clear doctrines, held by all; the same liturgy, with a minimum of variation in style or content. There is but one rule for monks, and one habit (Orthodox monks live according to a rule drawn up by St. Basil in the fourth century and there is no proliferation of different orders, such as Jesuit, Benedictine, Dominican, etc., each with its different rule and habit). And in spiritual life, there is a sense that unless your behavior lines up with your dogmas, there's a falseness to it. How do we evaluate all this? What kind of unity is more important for the Church?"

André and his superior invited me to stay with them that night; the time had been too short, they said. I agreed, but had told Stephanos I would meet him on the late afternoon boat coming around the point. As André walked me down to the sea, I asked him a question that had been troubling me. "The Orthodox Church that I have experienced outside of Mount Athos has been considerably more open in terms of things ecumenical. Which am I to take as the real interpreter of Orthodoxy?"

"There are two principles," he replied, *acribeia* (strictness) and *oikonomia* (latitude). The Orthodox Church in the world has to adapt itself to the reality of others around it, and so lives according to the principle of latitude. On Mount Athos the monks believe that the faith should be preserved in its purity and depth so that Orthodoxy in all its plenitude can be found somewhere in the world without any compromise. Thus life here is according to the principle of strictness. I think both are important and necessary."

I hardly had time to thank him as I got into the boat. I would have liked to stay longer, but it was just as well; my head could hold no more. The taxi boat puttered around the furthermost point of the Athonite peninsula. I leaned back on the bow of the boat studying the dreaded Karoulia for any sign of life. On these wild cliffs that rose sheer from the sea lived the ascetics and hermits, seemingly beyond any connection with the world, heedless of bodily needs. The sun glinted off the chain and metal ladders which led to the isolated huts, rickety structured cottages, and caves which ensure the hermits' peace and isolation by simulating the conditions of the desert where monasticism began. "There lived Maximos," a monk was pointing out, "a fourteenth century hermit who burned his hut every time he saw others preparing to live too close to him, replacing it with another higher up the cliffs."

"What do they do there all day?" asked a pilgrim in the boat.

"They entreat God day and night for their own salvation and that of all humanity," came the reply. The monks in the boat, moving the black-knotted rosary through their fingers as they wordlessly repeated "Kyrie Eleison" hour upon hour, lent credibility to a statement which in any other context would have sounded hyperbolic.

It was at Simopetra, the most daring building on the Holy Mountain, that both Stephanos and I had experiences which caused our blood pressure to rise. According to tradition, the first volunteer monks who offered their assistance to build the monastery on that spot were so frightened by the dizzying heights that they abandoned work in the middle. It was not the height which put Stephanos in a temper to leave.

After the Divine Liturgy one morning, a monk approached him and invited him to make his confession. The Byzantines seldom confess their sins to another, at least in the secular world, but Stephanos was willing. Confession is regularly practiced in the monasteries but is quite indistinguishable from a direction of conscience by the Spiritual Father. In Eastern ascetical literature it is nowhere evident that a priest's absolution is necessary to seal the act of repentance. Thus confession and penance, at least ideally, preserved more the character of liberation and healing rather than judgment.

But when Stephanos returned, he was not healed. Upon

learning that he was divorced and remarried, the monk with whom he had spoken had told him that he must leave his present wife and go back to his former. It was interesting for me to see that even a member of the Orthodox Church could find the Mountain more orthodox than Orthodoxy. For the Byzantine tradition approaches the problem of remarriage in terms of penitential discipline. Laymen, after a period of penitence and abstention from the sacraments, are readmitted to full communion with the Church, even after a second or a third marriage. The Orthodox Church accepts the possibility of an initial mistake and recognizes that single life, in cases of the death of a spouse, can be a greater evil than remarriage for those who cannot bear living alone. Absolute unicity as the norm of Christian marriage is also affirmed in that it is strictly required from the clergy. A man who has married twice, or was married to a widow or a divorcée, is not eligible for ordination to the diaconate or priesthood.

For laymen, an essential distinction between the first and following marriages is maintained. There is a special service dissociated from the Eucharist and penitential in character. It is understood that second and third marriages are not the norm, and as such are sacramentally deficient.

While both the Orthodox East and the Latin West have strongly emphasized the unicity of Christian marriage, the Orthodox Church sees the marriage bond as eternal. The West has been guided in its practice by the more legal notion of a contract which is automatically dissolved by the death of one of the partners. Remarriage of the widowed among the Orthodox is only tolerated, in the same sense as the remarriage of the divorced. This toleration does not signal approval, and implies repentance.

With regard to marriage and divorce, pastoral practice among the Orthodox has been guided by the following notions: sacraments require a free response which implies the possibility of a human rejection or mistake. After a sinful rejection or human mistake, repentance is always accessible and allows a new beginning.

The East considered divorce an inevitable factor of life in

the fallen world where humans can accept grace and refuse it. The Church's function is to find ways of showing compassion and mercy to human weakness without compromising the norms of the Gospel. This was the theological basis for the toleration of divorce in the early Christian Church as well as in Byzantium.

The response Stephanos had received from his confessor had not been characterized, to his mind, by the notes of mercy and compassion, and he was upset. I had my own little confrontation a few hours later.

There were ten beds in our guest dormitory, but only four were filled: by Stephanos, myself, and two lay Orthodox from the United States. One night we all took a break in our bedtime reading about the same moment and fell to discussing. The two Greek-Americans were interested in my motive for coming to the Mountain. When I had finished with a brief exposition, one of them rather casually reflected on what different religious worlds we inhabited. I asked him what he meant and invited him to go further. What came out was another version of Fr. Maximos' "We-worship-different-Gods-and-we're-as-different-as-a-bear-and-a-lion" analysis. Again it was late, but Stephanos and I were leaving the next morning, so there was no reason to save my energy. I had heard that analysis voiced on Athos once too often. It is a general misnomer that ecumenism is all polite concord and avoidance of anything resembling disagreement. To make my rebuttal, I set in mental order the points they had made: that we have a radically different approach to how we even know God; that the Trinitarian theologies of Byzantium and the West are sharply irreconcilable; that the West ignores the Holy Spirit; and that the decrees of the councils that have transpired in the West since the schism would never be acceptable to the Orthodox.

The West, it seemed to me, had been given short shrift. I set myself to put forth a different perspective, one held by a great many Western Christians.

How we seek to know God: Our common Christian tradition claims two ways. One says that we should eliminate all images and symbols for God because they are all inadequate. In this way (called apophatic), God is experienced in the quiet and darkness of contemplation. This has been, by and large, the Eastern way. The other way (cataphatic) says that God *can* be contacted through creation. Christ is proof; he is God's icon. And in him God is present in a real and positive way in creation and salvation history. But to place one way totally in the East and the other approach to God completely in the West is to oversimplify the situation, because Eastern and Western spirituality have always included both. They have *had* to. One's journey inward does not take place without benefit of Jesus Christ and the liturgy of the Church. Neither does the way of meeting God in history and creation end there; those points of contact are meant to lead us beyond to a superior, spiritual knowledge of God. The Incarnate Lord and the liturgy of the Church are the doors through which one passes. These different approaches to the knowledge of God do not amount to different statements of faith. Rather they represent development which from divergent perspectives make valuable contributions to our common quest to know God through every possible avenue available to us.

Our speculation about the Trinity: The most serious difference between the Byzantine theologies connected with Constantinople and the Church of the West concerns the formulation of the truth about the procession of the Holy Spirit being either from the Father alone or from the Father *and* the Son. Each way of thinking about the Trinity has its respective originality and merit. On the practical level between the Churches, this formulation of the *filioque* was used in parts of the West since the sixth century and for several centuries it never prevented the union of the Churches, nor should it impede their reunion. It was invoked as a problem when the drift had already widened through other issues. It does not represent an irremediable contradiction. Again, the different formulations are not at the level of faith. A better barometer than dogma whereby to judge whether there is any *real* difference between us is in the faith that is *lived.* And the faith that is lived and used in the spiritual life in both Churches is the same despite the difference in the dogmatic formulation. That is the

bottom line, the essential criterion. The too facile categoriza-
tions of theologies that differ in emphasis but not in orthodoxy
will have to disappear. As for the way the common faith is articulated, that can be and is being worked out.

*The Holy Spirit has been given little attention in the life
of the Church in the West:* That is true. For a long time we
have had an impoverished and underdeveloped sense of the
Spirit's role in the life and mission of the Church. But if there
has been a revolution in any area of the Western Church's life,
it has been here. Witness the charismatic movement which has
cut across all denominational lines. Witness the deeper awareness and respect for the *epiclesis* (a prayer calling down the
transforming power of the Holy Spirit on the eucharistic elements) in the Roman canon, stressing the importance of the
Spirit's role in what happens, and restoring a long-needed anti-
dote to an overemphasis on the words by which Jesus instituted the Eucharist. Even among the theologians there is a whole
new vocabulary. They used to talk about the Church as a con-
tinuation of the incarnation. Now they speak in terms of a con-
tinuation of the mission of the Spirit. The West is no longer
without anything to say when the Holy Spirit is mentioned.

*The decrees of un-ecumenical councils as a problem for re-
union:* On the face of it, the difficulty centers around those
councils held in the West and approved by the Pope *after* the
schism. Rome has already offered a solution. Pope Paul VI
demonstrated that Roman Catholic theology is willing to consider the notion of varying degrees of councils. Although general councils in the West have been called "ecumenical"
(which means including representatives for *all* Christians), that
just reflects popular usage. Pope Paul was ready to popularize
the notion that there are two sorts of councils in the patrimony
of the West: the early ecumenical councils of the undivided
Church and the later general synods of the West. Presumably,
in the event of reunion, the Orthodox would not be asked to
accept the conciliar decisions taken in the West after the
schism (for example: Trent, Vatican I) as binding on them, but
only to accept them as legitimate general councils of the West.
They would pertain to the Eastern Churches only insofar as

they proclaim the faith of the undivided Church. Western councils would thus not just be disregarded by the Orthodox, but they would be historically relativized and seen to be dealing primarily with concerns of the West.

As Orthodox writer Lev Gilet has discerned, there is no chasm between Eastern and Western Christianity. The fundamental principles of Christian spirituality are the same, the methods very often alike, and the differences do not bear on the chief points. There is, on the whole, one Christian spirituality with here and there some variations of stress and emphasis. The whole teaching of the Latin Fathers may be found in the East, and the teaching of the Greek fathers can be found in the West. The East has given St. John Cassian to the West, and Rome has given St. Jerome to Palestine. St. Basil and St. Benedict, founders of monastic life in East and West, were spiritual brothers. The lives of the wandering beggar St. Benedict Labre and "the poor man under the stairs," St. Alexis, are like mirror images. One finds the same inspiration guiding the lives of St. Nicholas and St. Vincent de Paul. St. Seraphim of Sarov would have seen the desert blossoming under Charles de Foucauld's feet and would have called St. Thérèse of Lisieux "my joy."

It will not help the re-establishment of full communion between East and West to form caricatures of theologies: the West is philosophic, the East is mystical; one is cataphatic, the other apophatic; one is liturgical, the other juridical; one is exemplified by Thomas Aquinas, the other by Gregory Palamas. These sorts of assessments that are still found in manuals of theology simply perpetuate the appalling ignorance of one another's traditions.

In the morning I bid farewell to my partners in dialogue and to a dear old monk with whom I had enjoyed some good conversations. I told him that I had learned much and was very grateful. "Athos," he said, "is a university in the spiritual life, and the monks are the professors. For those who live here, Mount Athos is a runway, a gateway to heaven. For the rest of the world, we are a lighthouse, battered by the waves, but still lighting the way, as we have done for centuries."

It had been apparent that not all the monks were equally learned "professors," and that some of them and their institutions had identified virtue with either primitiveness or pristineness. With regard to the former, the bareness and the frugality of life on Athos are not an end in themselves but a means toward an end. While this remains clear in theory, the same clarity was not always evident in practice. And relative to the latter, pristineness, it must be questioned to what extent the "early Church" was, is, and always will be the archetype of religious and ecclesiastical life. The seven great ecumenical councils are certainly formative moments in the life of the universal Church, but they are not, in the Western view, the only such moments. Tradition is indeed sacred, but care must be taken lest it become a frozen tradition. There is a need to distinguish *Tradition* from *traditions*.

Where does Athos fit in as a reflection of Orthodoxy? There is a pull upon the visitor to identify the two completely. But while the Holy Mountain is certainly an important place for Orthodoxy, it cannot be regarded as central or integral to it in terms of influence. Had monks never settled on the peninsula, it is difficult to say whether and in what way Orthodoxy today would be any different. Alexandria, Jerusalem and Constantinople play a larger part in the topography of the Orthodox Church, as indeed did Rome before the schism.

Orthodoxy is one integral strand of the entire Christian faith (for Orthodox the only such strand). And Athos is only a group of monasteries limited in time and space and contingent to Christianity as a whole. It is, to be sure, a focus of Orthodox monasticism. Those who have chosen to live there, who are drawn to the desert in the internal sense, can find at least relative seclusion and isolation from the inquisitive outside world for the pursuance of their monastic aims. But in the final analysis, they are living out the Christian faith in just one of several possible ways.

As Stephanos and I rode away on the boat, I looked back at this unfading flower where the hallowed practices are cherished, where the cultural contribution of Eastern Christianity is piously protected, and where the traditions of the Byzantine

Empire are still the daily ritual. It is indeed a storied place—one that deserves every letter of its mythology—where the way of life is that dictated by the transcendental truths of mysticism, of prayer, and of the life hereafter.

Athonite monasticism, like the granite rocks themselves, has withstood the incessant turbulence of history's waves. Staunch bulwark of Orthodoxy, it has resisted infiltration by any Western influence. The sense of the past is so intense that the visitor fast loses touch with the present and feels drawn into this world apart.

Like the mountain and sea which form its backdrop, life on Athos is austere and seemingly eternal. It is a phenomenon unique in the world.

Further Reading

John Meyendorff, *Byzantine Theology: Historical Trends and Doctrinal Themes,* London and Oxford, Mowbrays, 1975.

Timothy Ware, *The Orthodox Church,* Penguin Books, 1964.

Edward Kilmartin, S.J., *Toward Reunion: The Roman Catholic and the Orthodox Churches,* New York, Paulist Press, 1979.

Timothy (Kallistos) Ware, *The Orthodox Way,* London and Oxford, Mowbrays, 1979.

Stanley Harakas, *Living the Liturgy: A Practical Guide for Participants in the Divine Liturgy of the Eastern Orthodox Church,* Minneapolis, Light and Life Publishing Company, 1974.

Leonid Ouspensky, *Theology of the Icon,* Crestwood, N.Y., St. Vladimir's Seminary Press, 1978.

R.J.H. Matthews, "Reflections on the Holy Mountain," in *Diakonia,* Volume XV, No. 3, 1980.

Michael Fahey, S.J., "Son and Spirit: Divergent Theologies Between Constantinople and the West," in *Conflicts About the Holy Spirit,* Concilium 128, New York, Seabury Press, 1979, Hans Küng and Jürgen Moltmann, editors.

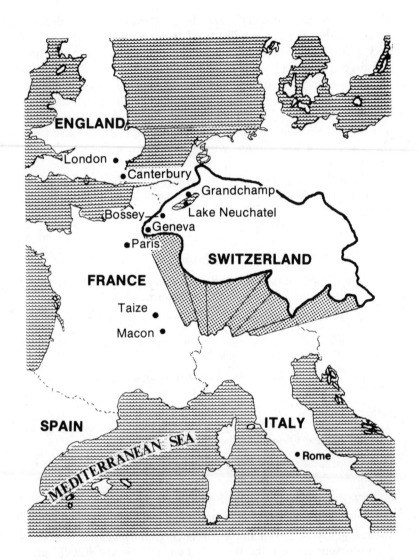

A GENEVA TALE

I approached Geneva from southern France by way of Hannibal's route through the Alps. Unlike Hannibal, I did not attempt the journey on an elephant. The vehicle of my election moved just slightly faster: a 1968 white Renault obtained for a pittance from a friend-of-a-friend who was happy to unload it. Thirty-five miles outside of Geneva, on the last in a series of taxing climbs that day, it simply lost power and stopped. Taking quick advantage of what little momentum there was, I guided the wheels off to the side of the road.

As the minutes ticked by, I waited in the fading light with the intense hope that a little breathing time would remedy the situation. It was but the first in a series of such experiences that would span the next several months. My Renault came to be recognized by all who climbed aboard as a contemplative who refused to voyage for long periods of time without stopping for prayer and interior renewal. It became clear with time that the mountains in particular evoked this inclination.

When eventually I crossed the border into Switzerland, darkness had fallen. Similar little dramas of travel were no doubt being played out all across the world as fifty-three comrades-to-be made their way from thirty-five different countries spread over every continent. Whether from Nigeria, Pakistan, New Zealand, Brazil, Canada, Holland, or Korea, all itineraries led to an eighteenth century chateau twelve miles outside Geneva lying in a tranquil plain between the Jura Mountains and Lake Geneva. As highways became country roads, or central train stations became village depots, or airplanes gave way to taxis and buses, we were all searching for the signs that read: Ecumenical Institute of Bossey. To say we were coming together as fellow Christians would have been to tell a truth. But to say that we represented twenty-one different denominations would have been to tell the truth more interestingly.

Over the next five months, from October to March, we would endeavor to live, study, pray, work, and play our way into an ecumenical community.

I arrived about 10:00 P.M. The reception desk was officially closed, but several of those already arrived who were testing out the chairs in the lounge knew where everything was. Roster. Folder. Room key. A colorfully dressed woman from Pakistan pointed the way.

Halfway down the corridor, I stopped. My eyes rescanned the list of participants. Funny—the possibility hadn't even occurred to me. I was the only Roman Catholic. "Think positive," I told myself. "Three years living in Washington, D.C. has taught you that the experience of being a minority (white) can be very instructive."

I turned the key in the door of Room 14 and flipped on the light, to get my second surprise: I'd have a roommate for the next five months. Two beds and *one* desk. Interesting . . .

I awoke the next morning to a vision framed by my room window: the blue waters of Lake Geneva and the French Alps. In the garden below was a fountain, and fall flowers bordering the closely manicured grass swayed gently in the breeze.

My roommate, Bill Raines, an Anglican deacon at Oxford, had arrived late in the night. We set out to explore the sixty-eight acres which were to be our home for the next near-half year.

The grounds of Bossey hold stories in their soil, which, could they speak, would signal a continuity of religious quest. In the early twelfth century it was the property of the Cistercian Abbey of Bonmont. The feudal castle buildings stood on the site of the present dining hall and sitting room. All that remains of it now is the tower of one of the outbuildings housing the winepress. At the time Bossey was above all a wine-producing property. In that regard all that has changed are the materials and the workers. The tower has become a chapel, and the effort to make one from many still goes on inside. The workers, clad no more in monk's cloth, wear the vestments from Christianity's universal wardrobe.

The present chateau, built in 1722, was acquired by the World Council of Churches (WCC) in 1946, and then the buildings and grounds in 1950. Bossey thus became the permanent home of the Ecumenical Institute, affiliated with the WCC, and used throughout the year for short courses, seminars, consultations, and ecumenical family vacations. The centerpiece in its program of offerings is the Graduate School of Ecumenical Studies open to all students, pastors, and laypeople—and that meant us.

Why had we come? The goals of the Graduate School told the story: to provide training for future generations of ecumenical leaders, both clergy and lay; to promote ecumenical theology within the context of inter-cultural and inter-confessional encounters; to share in an ecumenical spirituality which respects the diversity of liturgical traditions; to create a community in which ecumenism is *experienced* and shared.

For the next two days we all assembled in the modern conference hall for orientation and introductions. The three permanent staff (two Protestants, one Orthodox) and two provisional tutors (one Roman Catholic, one Protestant) and the librarian introduced themselves. Then it was our turn. The three interpreters in the glass booths at the back of the hall swung into action providing simultaneous translation in English, French, or German into our headphones. All we had to do was turn the dial on the desk in front of us.

Most turned to English. We had been asked to know two of the three official Bossey languages, but for the Asians, Africans, Latin Americans and Eastern Europeans, any *one* of the three was already a second or third language. If the one they knew was English, they would be able to communicate with everyone in the program except the four Africans who knew, besides their mother tongue, only French. For this small group of Africans it would be harder; the circle of people with whom they would be able to discuss over the next five months would be severely limited.

A minimal amount of organization had been done for us, said Program Director Dr. Karl Hertz, an American Lutheran. Monday and Tuesday would be lecture days on our theme, "The Bible in the Life of the Church." Dr. Hans Ruddy Weber, the WCC's biblical expert, would make the lion's share of the presentations, occasionally supplemented by other resource people from, for example, the Universities of Geneva or Freiburg. Wednesdays would be spent in Geneva at the WCC. Thursdays and Fridays would be seminar discussion group and special interest group days. Beyond that, we would have to organize ourselves. That meant menus, liturgies, social life, dishes, sports, cultural offerings, and desired academic supplements.

It was clear we were being thrown into the pool and told to swim. We didn't know how or which direction, but we would learn or swallow a lot of water. Drown? We were too filled with the air of idealism and good will. We would at least learn to float together.

The markers on the sides of the pool indicated the depths into which we were swimming and suggested risk and danger. "First world-third-world"; "men-women"; "rich-poor"; "communist-capitalist"; "political-religious"; "Protestant-Catholic-Orthodox," they read. But we were all near-sighted and had taken our glasses off upon getting into the water. We swam on, yelling and laughing with the high-pitched energy of a pool party.

Within the first week, those of us from the Western world began to realize that not everybody swims Western style. The Africans were having digestive problems with Western world cuisine; the Indonesians were freezing and sitting in the conference hall in winter jackets, scarfs, and hats on Indian summer days; several had sore backs because they weren't used to sleeping on beds. It hardly seemed fair. We Westerners had it all on our own terms: the food, the customs, the weather, the style of living. We could read with ease just about any book in the library that interested us, and we always had the upper hand in conversation and discussion because the going language was our own. What was more disconcerting was that we began to learn that this syndrome of life "on our terms" had imposed itself even on *their* turf through missionaries importing a Euro-American brand of Church life and multi-national companies holding economic sway. They were not in control even in their own back yard. In far too many cases we were to feel their anger at being kept financially dependent upon colonial structures whether Church or otherwise.

Meals were superb occasions for learning about situations in other Churches, different customs, attitudes, and ways of life. At supper one could learn from the pastors in Czechoslovakia and Hungary how they are in a sense "imprisoned" in their parishes. They can preach and teach within their own parish, but they are permitted no pastoral contact with anyone who is not a registered parish member or with any place outside of their own parish church. Milan told of a colleague who was imprisoned for visiting a parishioner in another parish. The state's minister of clergy determines who will be permitted to be ordained, and there are no objectifiable criteria. The state can, at any time, suspend the freedom to minister of even the ordained pastors or priests.

And at dinner the next day one could listen to the Africans defend the practice of polygamy in their countries. Nyogu: "There are more women than men, and it is unacceptable for a woman to be unmarried in our society. It is even more unacceptable for her to be pregnant and unmarried." Kesenge: "Having several wives and many children is a cultural sign of great prestige. A man must guard himself against the humiliation of a wife who may not bear children by having more than one wife." Bogango: "When the Christian missionaries brought the Gospel, we wanted to indigenize its message in terms of our own practices. The African tendency, for example, is to see polygamy as a good Christian act because it gives every woman a chance to marry and have children. It is a struggle for our people to see it otherwise and change their ways. In our culture, polygamy has never been a bad thing. We do not experience more godliness to come out of a person because he has just one wife." Nyogu, a Presbyterian minister, honestly admitted that he was not convinced it was right for Africa to give it up.

Our liturgy committee worked on formats for prayer that would leave no one feeling completely out of his or her element. It was not easy. Morning prayer succeeded; vespers failed. A weekly Thursday evening Eucharist took root and became a regular feature, with ministers from different Churches presiding in a celebration of their own rite. Several, after a Roman Catholic Mass one evening, said that it was different from anything they'd ever experienced. On alternating Sundays, the various confessional families organized a liturgy according to their own tradition for the whole community. On the Sundays in-between, we were free to participate with local congregations in Geneva or the canton. The Koreans were scandalized that we had a Eucharist twice a week; they were accustomed to only two or three a year, and each one was preceded by a period of intense preparation. Then there was always the language problem: how to rescue the aesthetics and flow of a service from the cumbersome necessity of having to do everything in at least two languages.

The "honeymoon" period lasted about a month. Then the initial fascination began to wane. When it came to meals, were you going to sit at a table where you would have to exercise patience in trying to get your message across and concentrate intensely to try to understand what the others were saying, or would you choose to sit with those with whom you had mother tongue, country, or religious culture in common? When it came to evenings and weekends, were you going to go with those with whom you'd been sitting at table, or leap-frog to another lily-pad? My journal entry of November 11 reads:

> I experience in myself the same tendencies that I saw and resented in others while learning French in France. There, when I was the one working at a disadvantage, I would often experience that the one with whom I was talking preferred to direct his discussion to others at table because they could express themselves better than I could and because it

took more concentration to listen to me, more patience. That was so frustrating. I had things I wanted to say and questions to ask, and I felt discriminated against. I catch myself now at table being more inclined to talk with other native English speakers than to a Korean or Czech who is struggling with English. It takes more investment of time and energy, and the return is often unsatisfying. The memory of my own feelings while being in their position helps me make the extra effort that the situation calls for.

The vein of gold to be mined each day was unquestionably there. The question was: Did you want it badly enough to keep swinging your pick even after you were tired?

The signs of the honeymoon's end were subtle, but they were there. We had brought the real world and its problems with us to Bossey. Some roommates (two-thirds of participants share a room) amicably separated. Some men knocked often on the doors of some women (there were eleven). And some people didn't do much of anything.

After six years of long days and nights ministering to university students, I was starved for reading and coveted the utter luxury of quiet hours in the library. One afternoon at tea, I asked Musanga, a Quaker from Kenya, what he had been doing. "Oh, I took a nap, played a little ping-pong, sat in the lounge . . . not much *to* do, really. What have you been up to?"

"I've been reading in the library."

"Oh, that boring place."

There was no mistaking it: we were a microcosm of the society we'd left to come here, with all its variance of values and vision. We were an entire universe of diversity melted down, the humanjfamily compressed, the universal Church cross-sectioned. And the Graduate School of Bossey was a reality test for our ecumenical idealism.

In the middle of the first month, we took a tour of Calvin's Geneva.

Located in the extreme southwest of Switzerland, Geneva lies on both shores of the lake whose charm and beauty have been celebrated by famous poets and writers drawn here by the reputation and prestige the city has enjoyed for centuries. Geneva is surrounded by magnificent country enhanced by rolling meadows and low hills whose distant horizons are outlined by the Salève and Jura Mountains. On the south shore of the lake soar the summits of the French Alps, crowned by the eternal snows of Mount Blanc, the highest peak in Europe. In every direction the scenery is grandiose.

A minuscule independent republic, Geneva became a Swiss canton in 1815. It has often been called the smallest of great cities or, if one prefers, the greatest of small cities. It numbers only 160,000, while the population of the canton is around 330,000. It offers its visitors all the advantages of a metropolis without the inconveniences. Elegant, clean, unpolluted, Geneva is safe by day and night. Sumptuous flowerbeds along the quays attract the admiration of strollers, while public parks invite those in search of repose. The soul of this ancient city is the Old Town where a maze of narrow, winding streets evokes the historic past.

Our visit began at the National Protestant Church of Geneva. We gathered in the Room of the Company of Pastors, the home of one of the continuing Church governmental institutions established by Calvin. There Rev. William McCormish gave us an introduction to the history of Geneva and the Reformation.

The sixteenth century, like our own, was a time crowded with surprises. A German miner's son (Luther) came out of a monastery with a message of God's wrath and love to begin a widespread transformation of the Church and the religious life of Europe. A patriotic Swiss humanist (Zwingli) became a zealous Church reformer and died in battle at the hands of his compatriots. A French humanist and law scholar (Calvin) underwent a "sudden conversion" and became a theologian and guide of Protestantism in its second phase of expansion. A Spanish aristocrat and soldier (Ignatius of Loyola), convalescing from wounds, discovered the secrets of spiritual discipline by which vigor was restored to the languishing Church of Rome. Luther, Calvin, and Ignatius had each a little less than thirty

years of public activity; Zwingli had only twelve. The significant labors of all these agents of religious change fell within
the short span of the years 1517 to 1564. This period witnessed
also the essential acts of the Reformation in England, Scotland,
and the Scandinavian lands. One would be hard put to find another period of history that shows a transformation as surprising, rapid, and permanent.

On the continent of Europe, the terms "Lutheran" and
"Reformed" refer to two clearly differentiated branches of
Protestantism. The Reformed Churches took their rise from
two distinct but similar expressions of the Protestant spirit.
The first was led by Zwingli who died when Luther was in
mid-career; this movement was primarily confined to German
Switzerland. The second was championed by Calvin, who had
never known Zwingli and who was active in French-speaking
Switzerland precisely during the crucial period of Roman
Catholic reform. This period consisted of thirty years from the
beginning of the pontificate of Paul III (1534) to the promulga-
tion of the Confession of Faith in the Council of Trent (1564).
The first of these dates is that of Calvin's conversion to Protestantism; the second is that of his death.

The year 1534 saw also Henry VIII's break with the papacy, and by 1564 the Elizabethan settlement of religion was
complete. During these three decades Lutheranism lost most
of its original energy, and in Germany and eastern Europe its
prospects were dimmed by the revived activity of Roman Catholicism. The expansion of Zwinglianism was limited to the
Swiss German cantons. Without Calvin and his disciples, the
survival of Continental Protestantism would have been imper-
iled. When Calvin died he left a series of Reformed Churches,
separately organized by nations and cities, but so closely associated as to form a new international Protestantism. The two
principal branches of Continental Protestantism continued in
separation from each other as the interpreters of Lutheran
theology repudiated elements in the Reformed teaching and
rejected proposals of union with the Reformed Churches.

Calvin himself had no hand in beginning the Reformation.
He appeared late on the theological scene when the early bat-

tles had been won and the Reformation was an established fact. By the time he was born in 1509, the monk Luther had already spent four years of anguished searching in his monastery. And Calvin was only a schoolboy when Luther took the step of publicly questioning the right of the papacy to levy indulgences. Although all this was taking place as Calvin grew up, he was untouched by it. He was sent off to the seminary to prepare himself through the study of theology to receive holy orders and take his place as a priest at the cathedral in his home town of Noyon, France. While he studied the nominalist theology in Paris that had long reigned supreme in Europe, he probably regarded the books and pamphlets that Luther was pouring out of Germany only as so much material for refutation by the subtleties of Scholastic philosophy.

When Calvin's father had a falling out with the cathedral trustees whom he served as a kind of diocesan registrar, he rerouted his son's career from theology to law, a background which would serve Calvin ably when he later came to the work of reshaping the Church in Geneva. His years in law school opened up a whole new world to him, a world of free inquiry and good writing. When after three years his father died, he now regarded himself as free to follow his own inclinations: he would be a humanist scholar after the pattern of the great Erasmus of Rotterdam. At some time between 1528–34 (when, precisely, we do not know—he was not a man to lay bare his soul) he had been converted to the teaching of the Reformation and had had an inner religious experience which was radical and decisive. In 1535 he handed over to the printers the manuscript of *The Principles of the Christian Religion,* more commonly called *The Institutes.* He was just twenty-seven. It was a stunning performance for someone who had been studying law.

When Rev. McCormish had finished his presentation on Calvin and the Reformation and fielded our questions, a group of Church members brought in sandwiches and pastries for lunch. We then walked from the meeting place of the National Protestant Church down the hill to the faculty of theology at the University of Geneva. There, in the library, I browsed through a copy of Calvin's *Institutes.*

He was born to write. Whatever course his life had taken, whether he had become a priest in the Roman Catholic Church or followed the footsteps of Erasmus, he would still have been a writer. When Geneva claimed him for the Reformation, he was left with immeasurably less time to give to writing and to the polishing of his sentences. Instead, the city council worried him about drains and heating devices, there were quarrels to settle with other churches, he had worries and sickness in his own home, and the like. Still, between the publication of his first book and his death he created by himself an entire and complete body of literature. In the definitive edition of his works, his writings fill forty-eight quarto volumes printed in double columns.

The *Institutes,* which grew through Calvin's constant revisions from their modest beginnings into today's large volume divided into four books, were not written as an abstract structure of ideas conceived in a mental vacuum. They sprang out of the contemporary situation and were adapted to serve a double purpose: they were a "confession" in the sense of being an apology to win immunity from persecution for those who held his opinions, and they were a book of instruction for religious inquirers. In later editions, the latter purpose becomes much more central and is responsible for the amplification of material. Thus, Calvin's book was expanded into a compendium of scriptural doctrine for student use and published in a format chosen for the desk rather than the pocket. Each of the 436 pages measures about 13 × 8 inches and has wide margins inviting the reader's notes. The topics of the Apostles' Creed provide its list of contents. The whole of his theology is epitomized here, and all his other writings emanate from or cluster about this work.

The work is a landmark in the history of French prose: no simjlarly elaborate and serious work of thought had ever appeared in that language, and, by common verdict of the scholars, it merited for Calvin a share in the honorary title of "the father of French prose" with Rabelais. The Reformation helped to form the languages of Europe. In England the Prayer Book and the Authorized Version of the Bible; in Germany, Luther's writings and especially his translation of the Bible; in Denmark, Christiern Pedersen, "the first Danish writer of importance": in each case it was as though the mother tongue reached within itself and discovered new resources for the treatment of the highest themes.

On leaving the theological faculty, we walked across the Promenade des Bastions toward the Reformation monument. There, in the center of the great wall in twice-human size, stand Farel, Calvin, Bèze, and Knox, carved in stone and staring sternly through and past the onlooker, their eyes seemingly held by a private, inner vision.

The story of Farel's conscription of Calvin into the Reformation cause sticks in the mind; it was the moment, wrote Calvin, when "God thrust me into the game." Calvin had set out from Paris for Strasbourg, hoping to resume there the life of a scholarly interpreter and inspirer, from a quiet nook, of the movement in which he preferred to let others take the posts of danger and power. A detour on the road brought him to Geneva, where he planned to spend one restful night and be gone. But William Farel, the big-voiced, red-bearded little evangelist and *agent provocateur* of the French and Swiss Reformation, learned of Calvin's presence in the city and called upon him, asking for help in the work of reforming the Genevan Church. Calvin, when he had heard of the state of things in this turbulent city, refused. He was, he said, a scholar, not a man of affairs. Besides, he had no aptitude for such work; he was shy and nervous with none of Farel's force and courage. Tomorrow he would be off for Strasbourg. But Farel, twenty years Calvin's senior and a man of flaming zeal, spoke with power: "You are simply following your own wishes. And I declare in the name of Almighty God that if you refuse to take part in the Lord's work in this Church, God will curse the quiet life that you want for your studies!"

"I felt," Calvin later testified, "as if God from heaven had laid his mighty hand upon me to stop me in my course . . . and

I was so stricken with terror that I did not continue my journey." Such was Calvin's call to Geneva.

Theodore Bèze, to the right of Calvin in the monument, was Calvin's friend, biographer, and successor in Geneva. John Knox, on the far right of the group of four, had been a Catholic priest, a Protestant preacher, an exile in England, and a galley slave in the French navy before reaching Geneva as a refugee. What he learned from Calvin during three years he took back to his native Scotland which since then has always been the main Presbyterian center. He opposed the Catholicism of Mary Queen of Scots and the Anglicanism of the English. He helped dethrone Mary and maneuvered the Scottish Parliament into establishing Presbyterianism as the state religion.

The tour continued. Next stop was the Reformation Historical Museum in the Public University Library. We looked at portraits and autographed letters of Calvin, Bèze, and other Reformation leaders, and examined the first printed version of the Bible in French. It is clear that Calvin's intention was to build his theology on the teaching of the Scriptures alone, to be guided in all his thinking by the Bible, and to refute all other guides. He reproached the Scholastic theologians for their elaborate and fruitless speculations and discouraged the intellectualism which reduced God to a fascinating problem. God makes himself known in a twofold revelation. He is known as Creator both through the outward universe and through Holy Scripture, but he is known as Redeemer through Scripture alone.

The simple effort to utter the truths of the Bible may have made Calvin hesitate to force its meanings to a consistent pattern. There is a problem of harmony among the elements of his theology. At times they seem more like a conjunction of opposites. If we try to represent the sovereignty of God as the main principle of his theology (as most do), we will have difficulty with his views of sin and evil. If we attempt to make his thought begin and end with predestination, we have to contend with a constant stress upon human responsibility and a recurring recognition of free will. Too facile attempts to classify his mind are to be shunned. Calvin was Calvin. To classify him with any group of his contemporaries does not explain him, nor do we gain much by associating him with any present-day theological school. His writings are first and foremost the utterances of deeply felt religious convictions that resulted from the experience of a sudden conversion in which he felt himself arrested and redirected by God.

The teaching on predestination with which he is most often associated in the popular mind was not new or original or even the most important thing he said. He kept adding to this section in his *Institutes* every few years, trying to explain it further because it was controversial. After his death, Bèze took over his work and gave the teaching on predestination a more iron-clad, formalized rendering. Today the teaching has become an historical curiosity for the average Presbyterian lay person, whose position is likely to be the same as that held by the pre-Reformation Roman Catholic Church. The Westminster Confession of 1648 is still the standard of faith for American, Scottish, and English Presbyterianism. It was modified by the United Presbyterian Church of North America to read on this question: "Concerning those who perish: the doctrine of God's eternal decree is held in harmony with the doctrine that God desires not the death of any sinner, but has provided in Christ a salvation sufficient for all. . . .Men are fully responsible for their treatment of God's gracious offer. . . .His decree hinders no man from accepting that offer. . . .No man is condemned except on the ground of his sin."

We headed back in groups toward Cathedral Hill, making a slight detour to walk down Calvin Street to see the place where he lived. The inhabitants of 11 Calvin Street formed more than a family; they were almost a colony. Along with Calvin, his wife (who had been a widow) and her daughter by a previous marriage, there was his brother who had four children by a first wife and four by a second. Thus Calvin did not pass his life in monastic tranquility, but in the midst of the pleasures and worries and noise of domesticity.

We proceeded to the twelfth century Romanesque and Gothic cathedral called St. Peter's. This was Calvin's parish. The portico was remodeled in the eighteenth century in the

neo-classical style, and the interior of the main body is presently undergoing extensive repair. Calvin's time was not spent sitting in an office and guiding the Reformation in Geneva with
intellectual blueprints. He was a pastor, busied with the common run of pastoral duties. So great was his personal ministry
that J.D. Benoit, in a book entitled *Calvin as Director of Souls*,
regards him as even more pastor than theologian. For the ten
years between 1550–1559 for which the cathedral has a regis-
ter, he performed about two hundred and seventy weddings
and fifty baptisms. But the center of his pastoral work, around
which all else revolved, was the preaching of the Gospel. Each
Sunday began with its service and sermon at daybreak, and
went on with catechism for the children at midday and another sermon at three o'clock. During the week sermons were
fixed for Monday, Tuesday and Friday mornings, until in 1549
they were increased to every day of the week. Calvin's method
was that of some of the Church Fathers. Rather than choose a
single text or isolated passage, he preached steadily through
book after book of the Bible. He wanted to bring the whole
message before his people, and he felt that it could best be
done by connected exposition. By expounding Scripture as a
whole he was forced to deal with the entire scriptural range of
ideas and, as an honest interpreter, he labored to represent the
thought of the Bible faithfully. He had a horror of those who
substituted their own ideas for those of the Bible when preaching. "When we enter the pulpit," he said, "it is not so that we
may bring our own dreams and fancies with us."

Next to the cathedral is Calvin's Auditorium. It was formerly the private chapel of the bishops of Geneva. At the beginning of the sixteenth century Geneva was one of many
independent city-states in Europe ruled by a prince-bishop.
(The city's coat of arms bore a key and half of an eagle, the former representing a bishop and the latter the Hapsburgs.) But
the rising standard of living, and an emerging literate, ambi-
tious, wealthy middle class was growing increasingly resentful
of ecclesiastical domination and interference. They revolted
and the prince-bishop was thrown out. Both the ecclesiastical
and the secular government had to have a new foundation in

the Reformation. The prince-bishop was replaced by a group of wealthy and respectable businessmen.

Calvin's treatment of the papacy shows clearly that he did not regard as an evil the development of the episcopal hierarchy during the early centuries. But from the end of the age of Gregory the Great (604) Calvin saw the papacy, with its "overweening monarchical claims," as the agent of a general corruption of the Western Church, in which corruption the bishops shared. Calvin would not reject all episcopacy in contemporary Churches—he recommended it, in fact, in the case of Poland. His primary concern was to guard against a condition in which one minister may lord it over others. The episcopacy that is admissible is that which is free from "dominion, principality, or tyranny." At the same time, any doctrines of a succession of bishops from the apostles as a distinct order is remote from his view. He held that the early episcopate arose by delegation of the presbyters for special duties connected with discipline and the holding of synods. Today, the Presbyterian Church takes its name from its form of government. Elected and ordained elders rather than bishops rule the churches. Churches in a given area come together through representation in presbyteries which supervise the Church-at-large.

Calvin's Auditorium is also called the John Knox Chapel because it was handed over to the foreign Protestant communities after the Reformation. John Knox preached there to English refugees. Knox was much taken with Calvin's city

> where, I neither fear nor am I ashamed to say, is the most perfect school of Christ that ever was in the earth since the days of the apostles. In other places, I confess Christ to be truly preached; but manners and religion to be so sincerely reformed, I have not yet seen in any other place.

We had come full circle in our visit to Calvin's Geneva and were now back at the National Protestant Church of Geneva headquarters, in the room from which discipline was administered to the medieval town. Calvin was not willing to abolish confession without substituting some form of discipline, for "if the preaching of the doctrine were not accompanied by private admonitions, reproofs, and other methods to enforce the doctrine, it would be altogether ineffectual." Calvin approached the cure of souls as a mutual activity of Christians and compelled no one to confess sins to his minister. It was, nonetheless, still an option, but the penitent was the judge of what he ought to reveal for the relief of his conscience. Thus the ecclesiastical importance given by Calvin to laymen is not only in the eldership with its disciplinary authority, but also in the enlisting of all in a lively attention to each other's spiritual state and needs. There was no thought of a separation in membership of church and citizenry. The Christian community was composed of the same people as the civil community. Calvin was well aware that environment forms character and habits, and he pressed for the extermination of the community sources of moral delinquency.

The attempt to apply this pedagogy provides many amusing stories in the history of medieval Geneva where moral conditions were indeed such as to invite drastic reform. Calvin and the authorities resorted to repressive measures to eliminate the numerous taverns and houses of prostitution. One attempt was made to replace the taverns by centers of "innocent entertainment," called *abbayes.* The keepers were to be watchful against excessive drinking, protracted games of cards, and obscene or irreverent songs. They were to keep a French Bible displayed, encourage religious discourse and conversation, serve no food to those who did not say grace, and close at 9:00 P.M. But the *abbayes* were boycotted, and in three months the taverns were reopened. Offenders noted by the watchful elders were haled by a police officer before the Consistory; oftentimes they had been privately admonished or counseled in advance by Calvin or another minister. The records of the Consistory show extraordinary minuteness in the offenses reported for correction, e.g., non-attendance at church and contemptuous deportment during services. Other entries indicate the ordinary misdemeanors of a medieval town: wife-beating, gambling, and adultery.

In many cases, the Consistory's prescribed penance seems

to have effected a real correction of conduct and attitude; in others, it was hotly resented and the issues raised convulsed the city. Not everyone was teachable; not everyone had been converted. Yet a city that had been a byword for rioting and immorality of many kinds was known as one of the godly cities of Europe. Geneva is oftentimes thought of as a theocracy guided by Calvin, but such was not the case. Calvin was dominated by the city council. He wanted, for example, Communion once a week for the people, but the city council ruled "No: every three months." Calvin was considered by many to be a French foreigner and a refugee. Nonetheless, he accomplished his task, securing the future of Geneva and making it at once a church, a school, and a fortress.

His portrait hung over the desk of the Consistory where we sat, his finger raised as if in the process of making an instructive point. The picture of Calvin that has come down to us is of a cold, severe man, restrained in his emotions and vindictive in his enmities. The man who comes across in the many volumes of letters preserved and on record is quite different. Reserved he certainly was, but not cold; hasty and impatient, but not vindictive. Sensitive, easily wounded, highly strung: yes. He was one of those scholarly and finely turned persons whose talents mark them for prominent leadership, and who shrink from but dare not shirk the duties involved. Such persons may become assertive even in overcoming an inclination to retirement. "God," he had said, "thrust me into the game." The game proved to be a series of battles in which blows were dealt and suffered. Plagued by a painful kidney stone condition and migraine headaches, he was seldom a healthy warrior. His temperamental inclination to anger and impatience, coupled with the infinite multitude and variety of Church affairs, often made this thin sickly figure peevish and difficult. But his intensity arose from a sense of mission and was not more pronounced than that felt by other men dedicated to a cause.

The secretary general of the Consistory was now addressing us from beneath Calvin's portrait. I wondered what kind of expression would have crossed that painted visage if it were able to hear the account of the present day state of the Church of Geneva: "The Church is national and Protestant. It was separated from the state in 1907. Fifty-two percent of the residents of Geneva list themselves as Roman Catholic, thirty-two percent Protestant, eight percent as other. One percent of those identifying themselves as Protestants attend church. . . ."

At the end of his presentation, there was a question from the group: "What about the 'Protestant ethic' that is spoken of—the notion that Calvin held the prosperity of believers to be proof of their benediction by God?"

The notables behind the Consistory desk discussed the question. Their consensus seemed to be that ideas which have been brought to expression by late Calvinists have been read back into Calvin to the confusion of history. Thus it is stated that Calvin set loose an individualistic business activity, sanctioned by the view that worldly prosperity is evidence of the favor of God. This notion has become the bourgeois heresy of the modern era. The fact is that, for Calvin, the elect differ externally in this life in no way from the damned. The view that "prosperity signals election" called forth from Calvin the most emphatic words of condemnation. He keeps repeating these judgments almost to weariness, but the impressive weight of the evidence has been largely ignored. The respondents granted that Calvin in his treatment of the providence of God (arguing against the notion of chance to explain the events of history) speaks of good success as the mark of God's blessing and calamity as his curse. But the treatment does not bear upon economic ethics. Capitalists who are in reality ethically Calvinist are those whose chief concern is not to gain wealth but to apply it to beneficient uses. "The Swiss aren't miserly," one of the officials said. "If there's a disaster somewhere, they'll collect millions of francs in a few days. But they want to know where their money goes."

The earthquake which struck southern Italy during our months at Bossey proved his words true. The Swiss quickly collected five million dollars for Italy's earthquake victims and donated so many clothes—six hundred tons—that Italian authorities had to ask them to stop sending more. This was the kind of Protestant or capitalistic ethic which would have been in harmony with Calvin's teaching.

There is much about modern day Geneva, however, that would likely give Calvin pause and cause his face to cloud and brow to furrow.

It is hard to believe in this elegant city today that, until the French Revolution, sumptuary laws decreed what each level of the population should wear. One of Geneva's historians talks about a "constant struggle against French elegance, fripperies and pleasure-seeking" that Calvinists despised, which helped to set Geneva apart from its French-speaking neighbors. But on the streets of modern-day Geneva, one receives the impression of a population more suavely attired than in Paris.

Geneva is the jewelry capital of the world, where even the serious business of time is marked on watch faces made of platinum and lapis lazuli. Yet, about three hundred years ago, Geneva inhabitants were forbidden to wear "chains, bracelets, necklaces, and pendants of gold . . . and any use on costume of gold and precious stones, whether they be beads, pearls, garnets or whatever." John Calvin clamped a specific limitation on women: "No more than four gold rings," he decreed. Brides were excepted—on their wedding day and the day after.

By the first half of the nineteenth century, however, Calvin's citadel was crumbling in its discipline. Luxury was the fever. Alexandre Dumas gave the palpitating report in his "Impressions de la Suisse" based on a visit in 1832: "Geneva represents the aristocracy of money; it is the city of luxury, gold chains, watches, carriages and horses. Its three thousand master workers all feed Europe with jewelry. A collection of one hundred thousand marvels to ensnare the feminine soul, to drive a Parisienne mad, to set Cleopatra quivering with envy in her tomb."

Today, nobody who can afford it seems afraid to drive to the center of the city in a Rolls Royce loaded with the kind of rocks an outsider can hardly believe are real. Swiss watches, in spite of Japanese competition, are alive and well, and when it comes to Swiss high fashion jewelry no stones are barred. In this town where tick-tock is big-time, a watch is required to do more than get you to the Bijou to meet Mimi before the second show begins. The Geneva watches are as personal as your signature or your visiting card. In some societies, if your visiting card cannot pass the thumb test you've irretrievably lost your place. With this implacable crowd your watch is the second gate and the judges are reading your wrist across the room.

If the Reformer's spirit still influences the old families when they talk of Calvin these days, they usually mean Klein. Over the past generation, the Calvinist attitudes that had distinguished Geneva have been slowly fading out. "When I was young," remembers historian Eugene-Louis Dumont, who is sixty-four, "we assumed that any older woman wearing make-up was French. The devil was behind it all, or so we thought. But today, things are changing. My son is now thirty-two and he no longer has the same reactions."

I asked a resident of several years in Geneva, "How do you find the Swiss?" That, he said, was precisely the question: How do you find them? Where are they? The Swiss are considered to be a private people. It is considered extremely difficult to penetrate the hard-shelled Genevese with the result that many a well-known foreigner has seen them only in a negative light. Lenin wrote that Geneva made him feel he was already in his coffin, and Voltaire sardonically advised that when you see a Geneva banker jump out of the window, jump after him because there is bound to be gold on the pavement. Stendahl, in his "Memoires d'un Touriste" in 1837, wrote: "I really like the Genevese until he is forty. Very often by that time he has put aside a small or a big fortune; but then appears the capital fault of his education. He does not know how to enjoy himself; he has not learned to live in prosperous circumstances; he becomes severe and puritanical; he takes umbrage against those who amuse themselves; he calls them immoral people."

Even if it is as Stendahl says, it seems harmless enough: "Their sweetest pleasure when young," he continues, "is to dream of the day when they will be rich. Even when they commit imprudences and let themselves go, they choose some simple, inexpensive pleasure like a promenade to the foot or summit of a mountain where they drink milk."

In the annals of its past, Geneva has been a Roman colony, a Burgundian capital, a city of fairs and an episcopal principality before bestowing upon itself, in 1536, the statute of an independent republic and adopting the Reformation. In the course of the years it obtained the reputation of a city of refuge, welcoming the persecuted men and women who were obliged to quit their native lands because of their faith or their political opinions. But Puritan morals came along with an openness to the world and a willingness to accept refugees of all persuasions. The combination brought prosperity to the town.

Back at Bossey, the days were dyed in the liquid gold that poured from autumn's cauldron over the oaks and maples along the path from the chateau to the conference hall and library. The fountain in the back garden splattered away contentedly like a child lost in solitary play. My roommate, Bill, and Gisela, from Holland, were falling helplessly but deliciously over love's brink. The Alps stood erect across the lake and arched their snowy backs, inviting weekend hikers. Even the geese in the pond seemed less willing to make their raucous sounds. It was late November, and we were still in short sleeves.

In the seminar groups, we spoke more freely as we came to know one another better. In my group we were from Zaire, Germany, Togo, Switzerland, Madagascar, Canada, Rumania, and the United States. We came together for several hours each week to discuss the themes we were studying in the plenary session biblical lectures. On this particular day, in the morning, the presentation had concerned a comparative study of the institution narratives at the Last Supper in the Gospels of Matthew, Mark, and Luke.

It came as a total revelation to me that the Protestant pastors in Africa customarily use coconut milk, or banana juice, or Coca-Cola in place of wine in the Eucharist. There are several reasons, they explained. Given the naturally-low African tolerance to alcohol, alcoholism has been a serious problem and the Churches are forbidden to use wine even in their Communion distribution. Roman Catholic churches continue to use wine, but Communion is only given under the form of bread to the faithful. Furthermore, using coconut milk or banana juice is a way of indigenizing the faithful in symbols that speak culturally to Africans. Wine is seen as a European import, and neither wine nor bread "speaks" to the people. Besides, both are too expensive.

That provoked a discussion on the universal value of symbols. Is it the bread and wine that are important, or the message they symbolize? Can the message be separated from the original symbols without losing something of its content? Can the message be communicated cross-culturally through use of other elements that speak the message more clearly to a particular people? Everyone agreed: care must be taken that new symbols express the meaning of the Eucharist, e.g., many are formed into one. How is this true, for example, with coconut milk or Coca-Cola?

The discussion revealed that there were some elements of eucharistic theology to which we did not ascribe a common value. From the Orthodox, Roman Catholic, and Anglican members came the point that the symbol must not only speak of "many become one," but of blood poured out, of sacrifice, since the Eucharist is inseparably tied up with the cross. The Protestant members indicated that their term for the Eucharist, the "Holy Supper," is such precisely because they do not attribute great value to sacrificial notions of Eucharist. Given that, orange juice or coconut milk could be substituted for wine without losing the symbolic dimension of sacrifice—for that dimension was not intentionally there to begin with. While the other side granted the meal aspect of Eucharist as real and important, the re-presentation of the bloody sacrifice on Calvary seemed to indicate that the wine could never be substituted for without losing some essential symbolic value.

It was the kind of discussion that popped up frequently and unexpectedly: one that necessitated examination of things taken for granted and hence a deepening of awareness concerning why we do what we do.

There lurked under the cover of almost every event at

Bossey, it seemed, some potential learning, some broadening or deepening of vision. Our liturgy committee met, for example, to plan a retreat day. It seemed like a simple enough task. I had planned numerous retreats of several days each before and wasn't expecting a great deal of difficulty in getting together with several others to chart out a single day's format. A little effective something here or there with lots of silence in between, and one has a retreat, right?

Wrong. Retreats may be standard practice in some Christian traditions, but by no means in all. We were at ground zero within the committee itself. What *is* a retreat, the representatives of the Free and Reformed Church traditions wanted to know, and what is it supposed to do? What are its components? There was one point in particular where I became very aware of how much I reflected the attitudes of my own background and had naively assumed that something which was a value there was a value everywhere. The point in question concerned silence as a milieu for prayer.

It had simply never occurred to me that silence was not a valued item in every Christian's toolbox. I guess I've just grown up with silence through grade school and high school retreat days, full weeks of retreat in the seminary, and various forms of Christian meditation. I don't even turn on the car radio when I'm driving alone. Silence has become through the years a good friend and comfortable companion.

And then Isaac, a warden in the Presbyterian lay training center in Ghana, said, "Silence? For one or two hours between talks? That is very strange! For my people a time of prayer means to gather together in church for a series of readings, songs, personal witness, and preaching."

It was as though I had been in the process of making a routine lane change and all of a sudden heard a horn off my back fender, waking me up to the fact that there was a blind spot in my vision.

The absence of monastic forms of life in Protestanism has played a large role in our different responses to silence. For the Orthodox, Roman Catholics, and, more recently, Anglicans-Episcopalians, monasteries double as lay retreat houses.

The lives of those who live there hold up silence as a positive value to us even when we're in the city, and when we want to resource ourselves spiritually, we generally join them in their contemplation. But as Isaac was reminding me, there were no monasteries, no convents, in his experience.

The retreat planning process took not one, not two, but several meetings. In the end, there seemed to be among the general community so much dis-ease with, suspicion of, and lack of understanding about the whole notion of a retreat that the planning committee appointed two of us to give an orientation to the retreat in a plenary community meeting and to explain the schedule step by step, and the thinking behind it all, to help people feel more secure with it. "For many," Isaac said, "it's an experimental step."

In the end, the retreat "day" was reduced to a four-hour period which opened and closed with structured half-hour prayer services and offered fifteen-minute meditation-sermons every three-quarters of an hour. And only two-thirds of the people elected to participate in it. But those who did seemed to genuinely appreciate and value the experience. I spent as much time planning those few hours as I have spent preparing a whole week's retreat in other circumstances. But I also learned a good deal more.

The night before the retreat, we had all been entertained in a cultural evening by those from the Pacific (each week a different geographical group prepared a cultural soiree). I couldn't help remark what a difference there was between the Australians and New Zealanders, on the one hand, and the "Islanders" from Samoa, the Fiji and Solomon Islands on the other. The latter were so at ease with their bodies, so musically endowed. There was a natural grace and rhythm to their most simple movements, to say nothing of the variety and skill of their acts. Enari's "mosquito slap" dance and performance twirling a flaming baton in the dark was the kind of first-rate talent that people used to tune in to the Ed Sullivan Show to see. Something very free, rich, inspired came across in all their numbers; their acts emitted sparks.

What was it that made the Australians and New Zealanders seem, by contrast, stiff, "proper," and self-conscious? The same cultural and educational forces, perhaps, that enabled them to feel perfectly comfortable in the lecture hall forming finely honed and penetrating questions, while the "Islanders" sat silently by, obviously out of their element.

These two back-to-back experiences, the cultural evening and the retreat, evidenced the riches we have to offer to one another. The evening before, my appreciation for what we were engaged in had become more pronounced with each act of the entertainment; the following morning, that same sense of appreciation deepened in the quiet prayer as we faced the Lord together asking him to give us unity in our diversity.

At the end of November we reached that point in the Bossey program where all participants are sent out into various parishes in Switzerland for the better part of a week. The first flakes of winter were falling as a group of us boarded the train north into German-speaking Switzerland. We traveled across a Christmas card landscape, singing songs to Caleb's guitar. At each stop along the way, one or two got off, warmly wrapped in hugs and well wishes for a good experience. Then the train pulled away again into the failing light, with people hanging out the windows and yelling good-byes from one of the cars in the train's otherwise silent and decorous line. The native Swiss aboard, too discreet to ask, clearly bent their brains trying to figure out what this group of many colors and tongues was all about.

Kesenge and I were among the last to debark. We were met at the station in a small town near the border of Germany by the pastor and one of his parishioners who took us to the families with whom we would be staying. I was met at the door by a ferocious German shepherd who had no intention of giving me entry. Mrs. Gruber, however, with apple pie aroma trailing in her wake, more than redeemed the temporary impasse with a generous offering straight from the oven.

Her husband spoke only German, she explained, and she spoke a little French. Their daughter Beatrice would be home from work soon, and she spoke German, French, and a little English.

After supper we all looked at picture books of Switzerland. Then Mr. Gruber brought to the table the ballot which he had to cast in the morning on some local issues. History and geography have conspired to create a political system that has not only held the country together but helped modern-day Switzerland adapt to a rapidly changing economic environment. Switzerland is the most politically decentralized nation in the West: its twenty-six cantons and half-cantons behave as sovereign entities in most areas other than defense, foreign affairs and communications. Every Swiss is a citizen first of community and canton, then of the confederation. He pays most of his income taxes to his canton and looks to it for such services as education, welfare and police protection.

The diffusion of power has been a key factor in preserving peace among people speaking four languages (German, French, Italian and Romansch, a Latin-based tongue used by fifty thousand residents of the mountainous Graubuden canton).

The following morning, before our program of Church activities began, Beatrice went to get Kesenge and took us both along a long walk through the forest that began right outside their door. The snow had been falling throughout the night, and the forest was a sacred temple transfigured in light, all its furniture adorned with fresh white linen and edges of lace. It was Kesenge's first encounter with snow. He was full of wonder and glee. I took pictures for his family in Zaire.

Dried out from our play, we spent the day at the parish bazaar and in the evening sat down with the pastor to help plan the services for the weekend. I thought that he was being very open and flexible on our behalf, trying to accommodate us by suggesting now one possibility, now another. But gradually I began to realize that he was genuinely planning the service from scratch, trying to remember how it went. The most recent Communion service in the parish, Kesenge and I learned, had been last Pentecost. As the pastor listed the parts of the service on his note paper, he stopped and reflected: "There seems to be something missing here." Then he looked at me across the table and asked, "What does your Church do at this point?"

A variation of liturgical rites can be a necessary and healthy expression of a faith that is truly catholic. That moment, however, was a microcosm of the unfortunate divergence of eucharistic theology and practice in the Christian Church in the West since the Reformation. Because the Eucharist is where the Church, in communion with its Lord, most realizes its own nature as his body, the belief that surrounds the Eucharist is always of critical importance whenever Christians seek to heal the divisions of that body.

From the beginning of the Reformation, the Eucharist was the critical touchstone of disagreement. Even the first two Reformers, Luther and Zwingli, could not reach accord on the expression of their eucharistic faith. That failure, in the Colloquy of Marburg in 1529, led to the split between Lutheran and Reformed Protestantism that endures to this day.

Zwingli believed that this sacrament is not the re-presentation of the sacrifice of Christ, but the faithful *remembrance* that that sacrifice had been made once and for all. He declined to accept Luther's teaching that Christ's words of institution required the belief that the real flesh and blood of Christ coexist in and with the natural elements of bread and wine. In the Zurich Consensus of 1549, Zwingli's characteristic theological opinions were set aside in Switzerland in favor of the more profound views of Calvin.

Calvin sought to build a sacramental theology of inwardness because in the previous centuries there was a great deal of emphasis on externals in the piety of the people. Eucharistic interest, for example, was centered on *seeing* the host at the elevation of the Mass (as opposed to receiving Communion) and carrying it in procession. Roman Catholic piety of the pre-Reformation and Reformation era did not stress enough the importance of the believer's personal interaction in relationship with the Lord, nor did it stress the believer's knowledgeable participation in the Mass as a presupposition to the reception of the sacrament.

"Romanism" was, as Calvin experienced it on the pastoral level, a clerical reality. Within the Church there was an elite to whom the most sacred tasks were entrusted. This clerical elect, who were supposed to perform their liturgical role within the community, became separated from the community. The result was that both they and their tasks became self-contained, self-perpetuating, having their justification in themselves, unrelated to the worshiping community of God's people. As the Church became identified with the clerical elite, so the worshiping activity of the Church became identified with clerical worship. The priest, having appropriated both word and sacrament, fed his soul with ritual splendor and liturgical mystery within the sanctuary; the faithful non-cleric, fed on neither the word of Christ nor the body of Christ, stood in reverent passivity, beholding from beyond the sanctuary grill the glory of the real "chosen people" at worship. Because the laity had need of the strong food of Christ's word and body and had not received it, they turned to the peripheral, to relics and pilgrimages and private devotions and indulgences. Meanwhile the cleric went on liturgizing in his self-contained world, content to speak to his God in Latin and to his people not at all.

Calvin could think of nothing more opposed to the theological understanding of the Eucharist than for it to be appropriated by the clergy and for the clergy to liturgize as though the Lord's Supper had been turned over to them. If the Eucharist was not the worship of the community, worshiping as community, participating as community, it was nothing. Calvin was bitter most of all over the neglect of the people; they were left unnoticed, uninstructed, and undisciplined. "For Christ commanded that stewards of his Gospel and sacraments be ordained, not that sacrificers be installed. He gave a command to preach the Gospel and feed the flock, not to sacrifice victims. He promised the grace of the Holy Spirit not to enable them to make atonement for sins, but duly to engage in and maintain the government of the Church" (*Institutes* IV, 19, 38). Calvin saw the priest saying his "private" Mass as a sacrificer who, "about to devour his victim by himself, separates himself from all the believing fold. The unity of which the Eucharist is a symbol is destroyed by the sacrifice of the Mass, and the Eucharist becomes a cause of fragmentation in the worshiping community" (*Inst.* IV, 17, 8).

Calvin's eucharistic theology is essentially pastoral. Instead of parading around with the bread of life or offering it up in sacrifice, it should be fed to believers who, weak and afflicted, need this bread from heaven. "We have not been commanded to adore, but to take and eat," he declared.

And as for the cup, from which only the priests partook: "The edict of the eternal God is that all should drink ('Take this and drink it, all of you'); man dares supersede and abrogate it by a new and opposing law decreeing that not all should drink" (IV, 17, 47). That both the consecrated bread and wine were to be received, as can be seen from the legislation and writings of the Fathers of the first thousand years, "was considered not merely a custom but an inviolable law" (IV, 17, 49). Calvin perceived the whole situation of liturgical clericalism as a ritualized form of excommunication, by means of which the community of believers is excluded from active participation in the eucharistic liturgy. Both the liturgy and the chalice were "clerical things."

For the laity, what was secondary and marginal had moved to the center, and hence the Catholic experience of God was defective because it was peripheral. That which was truly central and commanded by God, the preaching of the word and the right celebration of the sacraments, was forgotten. In its simplest form Calvin's efforts were directed toward giving centrality to what is central.

The Church in the centuries preceding the Reformation was indeed in a sorry condition because of a lack of preaching and an impoverished faith. The Reformers set out to fill that void. It was in the service of preaching, the effort to generate and confirm the people's faith, that Protestant theology developed. The general thrust toward preaching and the response of faith gave Protestant theology an orientation that was different from the Roman Catholic emphasis. The Scholastic theologians, in an effort to deepen the cognitive dimension of faith, had reflected at great length on the mysteries revealed by God for the sake of rendering them intelligible to the inquisitive human mind. Protestant theology tended to be more practical, edifying the faith of the common believer through preaching. Thus, in the Reformed Churches, there is an emphasis, not just on the presence of Christ in the bread and wine, but in the gathered community, the act of worship, the word, and the partaking of the elements. For it is in these "places" that any presence of Christ in the Eucharist makes its impact on the individual believer. The modern day Protestant and Roman Catholic will find these very emphases—almost the same words—in Vatican II's *Constitution on the Sacred Liturgy.*

The soil in which medieval Roman Catholic theology flowered was quite different, and that difference was reflected in a different orientation at that time. With the rise of the universities in the thirteenth century and with St. Anselm's understanding of theology as "faith seeking understanding" for a guide, Roman Catholic doctrinal statements tended to be descriptions of an objective world revealed by God, seen by faith, and articulated in the language of the time: Greek philosophical thought. Between these statements and the people in the street there was a whole intermediary role that needed preachers to transform the lofty notions and the specialized language into stimuli for the faith of the laity. But more often than not, an objective rather than applied approach was taken. When the people gathered for worship, Roman Catholic theology was naturally inclined to emphasize the objectively most important factor to which everything else was ordered in a hierarchy of importance. Christ present by virtue of his words pronounced over the elements, "This is my body, given for you . . . this is my blood, shed for you," was the focus of attention. The other ways in which Christ is present were not denied, but neither were they highlighted in theory or in practice. The appreciation of the richness and extent of Christ's presence in the Eucharist entered into official Roman Catholic teaching only with Vatican Council II where the Instruction on Eucharistic Worship says: "In the celebration of the Mass, the principal modes by which Christ is present to his Church are gradually revealed. First of all, Christ is seen to be present among the faithful gathered in his name; then in his Word, as the Scriptures are read and explained; in the person of the minister; finally and in a unique way under the species (appearances) of the Eucharist."

The tendency to emphasize only one manner of Christ's presence from the medieval era up to relatively recent times has resulted in a great deal of polemic around the Scholastic way of expressing how this presence happens: transubstantiation. Calvin objected to transubstantiation because in his view it made God a palpable object who could be "controlled" by man. The priest says the words and bread becomes God. This worked against the truth of God's sovereignty and man's utter subjection. "God cannot be commanded, nor contained, nor reduced, nor condensed to material physical accessibility," Calvin objected. Though truly, even substantially, present and truly given, Christ cannot be placed at man's disposal. The divinity a person relates to in the Eucharist is not a domesticated, attendant God who is conjured with a formula, summoned by clerical command and dismissed with digestion, a sort of "instant" God. The eucharistic Lord is the sovereign Lord, the uncommitted who is never so committed as to lose the freedom of his Lordship.

Calvin was wary of reducing the Eucharist to the "givenness of a thing." His intuition was on target: the sacraments are not God packaged, Christ condensed, ready for use. God is not to be reduced to a household God to be summoned and dismissed at will. At the same time, Calvin's evangelical passion for God's freedom and sovereignty made it impossible for him to conceive of God committing himself to a sacramental engagement of real incarnational dimensions. God is not bound, granted; but Calvin will not permit the possibility that God could freely bind himself. Consequently, the sacramental moment in his theology risks being too spiritual and lacks the concrete quality of the incarnation.

Reformed Christians regard the doctrine of transubstan-

tiation to be non-biblical, the elevation of philosophical speculation to the status of a dogma of faith. Recent discussions in
Roman Catholic theology have brought out that the doctrine
of transubstantiation is not the result of philosophical speculation but an effort to make explicit the doctrine of the real presence of Christ in the Eucharist and therefore, like that
doctrine, a matter of faith based on the Scriptures. The medieval theologians used the terms of Greek philosophy, which
was the matrix of theology in the Middle Ages, to express not
their speculations but their biblical faith's insight. Other Roman Catholic writers today use different terms to describe the
mystery of Christ's presence. That indicates how important it
is to distinguish between faith's insight and the language which
expresses it. Much of the disagreement is based on confusion
between faith and the *expression* of faith. Roman Catholics and
Reformed Church members have condemned each other's
words and concepts without endeavoring to appreciate the
faith which the words are feeble attempts to articulate. Roman
Catholicism is not at all tied to the term transubstantiation to
express its biblical faith. It can and does use other words to arrive at a clear expression of what is believed. What would be
the *most* adequate way of expressing the faith inherited
through tradition? History has shown that, as language and our
understanding of it changes, we need to be constantly seeking
out new ways to state old truths.

To say that a particular doctrine of the Eucharist is conditioned by a philosophical theory is not to say a great deal, because any doctrine of the Eucharist, whether Roman Catholic
or Reformed or Lutheran, is so conditioned. There is no de-
nomination that can boast of being in possession of pure faith
undiluted by metaphysical presuppositions.

The Reformed and Roman Catholic approaches can be
seen as complementary rather than antithetical. Roman Catholics can find in the Reformed doctrine a corrective to tenden-
cies to present the doctrine of transubstantiation in a too
materialistic or mechanical manner. Reformed Christians can
find in Roman Catholic teaching an emphasis to prevent the
mystery of the Eucharist from becoming overly spiritualized

and reduced to pious thinking about Christ in a manner that is out of line with God's way of dealing with humanity through the incarnation. It is worthwhile to observe that Roman Catholics have hung onto the terminology of transubstantiation throughout the past four hundred years to counter a tendency among Protestants to reduce the real presence of Christ in the Eucharist to the mere recollection of him or a presence in the minds of the worshipers. The conviction of the vast majority of Christians in the world and most Churches is that such a presence does not do justice to Christ's words declared in his name over the elements.

Nor could Calvin be counted upon for support of the "memorial" approach. In his *Institutes* he asserted: "The Lord so communicates his body to us that he is made completely one with us and we with him" (IV, 17, 38). In Calvin's teaching, the reality of the given body is not less real because the presence is "spiritual." Roman Catholics also believe that the Christ they encounter is Christ as he is now—risen, transcendent, glorified, i.e., a spiritual presence. As Scottish theologian Donald Baille has correctly noted, the Roman doctrine does not mean that the body of Christ is contained locally or spatially in the bread, inside it, so to speak, so that if the surface were peeled off, the flesh of Christ would be found.

In general the Reformed Churches today remain in agreement with Calvin's eucharistic teachings. But just as many Roman Catholics today would conceive of their own doctrine in a too materialistic way that implies a kind of cannabalism in Communion, so many Presbyterians conceive of the Eucharist as a memorial and no more. Both Churches will be enriched by a return to the sources of their espoused theology. That, it would seem, should be one of the starting points in a genuinely ecumenical theology.

The meeting that Kesenge and I were having with the Reform Pastor to plan the Lord's Supper for the next day illustrated that some Reform Churches, while espousing Calvin's eucharistic teachings in their confessional documents, have moved away from it in practice. Calvin wanted to return to the practice of weekly Communion in an attempt to restore values which Roman Catholicism had obscured and neglected for centuries. There was something ironic and regrettable about the fact that a Reform pastor whose congregation had not had Communion for five months was now asking a Roman Catholic what goes where in the weekly Catholic Sunday Eucharist. On one level, it was but another example of why all theology should be done ecumenically. At any given point in each Church's history it is either like a tortoise or a hare and needs the witness of where the other is to help it keep pace and on course. The Anglicans, Orthodox, Protestants, and Roman Catholics need each other's perspectives as correctives for their respective blind spots. None of them have perfect peripheral vision all the time.

Kesenge and I *both* preached the next day at the Holy Supper. Celebrated with comparative infrequency in most Presbyterian churches, the Lord's Supper is a spiritual banquet. For this reason the Supper has always had the character of a meal and the white cloth on the holy table is a *table* cloth. Many of the people never approached it; they departed for home after the readings and sermon and hymn. The pastor assured us afterward that it wasn't because of anything we had said; it was simply that the people were not accustomed to have a service of Communion follow that of the word. "I'm afraid we have some rediscovering to do," he said quietly.

That night the Gruber family's dining room was softly lit with candles, the largest flame being under the fondue pot. Of the six different kinds of Swiss cheese Beatrice proudly arranged on the table, gruyère and emmenthal were the specialties of the region. After dishes, we looked through family photo albums. Then Mr. Gruber got up and went to a closet and came back with his gun.

A mountain people at the crossroads of rival European powers, the Swiss have had to fight not only their neighbors but a harsh climate while eking out a livelihood from rocky, infertile terrain. During the Middle Ages, Switzerland was so poor that many youths signed up as mercenaries for the armies of warring dukes, kings and Popes. The work ethic was baptized by Reformation leaders Calvin and Zwingli and the country's fortunes steadily improved when it ceased to be an international battleground. After the defeat of Napoleon, the confederation in 1815 declared its perpetual neutrality, a status—later backed by its large reserve army—that spared Switzerland the carnage and destruction of two world wars.

But Switzerland's neutrality is truly armed. Every male is required to spend one hundred and twenty days in basic training at the age of twenty. From age twenty through twenty-eight he gives three weeks a year, and thereafter two weeks every other year until age fifty. He keeps his automatic rifle, live ammunition, and gray-green uniform at home. Mr. Gruber was now past fifty, but he was still proud of his gun and Swiss-preparedness. Though its neutrality has kept the country out of NATO, Atlantic Alliance planners have been known to say, only partly in jest, that Switzerland is one of the strongest links in Western Europe's defense. A key element in Swiss strategy is a network of nuclear bomb shelters that would ensure survival of ninety percent of the population in case of an atomic attack.

The pastor had confided to me upon my arrival at the train station that Mr. Gruber still carried some psychic scars from days of Catholic-Protestant animosity and that I was being deliberately placed in his home in the hope that some healing could be effected. When I was greeted at the door by an attack-minded German shepherd, I was ready to ask for a new placement. Healing is fine, but life is essential. If a thermometer could have been attached to Mr. Gruber's manner, it would have gone from about 38°F on the first day to 75°F on the last day. It was spring, not winter, and my sense was that summer wasn't too far around the corner. On my final evening with the family, he dug down into an old trunk and brought out two Roman Catholic prayerbooks that had been handed down on his side of the family. Then he told the story of why he had changed Churches. The two books he held were printed in old German script-type; one was dated 1703 and the other 1736. I told him that books like that would be on display in a museum in my country—they were half a century older than the United States! He grunted with pleasure.

Early the next morning the pastor was at our door in his hiking boots to take me along with him on his "weekly mental-health break." We set out through the woods, up and down the hills, high-stepping through knee-deep snow drifts and buttoning our coats against the sharp winter wind that whistled through the valleys. I quizzed him about the life of a pastor in Switzerland.

"The most difficult thing to deal with," he said, "is the prevalent Swiss attitude of 'I'm making good money, I have a home, a car, and a mountain chalet—who needs God?' Money is God here. The Swiss will do anything for financial security."

Possessing no more valuable natural resource than snow, lacking a coastline, clement weather or even a common language, and with one-fourth of its 15,941 square miles covered by barren rock and glaciers, Switzerland's 6.3 million residents have achieved the Western world's highest standard of living and, in many ways, its most enviable quality of life. Citizens of seven European nations polled by the French magazine *Le Nouvel Economiste* ranked Switzerland first among nations they would move to if they left their own. There are no slums. Even in the most remote mountain areas, villagers enjoy the amenities of urban life: modern appliances, color television, and telephones from which they can dial California or Singapore. Violent crime is so rare that it makes banner headlines when it occurs. Letters are delivered without fail the next day, and the post office earns a profit. Wealth oozes from the elegant window showcases of jewelers, furriers, and chocolatiers along Zurich's Bahnhofstrasse and Geneva's Rue du Rhône. Above all, everything appears clean and orderly, from the geraniums that adorn the windowsills of rural railway stations to the computer-operated traffic lights that keep Zurich's commuters moving during rush hour. Litter is no doubt left behind by a foreigner.

We passed by a turreted chateau that stood stalwart on the brow of the hill against the winter landscape. In about an hour and a half's time we emerged from a trail in the woods to arrive at a thermal bath health spa. The 85°F swirling pool waters turned our skin from frost to flush. Toward the end of the morning we retook the trail with new energy in our step.

As we hiked, we spoke about the importance of recognizing in deed as well as in word the possibility of the authenticity of each other's faith and doctrine. I gave him an example from the Lord's Supper at which he had presided the previous Sunday. After Communion he had respectfully disposed of the elements used in the celebration in a way that corresponded to the possibility that they were no longer ordinary bread and wine. Some Reform Church ministers will leave them there or put them on a table in the next room where they will be forgotten and found days later, bread drying in the basket, wine sticking in the cup. When someone from an Orthodox, Roman Catholic, Episcopalian or Lutheran Church witnesses that, it speaks more loudly than any intellectually expressed doctrinal positions of respect. It lands with a dissonant note against the achievement of unity and against the prospect of shared Eucharist in the future.

On the other hand, when Reformed Christians treat the elements used in the Eucharist with respect they are saying with their sensitive deeds that they acknowledge at least the possibility that the doctrine held by those who believe in the real presence of Christ in the Eucharist is authentically Christian belief. When that kind of action accompanies the ecumenically sensitive word, the goal of unity does not seem so far away. He granted the point and proceeded to make one of his own, concerning the non-reciprocity of Holy Communion practiced by most Roman Catholics.

"We believe," he said, "that the Lord himself invites us to his table. That is the reason why we think that the celebration of the Holy Supper must be open to all those who hear his call and wish to follow him. The Church has received this sacrament from Christ, and it is he himself who, through the Church, gives himself to the believer. The table is the table of the Lord. It is not ours. That is why we believe that we do not have the right to refuse the sacrament to a baptized Christian who loves God and confesses Jesus Christ as Lord and Savior.

We think that intercommunion could promote the community of the Churches among themselves. We have a great deal of difficulty to understand—even after all the explanations in this regard—why shared Communion at the table of the Lord remains in principle unacceptable.

"Another thing which from our perspective is still at an unsatisfactory stage of evolution is the policy of the Roman Catholic and Orthodox Churches in a mixed marriage situation. In many places in Switzerland the number of ecumenical marriages is higher than the number of those concluded within one and the same Church. On one level these couples are a sign of the kind of community toward which the Churches are moving today: unity in diversity. While the Roman Catholic Church has made its rules for mixed marriages much more flexible, the changes still do not represent to our view a satisfying solution. The necessity of a dispensation from the bishop, for example, remains for the non-Catholic partner, and for the Church to which he or she belongs, a requirement that rubs the wrong way. Here, in particular, a policy of mutual eucharistic hospitality would be a big help to a number of Christians in our country."

We took a bus the last two miles and arrived near his home. A number of people were already there when we arrived, for the pastor and his wife and family had invited Kesenge and me and our host families for a farewell meal of raclette, a Swiss speciality of melted cheese, boiled potato and condiments. Afterward they all saw us off on the train. "Tom," Kesenge suggested, "let's give thanks for these people." So there, on the train in the descending darkness, Kesenge, a black African Disciples of Christ pastor, and I, a white North American Catholic priest, joined our prayers for a Swiss Zwinglian Reform pastor and his congregation with whom we had just spent several days. "That," I thought to myself as the tracks sped by, "is a better definition of ecumenism than most."

Geneva was entering into a weekend of celebrating its liberty. The Genevese don't go in for merrymaking in the streets, but they do have their own festival in deepest winter, to recall the night in 1602, the longest and coldest in the year, when the city beat off an attack by the troops of the Duke of Savoy and finally established its independence. The festival is called "L'Escalade."

By the end of the fourteenth century the city of Geneva occupied a unique position. While most of Europe was under the domination of Savoy or the French or German Empires, Geneva's citizens had obtained a substantial measure of independence. Their rights, immunities, and liberties were officially specified in a document dated 1387. Attracted both by the consequent freedom of restrictions on the trade fairs held there, as well as by the central geographic location of the city, merchants came from all over the continent. The city prospered and its prosperity engendered envy. The Dukes of Savoy tried for over a century to annex this prize by intrigue, and, ultimately, by assault.

The ousted Prince-Bishop of Geneva, who was residing in exile in Annecy, France, in the wake of Geneva's embrace of the Reformation, plotted to retake the city. To this end, he enlisted the forces of the Duke of Savoy. On the night of December 11/12, 1602, several thousand mercenaries moved stealthily across the plains and approached the town.

A three-hundred-man commando group went ahead to make a ford of faggots over the three-foot-deep moat. Others were assigned the task of scaling the walls (hence the name Escalade). They carried sections of ladders which they assembled at the base of the city's bastions. Once inside, they were to open the town gates to admit the main army.

The Genevese were off their guard and weak in forces, but Geneva's armed citizenry poured forth into the streets to defend the tiny republic as the massive bells of the cathedral pealed the alarm. Fighting was fierce, and even the ladyfolk got into the act. By the mint, where fighting was especially bitter, Mère Royaume, wife of the master of the mint, was cooking late into the night. Hearing the alarm, she rushed to the window and poured her scalding vegetable stew over the Savoyard soldier mounting the ladder without; then, smashing her cauldron over his head, she knocked him out. By popular tradition, she is the heroine of the occasion.

Some Savoyards were trapped and killed inside the city walls; the rest fled. A mix-up in signals spelled total defeat. The main Savoy army mistakenly attacked its own retreating forces. The fratricidal slaughter that ensued ended forever Savoy's hopes of conquest. The victory was won at the cost of only sixteen Genevese dead.

Skeptics may wonder why the Genevese are still talking about the affair three centuries later, but it must be remembered that war is almost unknown in Geneva, and the incident is a patriotic symbol. Geneva's national hymn, played on the carillon of the cathedral throughout the month of December, tells the full story. Every good schoolchild knows at least the first, third, and last of its sixty verses. To this day the people of Geneva commemorate the event with a stirring torchlight procession through the streets of the Old Town. The costumes and weapons of the period (handed down from generation to generation), the decoratively harnessed horses, the huge bonfire in the cathedral square, and the solemn intoning by the massed citizens of the hymn describing these events make for an unforgettable experience in living history.

Calvinists, of course, abhorred carnivals and their papist connotations. Before the French Revolution the celebration of the attack was restricted to commemorative Church services and an anniversary banquet like the one first organized in 1603 by the families of the sixteen victims. Later, children were dressed in Savoyard costumes and sent in to watch their elders feast, and a masquerade aspect crept in. By the nineteenth century, *L'Escalade* began to be used as an excuse for having a good time, and, in the latter part of the century, turned into a full-scale carnival.

It is obvious that something is afoot in December, for the bakeries' windows begin to fill with chocolate versions of Mère Royaume's famous cooking pot, standing proudly on their tripods, and filled with engagingly look-alike almond paste vegetables: green and white cauliflowers, yellow chanterelles, pinky-orange tomatoes, brown pockmarked potatoes and even imitation cubes of bacon-like Neapolitan slices. Within each home, in hospitals, in children's homes or at parties, tradition requires the use of the chocolate marmite or cooking pot in memory of Mère Royaume's act of valor for her compatriots.

I was invited for the festive dinner to the home of the Fulpius family, long-time residents of Geneva. Tradition has it that at the end of the family banquet on December 12, the head of the household reads an account of the *Escalade* to refresh everyone's memory, and then asks the youngest member of the family to split the chocolate pot with sword (or breadknife). Bertrand, 13, spurned all weapons and preferred the bare fist. Standing up at table with both hands locked above his head, he cried, "So perish the enemies of the Republic!" and smashed the pot with one well-aimed blow. Mère Royaume would have been proud. The evening ended with a general consumption of the marmite and its contents.

On one level, the *Escalade* recalls an event in which the Protestant forces repulsed the Catholic effort to retake the city and reinstate the Bishop of Geneva. I asked Mrs. Fulpius, an official guide for the city, if she thought the religious element was still an undercurrent in the celebration. But no, she honestly thought not; it is rather a festivity in which the independence loving Genevese keep alive the tradition of liberty which they so long ago won and defended.

There was an extensive program of events throughout the weekend. Mère Royaume's soup was served at the Arsenal in specially baked clay pots; burghers were posted around the city to receive the public; children in costume had their own procession and danced the traditional *picoulet*. Everything, however, was just a warm-up for the Great Procession for which is sought the greatest authenticity possible. There is not a watch, or pair of spectacles, or pair of ski gloves to be found. There are fifes and drummers, hangmen with nooses, soldiers in their iron helmets and breastplates, long spikemen and halyards, women and children from all walks of seventeenth century life, bearded churchmen in long black robes and Reformation collars. Among those presented are Theodore Bèze (who is reported to have slept through the whole battle);

the four Magnificent Lord Syndics, Geneva's executive council; and, of course, Mère Royaume.

The result is by far and away the most stirring parade I have ever witnessed. There is a nocturnal poetry to the torches moving through the narrow streets of Old Town, and the costumes and music are so authentic that it *is* 1602. The procession ends in the square before St. Peter's Cathedral where a gaily-plumed rider on a restless steed unrolls his scroll and proclaims once again the liberty of Geneva. The bonfire is lit, and the anthem intoned. The voices are solemn and serious. After all, this is Geneva!

The glass walls of the Bossey lecture hall only served to transmit vibrations of Christmas drawn from the winter scene outside. It was a stroke of genius on the professor's part to save our study of the Infancy Narratives for this time, capitalizing on rather than competing with the natural orientation of our thoughts. Everyone would soon be departing to spend the holidays with various host families in Switzerland and Germany. I was vacillating between spending Christmas with friends in France or at the Protestant sisters' community of Grandchamp near Neuchâtel, Switzerland, where there was going to be a retreat from the 23rd through the 26th of December.

Grandchamp had strong appeal: to approach Christmas in a way that focusses directly upon the religious content of the feast, to take time to really reflect on the mystery of the incarnation. I could not count upon another opportunity to spend that usually hectic time in silence and prayer. The Christmases ahead would undoubtedly be taken up with the pastoral ministry that fills a priest's life at this time of year. There were still a few days yet before I had to decide.

At the Bossey Christmas party the following week, I was amazed at the number of people from Africa, Indonesia, Korea, and Japan who knew the North American-European Christmas carols. When I asked some of the Filipinos about it at the punch bowl, they told of how their missionaries taught them to put cotton on their trees to simulate snow. They were then instructed to stand around the tree and sing "I'm Dreaming of a White Christmas." Like the Africans, they regretted the failure of the missionary forces to leave them to figure out for themselves how to celebrate and give expression to the good news with their own cultural symbols and meaning-system. The pattern of teaching, catechizing, and including the new faithful in each local denominational Church bore the same unspoken assumption, regardless of the culture: that Western standards of faith were the norm.

For most of the participants at Bossey who had come from lands which had been heavily missionized, the trip to Europe was severely disillusioning. They expected to see the ideals which had been brought to them by missionaries from the West being lived in the West. Surely the people from whom their teachers came exemplified the Christian life to a high degree. They could not understand why the beautiful churches they went to on Sunday were largely empty. "If only I had a church like that for my people—how they would fill it," Kesenge had wistfully remarked during our days together in the Swiss parish.

But there was at least one church that was full that week: the large and uniquely decorated chapel in the World Council of Churches. It was impressive and inspiring to look around and see it overflowing with people from all over the world who were working together in the name of the Savior Jesus Christ to bring unity, justice, and peace to his Church. The song of the angels, "Peace on earth and good will to all," was writ large in the daily efforts of these women and men for a world in which "kindness and truth shall meet, justice and peace shall kiss."

As the days of December crept toward the holiday break, I sent my regrets to the family in France that I would not be with them for Christmas. When departure day came, Dan, an Orthodox theologian from Rumania whose room was next door to mine, had made a similar decision. We left for Grandchamp together. Both of us were mentally fatigued. "I've been studying for four years in the West," Dan reflected, looking out the window. "I feel a strong pull to go back to my own country because I've lost some of my joy in Western Europe. In the East, among the Orthodox, when we study theology, we spend a lot of time in prayer together. And we *sing!* In the dining room, in the hallway, in the chapel, outdoors—we *sing.* Here, people seldom sing or pray together; they just go to the library and fill their heads with ideas. I've lost some of my joy in the West. I think I must go home to regain it."

I was not in a position to doubt Dan's love for singing. His voice broke into liturgical hymns morning and night and carried through the wall that separated our rooms. We arrived at Grandchamp just before supper. The sisters in the little shop where visitors are welcomed had been watching for us.

For fifty years there has been a ministry of hospitality in this place. In 1931 a sorority of faith was born from the quest of a small group of Swiss women. They were searching for a style of life that lent itself to prayerful listening to the word of God. Their search led them to the great monastic tradition which, though rejected by the Reformers for its abuses and errors, was nonetheless in vibrant evidence in many places. Three of the women began joyfully living a life of common prayer, simplicity, and works of mercy according to the spirit of the Beatitudes. They called themselves sisters of the community of Grandchamp, and their door was open to anyone who wished to come and share their life for a few hours or days or months.

After the war was over in 1945, women began to arrive from several European countries, drawn by what they had heard. They came from the many different churches that had been spawned by the Reformation to find a common life together that sought an equilibrium between contemplation and action. Today, there are fifty. Half of them live at Grandchamp; the other half have gone out in twos and threes to Algeria, Israel, Lebanon, Holland, France, and Latin America, to simply share the lives of the people and to be among them a sign of the presence of Christ and his joy. Their membership blends several generations of women in one common life where evangelical poverty, chastity, and obedience are freely chosen and the plain but distinctive blue habit is worn by all.

Dan and I were among some fifteen others from Switzerland, France, and Germany who had come to make the Christ-

mas retreat and to live the festival days in silence. But the
silence, whether during meals or prayers or between the services, was not a heavy silence that separated us; rather, it was a
silence that united us because for each one it was oriented toward Christ. There were Protestants, Orthodox, Anglicans,
and Roman Catholics. We were all equally welcome and respected for what we were.

The sisters' community, in forming its life of prayer and
liturgy, has drawn from all the main traditions. Among Protestantism, their witness is particularly unique, for here are people from Churches of the Reform living a monastic life, singing
the office, venerating icons, and celebrating the Eucharist
twice weekly. The use of images by Protestants, for example,
witnesses to their Reform brothers and sisters that the icon
may greatly help the approach to that single Icon, not human-
made but painted within us by the Holy Spirit, of which each
ecclesiastical icon is but an aspect and a reflection. Their openness to and integration of the spiritualities of East and West
challenges Orthodox and Catholics as well. How many of either of those traditions have entered, by living experience,
into the deep emotions of Protestant consciences: the Lutheran emotion of salvation through faith, the Calvinist awareness
of the glory of God, the Baptist and Methodist emotion of conversion.

In any case, I passed the day of Christmas Eve after the
manner of a Quaker: seeking the "inner light" in silent worship. I wanted to be rested and focused for the Vigil service at
11 P.M.

There could be no more appropriate chapel for a Christmas Eve liturgy than L'Arche, as the Grandchamp chapel is
called. It is the literal equivalent of a hayloft that has been well
swept but no more. The imagination has an easy time of placing Mary, Joseph, and the Christ Child within its walls, for the
atmosphere of a stable is already there.

By the time 11 P.M. arrived, I was primed to "peak" with
the Vigil liturgy.

But it never happened.

When it was over, I remained where I was on the floor,

searching for reasons to explain my sense of "flatness." I was sure it felt like a retreat, but not so sure it felt like Christmas. My mind started taking the situation apart. Was it because the symbols which usually say "It's Christmas!" to me weren't there in the chapel: no crèche scene, no tree, no Advent wreath? Was it because the accoutrements of high celebration I'm used to on the main festival days weren't there: no full choir (though the sisters sang like angels), no musical accompaniment to the singing, no "smells and bells"? Was it because I thought the preacher's homily lacked joy . . . or was it just me? Was it because the liturgy was more contemplative than celebrative? Was it because I was far away from my family? Was it because I needed an emotional "fix," because I still had some adolescent need for symbols of security?

I was grasping for reasons to explain why I felt so out-of-sync with the occasion. It was Christmas! Why didn't I *feel* like Christmas?

Everyone had left *L'Arche* by now and all were gathering around the fireplace in the welcome room for hot drinks, cakes, and cookies. I wandered over, hoping for a miracle, hoping that somehow what I hadn't found in chapel I'd find in the happy voices around the hearth.

But my conversation reflected an inner disjointedness. My thoughts tripped over each other as though speaking were a strangeness. A couple of times in my efforts to converse, uncomfortable silences spectered forth. My heart wasn't in it. Something in me said: "Go—this is getting worse." But the idea of walking alone out in the fog lacked appeal. The part of me that was still looking for Christmas bid me stay and search on.

I was one of the last to leave. Dan and I walked back toward our rooms together. I stood on the stairway leading to our floor, tired, but not wanting to go to bed. "Dan," I said, "would you like to talk a while?"

We went into my room and I told him what I was feeling. He said that in his first Christmas out of his country, away from his family and parish, he found another Orthodox community but went away crying because he still felt like a stranger there.

This was his fifth one in a row. "I just don't look for so much anymore," he said quietly.

After Dan had gone to bed, I sat there a while longer. Things weren't supposed to work like this: I had shared it, but that hadn't taken it away.

At 6 A.M. I was roused from sleep by a brass ensemble in the courtyard playing a Christmas carol. They played just long enough to get me out of bed and to the window, then shouted "Joyeux Noël!" and got back in their cars and drove away. It was still warm between the covers, but now I couldn't get back to sleep. At 7 A.M. I heard the voices of the sisters singing carols in the hallway. I got up again, slipped on my robe, and went out and sat huddled in the corner, happy for their joyful presence. When they realized I was there, they looked surprised and acknowledged me with smiles. When they moved on to another building, I decided that I'd follow their *chemin de joie,* quickly changed, and caught up with them again, this time providing a little bass harmony. We sang together until matins at 8 A.M. and then went to chapel.

Normally, I would not have noticed the cross in a church on Christmas Day, but this time I was very conscious of its presence. Indeed, there was little else to look at. Maybe this Christmas is a "growing up" experience, I thought, to move me from the flowery sentiments of a child and a star to something more substantive. It's easier to rock a cradle than to carry a cross, to follow a star than a grown-up from Galilee who asks big things. I was still searching for the answer.

When I came down the steps out of chapel, Sr. Edith was standing by the door motioning to the Roman Catholic retreatants. She had information about Christmas Day Masses in neighboring parishes. We asked for the biggest, liveliest liturgy in Boudry.

The so-called "Grande Messe" at 10 A.M. wasn't so grand. Obviously, their main celebration had been at midnight. If it wasn't, this parish was in trouble.

On Christmas Day afternoon, the "missing piece" in my puzzle was handed to me.

I was sitting in the Jubilee Room listening to Handel's

Messiah and making a papercut. Sr. Heidi came in and sat down at my table. "We'd like to have a Eucharist tomorrow on St. Stephen's Day," she began. "Could you help plan it and preach?"

"Of course," I said. "I'd be delighted."

Within minutes, I noticed that I began to feel excited.

The next morning when I awoke and went down the hallway, I saw the candles burning in the darkness, surrounded by evergreens, on all the stairway landings. Their flicker seemed warm and friendly.

In the middle of the liturgy of St. Stephen's Day, it all came together. My Christmas Eve "funk" wasn't because I was out of North America or in a foreign land. It wasn't because I was with a Protestant rather than a Catholic community. It wasn't even because I was far from my family, who I have always felt to be God's greatest gift to me and who normally translate the meaning of home and Christmas for me. I had been depressed because I am a priest and there had been little opportunity to be who or what I am all during Advent and Christmas until this moment. Without the chance to give at Christmas—our own gifts and in our own way—we can't complete the cycle of the season.

That morning, in proclaiming the Gospel and preaching, I felt joy and gratitude and *energy*. When was the last time I had awakened with an eager start and a sense of excitement because in a short time I would be able to do what a minister does? It had been a *long* time, because the opportunities for sacramental ministry were always there and came to be taken for granted. Sharing faith and hope and joy through the celebration of word and sacraments grows on one. It had been precisely the absence of opportunities in this very pastoral season to do that, and my reaction to that lack, which made me realize how deeply the ministry takes root. It had gotten in my blood, and the experience of being on the sidelines, away from a community which gives that special ministry, left me feeling very unfulfilled.

Yet that experience had been, by reverse action, a tremendous grace. It helped me to prize the ministry all the more. As the day went on and I realized these things with greater and greater clarity, I became increasingly happy. On the twenty-sixth of December, I felt the joy of Christmas.

I couldn't even wait for the retreat to end to express it. I had to explode somewhere, *now,* in greens and reds. The mountains were literally just across the road and it was snowing. I grabbed my cross-country skis and was on my way.

There are days when one skis one's brains out because one is full of mental fatigue, and days when one skis one's heart out because one is full of joy. I was going to leave bright red valentines all over the snow. On my map I located a trail along which were threaded several villages like intermittent cranberries on a popcorn string. La Tourne was the first. I clamped on my skis and disappeared into the pines.

The benevolent mountain silence swallowed my whoops and yelps and smiled. Kick, glide. Kick, glide. My legs drove harder, fueled with the exaltation that geysered within. Through La Tourne, through Les Petites Ponts, through Brot Dessus. Finally, at Martel, I felt the implosion residing, and my energy surplus near spent.

The waiting room in the tiny train station at the edge of the village was empty. I took off my shoes and put my feet up on the radiator. The snow was falling harder now, and the wind was coming up. Through the window I watched a little toddler come down the road, shuffling along on his miniature skis. He'd probably received them the day before. A man with a wheelbarrow full of chopped wood stopped and put down his load. He stood behind the little tyke and, taking his arms, showed him how to move them in rhythm with the stride of his legs.

How important it felt to take time. To be attentive to all the experiences of life and to reflect on them. A particular hazard of this year was to pile experience on top of experience until the wheelbarrow was full, never leaving myself enough time or reflective space to stop along the way and attend to rhythm.

The silent days of Christmas had helped me to discern a rhythm, a style, a form that worked well for my life. I had seen it better through losing it, through feeling very uncoordinated. During Advent and Christmas, all my developed pastoral instincts had been standing on tiptoe, ready to run. But there was no track.

When we are living and being in such a way that what is deepest and truest in us has free expression, our lives are like an art form—they have rhythm, balance, harmony. For my mom and dad, my brothers and sister, marriage, family, their careers, and the way they live them is their art form. Our foundational values are the same, but our art forms are different. There are values and convictions which are common to us, but my way of expressing them is being a priest. Our art forms are the different ways by which we live the same vocation: to be available for service in love—whether to a spouse and family, or to a fraternity and Church community, or both at the same time.

The reaffirmation of my life's choice was God's Christmas gift to me.

The snowfall was turning into a first-rate mountain storm and visibility was rapidly dropping. I reached for my shoes.

But it was difficult to feel either anxiety or hurry.

Dan and I left the following day on a trip through the northern half of Switzerland and then doubled back through the Black Forest in Germany to Freiburg in Breisgau where we stayed two nights with the Sacred Heart Fathers. For Dan, it was a homecoming. He had lived in the priests' community the previous four years while doing his doctorate. His dissertation study dealt with the integration of Eastern and Western forms of the Christian spiritual life. Topics relative to his studies and the subject of unity occupied many of our hours on the road.

"The solution for the course of unity that I see is this," Dan said one afternoon as the countryside passed by outside the window. "We must return to the essentials that we agreed upon in common and accept them anew. And anything that has been decided unilaterally or developed since then is not forced upon the other but is seen as proper to that tradition—for example, celibacy for the clergy. At one point we agreed on a common discipline for celibacy, but the West later made it mandatory for all.

"The Orthodox believe in the infallibility of the Church and in the importance of a central figure of unity. They recognize from antiquity the primacy of the See of Rome. But Rome, being the only patriarchal see in the West after the schism, developed in the direction of a monarchy, while the Oriental and Orthodox Churches preserved the accent of conciliarity. Each needs to an extent what the other has. The West needs to give more autonomy to the local Churches. And the Eastern Churches—who have developed so deeply in the direction of autonomous national Churches to the point that it is a problem among themselves—need a stronger principle of unity.

"But when you consider the dynamics involved among the people of each tradition in a change, you begin to understand why unity isn't yesterday and won't be early tomorrow. The Roman Catholics have been so trained to look to Rome, to lean upon the authority of the Pope, that if that were downplayed and the authority of local Churches emphasized, wouldn't you become just like so many more national Churches? And if the Orthodox were asked to accept an authority that comes from outside the local Church, you can't imagine how difficult that would be for us. We don't even dare call a council 'ecumenical' until several years after it has happened—and only then if it has been accepted by all the independent Churches and thereby earns the title. We could never just convoke an 'ecumenical council.' 'Ecumenical' represents a judgment made by all the Churches *after* they've each seen the council's proceedings and recognized their faith in them."

One of the things that struck me most about Dan was the way his faith was integrated with his daily life. One evening while at the Sacred Heart Fathers' residence we were sitting in his room talking. He wanted to finish off a carton of juice we had begun, but I suggested that we save it for the next morning. "No," he said. "Tomorrow is Sunday and we fast before the liturgy!" But what we both knew was that it would be a

Mass and it would be I and not he who would be receiving Communion.

We returned to Grandchamp for the New Year's Eve and New Year's Day celebrations of the feast of the Holy Name of Jesus. By January 3 we were back at Bossey.

One of the highlights of each week was the day at the Ecumenical Center in Geneva. Some visitors to the Center expect to be received in large impressive buildings, similar to the Vatican State in Rome. They soon discover that the headquarters of the World Council of Churches looks much like any modern office building—a functional concrete structure four stories high, inconspicuous among the other organizations located in Geneva's "international area."

On a slight rise above the United Nations, the World Health building, and the new headquarters of the International Labor Office, the buildings of the Ecumenical Center house the Council. The main block with three wings consists primarily of offices in which some two hundred and seventy-five people on the Council staff work each day from 8:30 A.M. to 5 P.M. The complex, surrounded by trees, lawns and car parks, also contains a chapel in which the staff meets weekly for worship and daily for intercessions on behalf of the Churches. There is also an exhibition and conference hall, smaller meeting rooms, a bookshop, cafeteria and library.

The World Council of Churches is a fellowship of over three hundred churches in over one hundred countries "which confess the Lord Jesus Christ as God and Savior according to the Scriptures and therefore seek to fulfill together their common calling to the glory of the one God, Father, Son and Holy Spirit." The four hundred million Christians represented in its ranks embody all races, worship in hundreds of languages, live under every kind of political order and disorder, and yet commit themselves to sail through the storms of contemporary history in the same boat. The Council is not a super-Church or universal authority controlling what all those Christians should believe and do. Each member Church commits itself, whatev-

er its understanding of its own authority and organization, to
the search for an expression of visible unity and obedience
through theological study, common encounter, witness and
service. The member Churches must remind each other that
membership is meaningless if commitment to the basis disap-
pears. The main elements of that basis are confession of the
Lordship of Christ, fellowship of the member Churches, acceptance of biblical authority, common witness and service, and
the worship of the Trinity. How seriously the members' constituencies take their membership in the world body is not a
matter that can be legislated. Most Reformation and Orthodox
Churches belong.

The Council exists to serve the Churches, to enable them
to serve God and one another and people in need. It is the
most visible international expression of the ecumenical movement which seeks to promote the unity of the Church and the
unity of humankind. Its main task is to enable the Church in
each place to *be* the ecumenical movement. As servant of the
Churches, it calls them to the goal of visible unity in one faith
and one eucharistic fellowship. It facilitates and supports their
effort at common witness, and expresses with one voice their
concern for the promotion of peace and justice. It fosters the
on-going renewal of the Churches in unity, worship, mission,
and service.

The policies of the WCC are determined by delegates of
the member Churches meeting in Assembly, normally every
seven years. The most recent Assembly was held in Nairobi,
Kenya in 1975. The next Assembly is in Vancouver, British Co-
lumbia, Canada in 1983.

There is a large painting on the wall of the Ecumenical
Center's lobby which charts the birth, growth, and development of the WCC. It was the missionary expansion, most notably in Africa and Asia, which gave birth to the twentieth
century ecumenical movement. This movement is generally
reckoned to have begun at the world missionary conference in
Edinburgh, Scotland in 1910. Its vision gave birth to three re-
lated movements. The International Missionary Council, established in 1921, brought together foreign missionary societies

and national Christian councils for study and common action. Following the First World War, the Life and Work Movement held a universal conference in Stockholm, Sweden in 1925, at which leaders of the Churches began to explore together the responsibility of Christians for the great social questions of peace and justice. The Faith and Order Movement held a world conference in 1927 in Lausanne, Switzerland on the thorny questions of doctrine and authority underlying Church divisions. The second meeting of these two latter bodies proposed the setting up of the World Council of Churches.

After the interruption of the Second World War, the WCC was finally constituted by one hundred and forty-seven Churches at Amsterdam in 1948. In the early years the Council was still very much a European/North American affair. Since then, however, it has become steadily more a *world* Council in fact as well as in aspiration. The 1960's and 1970's saw many Asian, African, Latin American, Pacific and Caribbean Churches taking up membership. In recent years, women, laity and young people have had more prominence in its leadership. At present, the staff represents forty-two countries and many different Churches and Christian traditions.

From my first visit to the WCC I was impressed with the sense of dedication, faith, integrity and openness that the staff manifested. Early in the fall I sat in on the orientation sessions for new staff who had only been working at the WCC for a few months. It was a valuable experience, not only because it gave me some insights into the inner-workings of the WCC but also because it demythologized the whole operation. Various staff members wanted to know why there was not more communication between executive and secretarial staff, why there was not more sharing within the WCC itself ("If we can't live ecumenism here, where can we expect it to be lived?"), why there were not more people at the daily prayer sessions, why orientation did not include the opportunity to familiarize oneself with the good library, and so on. It all seemed pretty normal. Like every other big organization, it has difficulty in living its rhetoric.

To be sure, the WCC is peopled by men and women with

ideals and vision, but they are flesh and blood nonetheless. The candidness of the staff consistently impressed me; there was never any sense of a united "front" for the sake of image. The responses to questions were very *real* and, by that token, quite acceptable, even if not always bearing good news. The Director of the Department of Communication offered this description of the WCC: "The WCC is a chaos in which one tries to accomplish a lot with a little, in which one is permanently overworked, in which one doesn't often get feedback for what is written or produced, and in which one has to struggle for communication within the offices of the WCC itself." *That* from the Director of Communications!

As regards communication, perhaps the most important half-hour of each day is tea-time in the middle of the afternoon. Everyone gathers in the cafeteria, and the relationships begun or kept up to date, the information exchanged, and the sense of camaraderie in an effort that binds all together make for thirty golden minutes.

A person walking into the Ecumenical Center with a sense of who he or she wants to see, and about what, is likely to emerge glorifying the virtues of centralization. The Lutheran World Federation, The World Alliance of Reformed Churches and the World Methodist Council all have their offices with the WCC in the Ecumenical Center. Offices are also provided for the Conference of European Churches, the representatives of the Russian Orthodox Church and the Ecumenical Patriarchate of Constantinople. The number of key people that one can see and talk to in the span of a single working day all within the confines of one complex is a time-and-energy-saver's dream. The people on whose doors I knocked were always busy but welcoming and ready to take time to talk.

For all its ecumenical services over the last thirty-four years the World Council is not itself the ecumenical movement. Being the only participant in the Bossey program whose Church did not belong to the WCC, I found myself the object of my colleagues' questions as to why the Roman Catholic Church is not a member. I didn't have a good answer. I had often wondered myself why it was not. So I passed on the ques-

tion. What I found particularly interesting was that nearly everyone I asked had a different answer. When I put them all
together, I felt as though I understood better some of the com-
plexity of the situation.

The Council's Honorary President said that at Vatican II
the Catholic Church was shot into an orbit of experiment and
change. It was presently occupied with the task of re-entry and
had its hands full right now trying to hold the spaceship together against the various forces of friction and stress. It was
not the opportune moment to present its people with another
change to assimilate.

The answer that one of the staff members at Bossey offered was that because of its hierarchical structure and its
sheer numerical weight, the Roman Catholic Church would
create a whole series of administrative and psychological problems, not to mention theological ones, if it entered as a full
member into the WCC. It would require a change in the
Council's constitution, alter the Council's character, and create
an entirely new situation. He wondered how eager the other
member Churches were to have all that happen.

But the acting General Secretary of the Council did not
agree with that implication. The size was not the problem, he
said. Granted, it would be like an elephant coming in to pas-
ture with a herd of horses. But the WCC had drawn up a formula to accommodate that in 1971 when the two bodies were
looking at the possibility of the Roman Catholic Church's entry
as a full member. The WCC had been ready, and the Roman
Catholic Church was welcome then as it is now to join. The
crux of it, he felt, was the Roman Catholic Church's perception
of itself as the place where unity already subsists in the
Church. To enter the WCC as one Church among others seeking the unity of the Church would necessitate watering-down
or letting-go of or interpreting differently that conviction.

A member of the Vatican's Secretariat for Promoting
Christian Unity offered several more points of consideration:
membership in the WCC is by National Churches, e.g., the Lutheran Church of America might decide to join, but the Lutheran Church of Germany might not. However, the Roman

Catholic Church is an amalgam of national Churches in an international universal Church with a strong center of authority. It does not relate to world organizations through its national Churches, but with its universal voice. Thus it would be committed in a way that the other member Churches of the WCC are not. Second, the staff of the WCC, who are members of many different Churches, serve the WCC as a separate entity independent from the administration levels of the churches to which they belong. But the Roman Catholic Church's tendency, if it participated, would not be to see the people who represented it at the WCC as one step removed from itself. Third, back in 1971–1972 when membership was being looked at, the Roman Catholic Church just felt that it had not accumulated enough experience yet in working with the WCC. "The years that have transpired between then and now," he said, "have been very valuable and there is a real commitment to one another. We know we cannot live without each other."

The problem in the main seems to be how to relate the right kind of diversity to the right kind of unity. Put a different way, exactly how can the WCC, as a council of autonomous Churches, relate in formal and institutional terms to the centralized authority of the Vatican? Another Bossey staff member provided a concrete example of the kind of potential problem that could arise under present circumstances. "Suppose the Roman Catholic Church were to join the WCC as a full member. The next General Assembly of the WCC in Vancouver would be the first Assembly since the fifth century in which all Christians of the world were represented. Such a gathering would merit, in fact, more so than any other assembly which has called itself such in the past fifteen hundred years, the title of an ecumenical council ('ecumenical' comes from a Greek word meaning 'the whole inhabited world'). There would be the natural implications of authority proper to such a unique gathering. But suppose the Assembly made a statement that didn't exactly square with some moral teaching of the Roman Catholic Church. Which would the Roman Catholic in the street be expected to take more seriously?"

The bottom line is that the vision, methodologies and

timetables of the two world bodies do not yet coincide. Yet both are dedicated to and striving for the unity of all Christians, and there is a great deal of collaboration. Given all that has happened in the last twenty years, nothing should seem impossible. Roman Catholicism has radically changed its attitude toward the ecumenical movement since 1960. The decisive turning point came with the Second Vatican Council and the great influence of Pope John XXIII. Before that time the official position of the Vatican was negative toward rapprochement with other Churches. Pope John XXIII created in 1960 the Secretariat for Promoting Christian Unity which coordinates all ecumenical relations with other Churches. From 1965 onward a Joint Working Group of members appointed by the Vatican Secretariat for Christian Unity and the WCC has met annually to discuss common problems and concerns among their members. The Week of Prayer for Christian Unity is annually prepared by a group of World Council and Roman Catholic representatives. The Faith and Order Commission of the WCC includes twelve Roman Catholic theologians. And for more than a decade, any important World Council conference or consultation has been attended by a number of official and fully participating Roman Catholic delegates. In addition, there are ad hoc contacts in regard to many programs and projects of common interest.

Since the Second Vatican Council, mutual understanding and collaboration between the Roman Catholic Church and the member Churches of the WCC have steadily grown. Dialogue has led to the discovery of unexpected convergences and common perspectives. Bilateral conversations have made possible the formulation of significant agreement on issues of doctrine. The findings of the dialogues, though, need to be communicated to, and appropriated into, the life of the Churches. There is not yet sufficient communication with the Churches at the national and local levels. The Joint Working Group, for example, has not been able either to benefit as it might have from their experience or to share with them its reflections.

While collaboration between the Roman Catholic Church

and the World Council of Churches extends over a wide range of issues and concerns, it is evident that in certain respects collaboration remains limited. The emphasis, on the whole, has been on study programs rather than action programs. One action program that was entered into jointly—Sodepax—was phased out in 1980 because of different priorities and methodologies on the part of the two sponsoring world bodies. The Joint Working Group has not succeeded in discovering ways of responding together to political issues. Clearly, the differences between the Roman Catholic Church as one Church and the WCC as a fellowship of Churches must be recognized in evaluating the progress of collaboration. The different structures existing on both sides must also be taken into account.

The transition from dialogue and collaboration to unity can only gradually be achieved. There is, therefore, a need for intermediary stages on the way to unity. Unity cannot be achieved on the basis of theological and ecclesiological designs alone. Churches need to become acquainted with one another and begin to share their daily lives. They need, therefore, effective ecumenical structures which enable them to give full expression to the partial communion existing between them. One promising sign is that the Roman Catholic Church now has full membership in the National Council of Churches in twenty-four countries.

One of the fall-out effects, however, of official Roman Catholic Church non-membership in the WCC is a low-level of participation by Roman Catholics in the programs of the WCC's Ecumenical Institute at Bossey. It is only when the Roman Catholic Church joins the WCC, hypothesize former Bossey co-program director Alain Blaincy and Fr. René Beaupère of the St. Ireneus Ecumenical Center in Lyon, France, that both Roman Catholics and Latin languages (French, Spanish, Italian) will be found in greater evidence in the WCC's programs. While it cannot be denied that Roman Catholic membership in the WCC would make WCC programs more widely known among Roman Catholics, there is absolutely nothing to prevent more active recruitment toward a fuller Roman Catholic participation in the present situation. The plain fact is that

Bossey does not seem to be very widely known in the Catholic (and, one might add, Orthodox) community. The staff at Bossey is solicitous to change this. The WCC (in spite of Orthodox membership) and hence Bossey are still popularly perceived, it seems, as an Anglo-Saxon Protestant institution. Finding ways of soliciting greater Orthodox-Roman Catholic participation is one of the challenges facing the Institute in its quest to be truly ecumenical.

January found more people in the library than usual at Bossey. At the end of the month a twenty-page paper was due from each of us on some aspect of our biblical studies. It is perhaps misleading to advertise the program as a "Graduate School." Not all participants would strictly qualify as graduate students and the level of academic endeavor is not that to which a Westerner normally concludes upon hearing the term. The academic question, given the linguistic difficulties, is how much "heavy work" it is realistic to ask for. Academic credit is possible, however, through matriculation at the University of Geneva—and justifiably so, if credit is to measure learning, and learning is not to be restricted to what is in books. The cultural evenings alone, put on by the various national groups throughout the semester, are, together, worth a course in geography and culture. Ecumenical education with worldwide perspectives in a global context, one of the Institute's goals, need not be seen only in terms of the lecture hall.

The last of the cultural evenings was that presented by the North Americans. The Europeans had been razzing us for several weeks, saying that if it was indeed to be an evening of North American culture it must necessarily be a short program and thus they could make other plans for the second half of the evening.

Undaunted, we worked up a series of skits that featured the Wild West, the South, French Canada, and immigrant ethnicity. One of our themes was: "There's no such thing as a 'typical North American.'" At intermission we served the national staple of popcorn and coke. Act II presented jazz and disco dancing, engaged the audience in Halloween party games, and offered a live demonstration of how football is played. The line-up was the most international in the history of the game, and the three point stances confirmed the findings of anthropologists everywhere: there is no one single approach to *anything*. The center, a professor from New Hebrides, crouched over the ball and then suddenly turned all red and straightened up again when, as the quarterback, I put my hands on his rump to receive the snap. We ended the entertainment with— what else—Charlie Brown and the Peanuts gang singing "Happiness" (with the words changed to fit the situations of life at Bossey). A party and dance followed, with every woman on campus being conscripted into action. As we found out, such social constructs weren't necessary: many of the men were quite spontaneous in just getting up and moving to the music with or without a partner.

January 18–25 brought the Week of Prayer for Christian Unity and special services each morning. On the closing Sunday, all the local Protestant and Catholic parishes highlighted the importance of unity by canceling their respective Sunday services and holding a common service at Bossey. There was standing room only in the largest hall on campus. Afterward, a snack and drink was available and everyone mixed and talked. I wondered if such an idea could be viable in America: the designation of a site large enough to hold all local communities for a common service followed by fellowship.

The day after everyone's paper was handed in, the whole community climbed on the bus and headed into the Burgundian hills of France for a long weekend in Taizé.

Taizé is so small that it is not even on most maps of France. I had been there twice before and each time found it necessary to first locate Cluny, the Benedictine monastic foundation whose reform movement embraced a thousand monasteries throughout Europe at the end of the twelfth century and whose artistic achievements were unparalleled. The largest church in Christendom once stood on the monastery grounds; all but one-tenth of it now lies in ruin in one of the French Revolution's most unforgivable destructions.

There are still thousands of pilgrims moving on the Cluny

road today, but their destination is a tiny village of no more than twenty stone buildings six miles further down the road past Cluny. Here, in Taizé, the son of a Swiss Reform pastor and French mother from this Burgundian region bought a house in 1940 and looked after Jewish refugees swept from their homelands by Hitler's broom. His name was Roger Schutz.

In 1942, three like-minded men from Reformation Churches, one of whom was Max Thurian, joined him. Prayer and an open door for their neighbors were characteristic of their life together. By Easter 1949 their number had grown to seven, and they committed themselves for life to celibacy, community possessions, and a life of service and obedience to Christ and the Church. They called themselves the brothers of Taizé.

Four years later, Brother Roger had written the Rule of Taizé to guide their common life. It was adopted as well by the sisters of Grandchamp. For two decades the seeds of prayer and Gospel living took root in this socially impoverished and economically depleted area. Then, as always happens, the aroma of Gospel-living went out on the currents of the air. The people seemed to "smell" the fragrance of something extraordinary being lived in the house on the hill. They came from far and wide to taste of it personally. In 1962 a new church had to be built to hold them all. Over its doors is painted in five languages:

Church of the Reconciliation
Be reconciled all you who enter here
parents and children
husbands and wives
believers and those who cannot believe
Christians and their fellow Christians.

As for lodging, huge army tents were set up in the fields on the edge of the village.

The community of brothers now counted among its fraternity Anglicans and Catholics. In 1966, members of an international Roman Catholic congregation of sisters took up quarters in the next village and took on responsibility for a large part of the work of welcoming people to Taizé. People described what was happening here as a "parable of community." The young, impatient with doctrinal divisions inherited from past centuries, responded to this working model of reconciliation.

In 1970, twenty-four thousand youths from forty-two countries attended the announcement of a "Council of Youth," a reality that would involve and gather youth from every land to open up new ways of reconciliation. The preparation of the Council of Youth lasted four and a half years; it was an "inner," spiritual adventure of personal and parish renewal before it was an "outer " public international gathering. In 1974, from August 29 to September 1, forty thousand youths gathered at Taizé, coming this time from one hundred different countries. Six circus tents arranged like the petals of a flower formed an immense provisional church in the camping area. All those inside sat on the ground and were challenged to be a "people of the Beatitudes." From then on, Brother Roger and an intercontinental team began to draft texts called "Acts of the Council of Youth" while sharing the conditions and lives of the poorest of the poor in Calcutta, Kenya, Brazil, and on the China Sea, Belfast, and other similar locations.

Brother Max Thurian, now one of Europe's most respected theologians, came to tell us about Taizé and to respond to our questions. "Taizé does not want to be a place of pilgrimage but a stimulus to reflection," Brother Max said. "Taizé doesn't want to be a movement; it wants to inspire and encourage involvement on local Church levels. It wants to get the people who come here from different countries to share with one another what they are doing, to cross-fertilize one another. Taizé does not want people to focus on this place but on their local situations."

"Is Taizé too 'successful'?" asked my roommate Bill, who had spent the better part of two summers at Taizé several years ago. "Do numbers and popularity begin to work against you after a certain point?"

"Can we be 'too successful' in Christ?" Brother Max responded rhetorically. "We're not looking for numbers, but we have to face up to the fact that there is a danger in numbers. Right now the numbers are just a fact, a reality that is there. If even a few young people find their way to Christ again, it is worth all our efforts."

Many of the brothers had just recently returned from a four-day meeting in Rome which had drawn some thirty thousand young people from all over the Western world. A much publicized aspect of that gathering had been the meeting with Pope John Paul II in a packed St. Peter's Basilica. On that occasion Brother Roger called for an openness on the part of everyone to the ministry of a universal pastor. The implications of his statement seemed to be on the minds of many in our group. Schatzi, a Lutheran pastor from the United States, gave voice to it: "Brother Roger has been urging closer relations with the Pope and speaking about the need for one spiritual father. Would you discuss that a bit?"

"In the approach to the unity of the Church as a community that we and the young people who come to Taizé are hoping for," Brother Max replied, "I would say that there is room for a service-function for visible unity. Certainly the instrument in the great tradition of the Church is the bishops' council. It would be in this conciliar form that visible unity would be best maintained. But we cannot deny that the Church in the West has had a special relationship with the Bishop of Rome. Rome was a Church which had a leadership role in 'presiding over charity' and its bishop evolved as a universal pastor or servant of the servants of God. The Bishop of Rome could today play a positive role in encouraging all Christians to come to unity. Of course this presupposes a terrific amount of development on all sides in the papacy to begin with, for it is not immediately comprehensible or acceptable to all Christians.

"But I was particularly struck by a message which the Methodist Church sent to Paul VI when he went before the United Nations that it (the Methodist Church) felt it was represented in front of these members of universal political bodies by his presence there. I think it's true—there are certain moments when the Church needs to be expressed in a sign by a representative. It may be a council, or sometimes it may be a particular person in whom a charisma for this is recognized. On the side I might add that the best argument for the papacy in the Reformed understanding is not the theory of succession from Peter, but Popes who show in their own personal lives a love of the Gospel and a desire to serve the needs of the world.

"The idea is of someone in certain cases being able to exercise a universal responsibility for the Church—but a responsibility that always has the nature of service and is collegial, having a reference to the college of bishops, the councils, and the Church as a whole. The Pope cannot just act completely on his own. So I would say in general that that is the sort of feeling in Taizé about the Pope.

"We have all read no doubt that this particular Pope, John Paul II, is very doctrinally conservative. But we must be careful not to sell him short. He is a very dynamic and apostolic man. He has a will to make progress. When he met some people very involved in ecumenism, he said to them, 'Help me to know more.' For the average Pole, an Orthodox is a Russian and a Protestant is a German. Given the history of Poland, there is not a natural inclination in either direction. That's a non-theological problem, but it's a problem nonetheless. Yet the things John Paul said in his recent visit to Germany about Luther—well, no Pope has ever talked about Luther in a positive way before. And no Pope has ever spoken so much about ecumenism. No Pope has dared to call the non-Catholic Churches 'Churches.' He completely gave up the very careful language of Vatican II which reserved 'Church' for the Roman Catholics and the Orthodox and perhaps the Anglicans, but then called the others 'ecclesiastical communities.' He talks about the Lutheran Church, the Baptist Church, and so on. I think he's a rather surprising man."

Judy, another Lutheran pastor from the United States, spoke up: "In 1949, seven brothers took their vows to celibacy, community possessions, and a life of service and obedience. I presume those brothers were Protestant. I'm wondering about the theological implications of the taking of vows because in the Augsburg Confession and in the Reform Churches in gen-

eral there is great exception taken to the traditionally Roman
Catholic vows. Both Luther and Calvin condemned the monastic way of life."

"We had to discuss this question very thoroughly," Brother Max said, "with members of the Lutheran and Reform
Churches in the 1950's. The condemnation of the taking of
vows that you referred to in the Augsburg Confession flowed
in large part from a desire during the Reformation to recognize the priesthood of all baptized believers, and not for this to
be reserved for just certain ones. Monastic life and the episcopacy had lost their sense of service. Today these problems and
situations are past. It's necessary for us Protestants to be open
to the Holy Spirit to see anew if the vows are viable. One can't
know this theoretically. It has to be lived. We thought it was
possible for us today to restate this way of Gospel life. We can't
just raise the problems of the sixteenth century on a theoreti-
cal basis and think that that settles it."

Gisela, a theological student in the Reform Church in Holland, had only days before received a letter from her father
who had been reading the accounts in the newspapers of the
Taizé meeting in Rome. "Taizé seems to be becoming more
and more Catholic," he had written, "and I feel more Protestant than ever." Gisela passed on her father's sentiments to
Brother Max and asked, "How Protestant is Taizé at the moment, and what would you say are its Protestant characteristics?"

"That's a good question you pose," Brother Max answered.
"What does it mean to be a Protestant? I can only give you my
own answer, and you can tell me whether you think I am on
the right track or not."

Early in the year I had participated in a five day meeting
of the Group of the Dombes, theologians from France, Belgium, and Switzerland who work together on ecumenical
problems. Time and again at that conference I had witnessed
Brother Max's humble manner and irenic spirit rescue the proceedings and keep things moving forward toward reconciling
solutions. I found myself impressed once again by his accepting, non-threatening, and gentle manner.

"As far as I am concerned," he was saying, "to be a Reformed Church or Lutheran Church member means to have the freedom in the name of the word of God, understood in the community's reading of the Scriptures, to have the freedom to open yourself up to the genuine movement of the Spirit. If union with the Roman Catholic Church, for example, means abandoning the liberties and rights of conscience which were achieved in the struggle of the Reformation, then a Protestant will not seek it.

"But for me, Protestantism is a tradition which has no option but to be ecumenical. It lives in the name of the word of God which is never closed, always active. That's why Protestantism cannot lay down limits on the word of God, limiting it to a particular expression in a definite, final, unchangeable way. That's what Protestantism is: the freedom constantly to listen anew to the genuine movement of the Spirit.

"So if today there is a possibility of really serving unity through the Bishop of Rome, if there is value to this service in a practical way, then Protestantism in the name of the word of God and the freedom of the Spirit has to pay attention to this possibility. It must discern how this service is still not appropriate, whether it can be reformed, if it has developed from where it was. We must always resist the Roman tendency to dominate, to have a universal jurisdiction. But the spiritual leadership that could be offered—that would be salutary and a value.

"It is along these lines that I and the Taizé brothers who are Protestant remain Protestant. That, of course, is my personal answer. I would not want to commit the other brothers to it. Does that answer your question?"

Gisela's face contorted as though she were searching to make some connections inside her head. When she spoke it was a long, drawn out: "Well . . ." And then: "I guess I'm still not satisfied."

"We can go further," Brother Max said, laughing. "I am here for your service." But Gisela decided to let it go for the moment. There was time for two more questions.

Godfrey, a Presbyterian catechist from Nigeria, jumped

into the breach: "How do the Taizé brothers handle the question of intercommunion?"

Brother Max replied: "We respect the doctrine and discipline of the various Churches of which the brothers are members. When a Protestant presides at the Eucharist, the Catholic brothers take Communion from the eucharistic reserve. When a Roman Catholic presides, the Protestant brothers have the permission of the local Catholic bishop to receive Communion if they so choose. The bishop was guided in his decision by the Instruction of 1972. 'Concerning Cases When Other Christians May Be Admitted to Eucharistic Communion in the Catholic Church.' Obviously it is not a comfortable situation for any of us. We find it very painful, and we see where we are now as a provisional solution; we hope to evolve into a better one. We feel, however, that it is very important for us to abide by the official discipline of each Church in this regard because of all the people who come here and watch what we do. We want to be a help to local Churches, not cause problems for them.

"Members of Reform Churches need to resist trying to hurry things along too much. I have consistently had the experience of ecumenical meetings at which the Protestants are always trying to promote intercommunion. 'Well, why not,' they say; 'we're all here and we're all brothers and sisters—why can't we all have Communion together?' But when you ask more precise questions about their own eucharistic practice, they rarely or at least infrequently have Communion. Questions like the real presence and who presides over the celebration are secondary questions for them. And you immediately see that this demand for intercommunion is based on something which is really only a minimum, whereas if one day we really were to have reciprocity in the Eucharist, it should be based on a maximum. It should be based on a common, real faith with a clear structure. Otherwise you will never have a real unity. You won't have unity with just a minimum of common faith."

The last question was Jorge's, and concerned the liturgical style of Taizé. During our days in Burgundy, we had spent one afternoon and evening with a Carmelite contemplative community of sisters in nearby Mazille. Ironically, my Protestant mates felt much more at home in the Catholic sisters' stark, cinderblock chapel, with lots of light pouring in through the clear windows and no decor save for a simple cross, than they did in Taizé's Church of the Reconciliation. By contrast, I found Taizé's church with its soft candlelight, icons, stained glass windows, and semi-darkness more conducive to prayer. The irony was that the sisters' chapel fit Calvin's criteria for a liturgical environment to a "T" and Taizé fit it not at all. Calvin desired a completely spiritual worship ascending toward a completely spiritual Reality. He rejected all sensible signs by which we are led to express our adoration of the unseen. Unlike Luther, Calvin was hostile to the medieval embodiments of worship; hence he cast away its liturgy and symbols. No organ or choir was permitted in his churches, no color, no ornament but the tablets of the Ten Commandments on the wall. The bleak, stripped interior of the real Calvinist church is itself meant to be sacramental: a witness to the inadequacy of the human over the Divine.

Jorge's question had taken formulation during our participation in the "weekly Easter" at Taizé. On Friday night there is a prayer of adoration around the cross. Saturday night is a celebration of the light of Christ. On Sunday morning the week culminates in a celebration of the Eucharist. Jorge, a Methodist pastor from Argentina, found the prayer-posture used by many at Taizé (sitting on one's heels and touching one's head to the floor—there are no pews or chairs), coupled with the low-lighting, reminded him of a fetal position, a return to the dark, silent womb. He wondered if the prayer at Taizé was moving forward toward independent maturity, or backward toward self-centered infantilism, seeking escape from the problems of the real world. What came through to him most strongly was not freedom but security, not commitment but withdrawal.

Brother Max reflected for a moment. "Your observations are challenging," he said, choosing his words carefully, "and we need to be always looking at those questions. I think your analysis is disproven, however, by the overall life in Taizé.

Those who come—and they are not just young people, but also senior citizens, and husbands and wives with their families—all join a discussion group which meets three times each day to try to discover how, concretely, to link struggle and contemplation in day-to-day living. They start from the questions encountered by men and women immersed in the contradictions of the human family, and they try to come up with the beginnings of a response which can be applied to daily life in the real world. They try to imagine ways in which this same quest can be continued locally, in their Churches at home.

"We are not interested in organizing those who come to Taizé into a 'movement.' Instead, we try to understand, together with them, the realities of the Christian community in the local situation where all the generations are present. At Taizé we wish to be nothing other than a place of prayer, where people come to search for the basic sources which give meaning to their lives, and to rediscover that the human being only finds fulfillment in the presence of God.

"There are also silent places at Taizé for those who wish to make a retreat in solitude. But even in this case, they must meet for an hour each morning with a brother who gives them certain biblical passages to help them confront their life with the Gospel and to reflect on their commitments.

"Then, everyone shares in the office prayed three times daily by the brothers. The hill here has always been an antenna attentive to the events of the globe and the cries of suffering humanity. A famine in Africa, an uprising in Asia, a coup d'état, someone condemned to death for political reasons: all of this finds an echo in Taizé. And good news, too: people coming together, walls falling down. There is no desire to separate ourselves from the world, but to place ourselves at its heart, to concern ourselves with its deepest needs.

"Praying around the cross each Friday night is a way of being in communion with all those who are suffering, prisoners of conscience, and also the sick, the handicapped, all those whose solitude is a real martyrdom for Christ. You have seen how those who wish to approach the cross place their forehead upon it. By this gesture they commit to Christ those whom they love dearly or the suffering of people about whom they are particularly concerned.

"As a final example, there is the fact that all the brothers do not always remain in Taizé. Some live in small fraternities among the poor in Brazil, Kenya, the Philippines, Bangladesh, Hong Kong, Japan, and New York."

We thanked Brother Max for coming to talk with us. "I am grateful for your questions and your criticism," he said. "You can help us a great deal by your prayer. Our life is a difficult one and we need your prayer."

February flew by. A Solidarity Day (of education, prayer, and fasting) with the oppressed blacks of South Africa and Namibia. An outing to the other end of Lake Geneva to visit *L'Abri*, the Evangelical Fellowship founded by Francis and Edith Schaeffer, authors of many inspirational books from a biblical perspective. A party for Bill and Gisela who announced their engagement and a June wedding. A day of solidarity with the people of El Salvador. And the Bible Festival: four days of our own personal creative responses to the riches of the Scriptures through skits, songs, poems, meditations, expositions of biblical study materials, and experiential approaches to different forms of biblical prayer.

One group's contribution to the Bible Festival was to hold a session in which various problems of the world would be viewed from a biblical perspective. The group had met several times in advance and intended to make a presentation. When the time came, one of the group's leaders, Anglican priest Bill Richards from England, stood up and spoke:

"We have labored like a woman in childbirth until we realized that we have no baby to present to the world. We have been forced to accept that the world's problems are our problems. We were united in hating apartheid but we were separated in how to respond to it. We suspect that this separation is more than simply a matter of procedure. It has something to do with us.

"In our desire to see justice in El Salvador we are unhappy to see decisions made which oppress people. But then within our own community we are aware that decisions have been made which have been 'oppressive.'

"We look for openness between people of different races and cultural background and yet we have found, even within our own small community, that we have often shrunk back behind the walls of our own differences and into our particular groupings. This is not a criticism, but an observation.

"In these and in other ways we have learned that the poverty in human relationships across the world is deep within each one of us. We have enjoyed the challenge to overcome this poverty, but whenever we have given way to it, those little moments of surrender show us our part in the sin of the world.

"Therefore we are convinced that the best political attitude starts with a sense of shared responsibility. We need now a 'crucified' mind, not a 'crusading' one. Our solidarity is with the poverty in the soul of humankind. We struggle against it from inside it, not from outside.

"This statement is a surprise to us. We feel ashamed because we had planned a different presentation. But the present one was forced upon us by our own experience of trying to present to you something which could be true to the world and yet no less true to our own experience inside our own community.

"When all this is applied to Christian unity, our conclusion is that the division in the Churches across the world is deep within each of us as well."

The semester ended with a week in Rome as guests of the Vatican Secretariat for Christian Unity. It was an unspeakably rich combination of discussions with members of the Secretariat for Unity and the Secretariat for Inter-Faith Relations and with heads of religious orders; tours of St. Peter's Basilica, underlying excavations, and the Vatican Museum, highlights of Rome with special guides; introductions to an ecumenical Church renewal movement (Focolare), the Waldensian Church, and an experiment in Christian community (St. Egidio's). One has to have gone to Rome alone and struggled as a tourist to fully appreciate our accommodations (a ten minute walk from the Vatican), guided tours, and all the doors that opened to us. It seemed to be the general feeling of our whole group that the members of the various Secretariats took us seriously and in each of our discussions with them sent in their "first team." A private audience with John Paul II had been on the original agenda, but our trip to Rome coincided with his to Japan.

In the final hour I was grateful for everything and everyone in my life who ever helped me believe that crying is all right. There were embraces all around and promises to write and keep in touch.

For a few, with whom much was shared through many unforgettable experiences, my feelings were and are profound. They are people who, in the passing of time since Bossey, my heart has yearned to see and be with again.

The truth that deepened in me in that moment of goodbyes is that once one has lived and laughed, played and prayed together, once Protestants, Anglicans, Orthodox, and Roman Catholics have become one's friends, one can no longer be indifferent to the question of Christian unity.

Further Reading

John Calvin, *Institutes of the Christian Religion,* Library of Christian Classics, Vol. XX, ed. by John T. McNeil, tr. by Ford Lewis Battles, Philadelphia, The Westminister Press, 1960.

T. H. L. Parker, *Portrait of Calvin,* London, SCM Press, 1954.

John T. McNeil, *The History and Character of Calvinism,* Oxford University Press, 1967.

Kilian McDonnell, *John Calvin, The Church, and the Eucharist,* Princeton, Princeton University Press, 1967.

Leonard Swidler, ed., *The Eucharist in Ecumenical Dialogue,* Ramsey, N.J., Paulist Press, 1976.

Ross MacKenzie, "Authority in the Reformed Tradition," in *A Pope for All Christians,* ed. by P. J. McCord, Ramsey, N.J., Paulist Press, 1976.

A CANTERBURY TALE

When in April the sweet showers fall
And pierce the drought of March to the root, and all
The veins are bathed in liquor of such power
As will bring on the engendering of the flower . . .
Then people long to go on pilgrimages,
And palmers long to seek the stranger strands
Of far-off saints, hallowed in sundry lands,
And specially, from every shire's end
In England, down to Canterbury they wend . . .
Some nine and twenty in a company
Of sundry fold happening then to fall
In fellowship, and they were pilgrims all. . . .
By speaking to them all upon the trip
I soon was one of them in fellowship.

Geoffrey Chaucer in *Canterbury Tales*

The members of Chaucer's company derived from their experiences a traveler's truth: some of life's best story material is culled, not upon or after arrival, but along the way. A pilgrim's acceptance of the unexpected is of the same paramount importance as a comfortable pair of walking shoes.

In my case, if it was not an airline strike in Rome, it was the idiosyncrasies of an aging Renault in the Alps. Boat, car, train, plane: none can promise the idyllic passage. England was not without some mischief of its own.

After a channel crossing that was first threatened by strike, then postponed due to stormy seas, and finally negotiated via a different port, my belongings were lost for two days in baggage transit. Such is but the modern pilgrim's fare. The secret, I discovered, lay in concentrating upon arrivals and departures as potential snake-pits and being psychologically ready to deal with their challenges. Reflection upon my now mounting catalogue of travel plans gone awry taught me that upset is more often than not the result only when something happens for which I am in no way prepared.

The train ride to Canterbury, apart from the fact that I was nearly cut in half by a hydraulically closing door which I was doing my best to resist while pulling in a late-comer as the train started to leave the station, was really comparatively uneventful. And my belongings would, I trusted, eventually catch up.

A glance at the map shows clearly enough why Canterbury has never lost importance, even when national affairs have been centered far away. It is positioned in the center of a southeast projection of England and stands on the shortest route from London to the continent of Europe. In the early days it was the meeting place of three important roads leading to Roman forts and it lay on the direct route from London to Dover, which grew to be the main port in the area. Today, with a population of thirty-two thousand, it is the third largest of England's walled cities, after Chester and York.

From the station in Canterbury, I boarded a taxi with two others. "Christ Church College," the woman seated next to me said to the driver. "It appears we're going to the same place," I said. "Are you by any chance participating in the Canterbury Ecumenical Summer School?"

She was. And furthermore she was coming from my home state of Minnesota where she served as an Episcopalian priest at the Cathedral Church in Minneapolis. "Mary Belfry is my name," she offered, smiling.

We arrived at Christ Church College in ten minutes, registered, picked up our folders and headed off to find our rooms with a promise to talk further at the afternoon tea. "It is," she called over her shoulder, "the most holy hour of English life!"

I entered into the ritual reverently. An enticing platter of shortbreads blessed the table nearby and offered me communion with the others, but my reach was interrupted in mid-air: "Oh, so it's you who answer to the name of Tom Ryan, is it?"

I heard the words, but found my attention fixed more upon a wonderfully craggy and weatherbeaten Irish face than upon my response. His name tag read "Brian Snow" and seemed more like a large button off-center on his six-foot-two frame. His coarse, grey-white hair, brushed straight back, stood slightly up like a rooster's cranial feathers, and bobbed amicably as he spoke. His was the look of a man concerned with other things than physical comeliness. He wasn't unkempt, mind you, but homespun. One knew that his vigil before the mirror was no more prolonged than several scrapes of the razor and a few strokes of the hairbrush required.

"I saw your name on the room next to mine," he said, "and, noting in our list of participants that there aren't many Roman Catholics here, I decided to establish good neighbor relations immediately. Where I come from, the local Catholic priest and I are over at each other's places often enough that our people aren't quite sure who belongs where."

A priest in the Church of Ireland, one of the national member churches in the Anglican Communion, Brian pastored a congregation in the little town of Kilmallock in County Limerick. He added, "This is Ian McDowell from Australia; he's just down the hall from us."

And so it began. One hundred and sixty of us "to Canterbury had wend . . ." to share in a study program entitled "The Servants of God," to seek insights into Christian thinking, to join in fellowship with Christian people from many parts of the world through worship and leisure in a city that has welcomed the pilgrim for seven hundred years. From the United States, Canada, South America, Australia, Ireland, Scotland, The Netherlands, West Germany, and, of course, England, we came. There was no mistaking from the start that the two week summer session was essentially an Anglican* gathering, but the twenty or so of us who were in the Presbyterian, United Reformed, Baptist, Lutheran, United Church, Roman Catholic, and Disciples of Christ traditions were warmly and hospitably welcomed.

The theme for the summer school, "The Servants of God," gave all of us the sense that our community is the Christian Church; one of the greatest influences in making it what it is has been the lives and teachings of its leaders in the past. Those whose teachings and example we were to survey in the next two weeks—Augustine, St. Francis, St. Anselm, Martin Luther, John Wesley, Cardinal Newman, Karl Barth, and Teilhard de Chardin—belonged to all of us.

"There's a service of Holy Communion at the cathedral tomorrow morning at 8:00," Brian offered as we walked toward the opening orientation session. "Ian and I will be going. Would you like to join us?" Though the summer school community was going to have a morning service in the Christ Church College chapel, the cathedral was a holy place, Brian informed me, and one couldn't be in Canterbury without breathing in its sacred air at every possible opportunity.

The cathedral's Bell Harry Tower was impressively framed in my dorm room window, and I was eager to see more. Brian's light rap on the door the next morning needed no words, and I stepped out into the hall at the same time that Ian was emerging, sleepy-eyed, from his room. Brian had the air of having spent the night in the hallway, just waiting for the moment of departure. We shuffled down the four flights of stairs and out into the bracing morning air, briskly traversed

---

*The term "Episcopal" is used to identify the Anglican Church mainly in the United States and Scotland. In both of these countries, the title "Anglican" is recognized. For example, the *Anglican Theological Review* and the *Anglican Digest* are names of two Episcopalian publications in the United States. In Canada, the Church is generally called the Anglican Church, except for a few French-speaking Canadian parishes where "Episcopal" is used to soften the English identity of the Church. For the sake of simplicity and consistency, I will use "Anglican" throughout.

the inner college courtyard, turned left around the tennis courts, skirted the ruins of St. Augustine's Abbey, and passed through a gate in the north wall of St. Augustine's College where we were confronted by the imposing fortification wall still enclosing Canterbury's east side. With Broad St. running along its borders like a modern-day moat, we waited for the light on the drawbridge to turn green, and crossed over into what felt distinctly like another, older world. As we mounted the half-dozen steps leading toward a tiny doorway virtually lost in the mass of the fortification wall, Brian could contain himself no longer. "This is Queningate," he announced in a respectful tone. "Queen Bertha, wife of King Ethelbert, used to go through this little entrance in the city wall to morning Mass at St. Martin's Church."

On a spring day in the year A.D. 597, watchers along the Kentish shore might have seen a long-awaited vessel approaching from the coast of France. On board was a company of forty Benedictine monks who had journeyed from Rome under the leadership of their prior, Augustine. Their long and perilous journey had been undertaken at the command of Pope Gregory the Great (himself a Benedictine monk and the founder of their monastery) who had heard that the Saxon king Ethelbert would welcome Christian missionaries. Ethelbert had married Bertha, a Christian princess from France, and had granted her the right to worship God in a small oratory outside the walls of Canterbury, still surviving as part of the fabric of St. Martin's Church. There had been Christians in Canterbury in the late Roman times.

How did the faith come to England? No one knows for sure. Perhaps some legionary who had become a follower of the way in Italy had married one of the village girls in Kent and settled in the region. Or maybe the builder of that Roman villa whose tiled floor can still be seen on Butcher St. was a well-to-do Christian from Gaul who had fled here to escape the persecution raging in Lyons and Vienna. Or was it that some merchant traveled south with dusky British pearls and there found the "pearl of great price"? In these and many other ways, Christianity filtered into the country, took root, and sprang up. All that is known for sure is that, by the beginning of the third century, Christians in distant lands—Tertullian in Africa, for example (A.D. 208), and Origen in Asia (A.D. 239)— write of the Church in Britain as already in existence. And in the fourth century, three bishops are recorded as attending the Council of Arles in 314.

The first Christian emperor, Constantine the Great, was actually proclaimed emperor while he was in Britain in 306, and when Christianity became the official religion of the empire, no doubt churches were established in Canterbury. The chief authority for this period, the Venerable Bede, states that there was a Christian church on the site of the present cathedral and that the Church of St. Martin was built outside the walls. It is on this account that St. Martin's claims to be the oldest parish church in England.

But the young plant of Christianity in England was soon to undergo a period of darkness and wither. The mistress of the world, Rome, was fighting for her life at home as Alaric and his Goths were pouring into Italy. Rome had no troops to spare to defend her distant colonies. First one legion, and then another, marched toward the sea, and in 407 the last Roman legion set sail, leaving Britain to protect itself as best it could. Even before the Romans withdrew, two sets of marauders had been giving trouble. The Picts, or painted folk, of Scotland were ever swarming over the wall and having to be driven back, while pirates from Denmark and North Germany were constantly raiding the coast. When the legions left, these raids naturally increased in frequency, and at last, in 447, the government of Kent, in despair, adopted the fatal policy of trying to hire the sea-roving pirates from Jutland to repel the Picts. When the inevitable disputes arose over pay and rations, the pirates turned on their employers, and within a few years the Jutes had conquered the whole country, putting large numbers of Christian inhabitants to death and sending survivors scurrying into the forest or enslaving them to till the ground. Northward in Essex, westward in Sussex, bands of Saxon sea-robbers did the same thing. Further north the Angles were winning all the East coast. More Saxons seized the district which they named Wessex. By 580 half of Britain had passed into possession of the pirates, and in that half all outward observance of the Christian faith had been stamped out in fire and blood.

All of this helps to explain why the old Church of St. Martin had been standing roofless and ruined when Ethelbert married the daughter of the king of Paris. Bertha had brought with her a bishop named Luidhard, and the king had restored the old church and given it to her to worship in. Soon some of the men of Kent began to wish to learn more of the queen's religion, and letters were written to the bishops of Gaul asking them to send teachers. Enter Augustine and his whole priory of monks in response to the king's wishes. It was, as Sir Arthur Bryant said of this mission, "the most important of all the invasions of England and the most peaceful."

The king gave the monks a house in Canterbury and they were preaching daily in St. Martin's. When the king himself became Christian, tribal loyalty prevailed, and the people, on the conviction that it was impossible for king and people to serve different gods, followed suit. Gregory had given the missionaries instructions to make as few changes as possible in the customs of the people. They were to retain and Christianize even the heathen festivals. Thus the Teutonic high festival at the beginning of winter was christened Martinmas, and the geese were slain and eaten, but now in honor of St. Martin. The mid-winter revelries, with the burning of the yule log, and the hanging up of the mistletoe bough in memory of Baldur the Beautiful, were boldly claimed as rejoicings over the birth of Christ. The spring feast of the goddess Eostre with her (Easter) eggs became the festival of the resurrection. Rogation days were merely the continuance of the mid-May heathen processions, and the leaping through bonfires on midsummer eve was retained to the glory of St. John the Baptist. Even the most sacred symbol of all, the mighty hammer of Thor, needed but little alteration, and it became a cross.

The sole result of Augustine's mission was the conversion of Kent. The other kingdoms were won in various ways. Wessex was converted by Birinus, a free-lance missionary from north Italy (634). Felix, a bishop from Burgundy (636), won east Anglia for the faith. The three largest kingdoms were evangelized by Irish monks. The Church of Ireland was a sister of the British Church. The Church in Ireland had grown up entirely apart from the influence of Rome, and it stood at this time without a rival in its love of learning, its passion for holiness and its boundless energy. It had made its own country an island of saints and now was flinging itself into battle with heathenism abroad.

Columban had carried the Gospel to Burgundy, St. Gall had gone to Switzerland, and Columba had built (536) a monastery on the island of Iona from which he could work among the Picts of Scotland. From the monastery (635) came Aidan and a party of monks to the island of Lindisfarne off the coast of Northumbria; and from Lundisfarne they began those mission journeys which won back the northern kingdom for Christ. They sent out Cedd, who reconverted the apostate kingdom of Essex. By 660 all England was nominally Christian, except the little kingdom of Sussex, shut in between the forest and the sea.

I passed through "Bertha's door" in Brian's footsteps, mentally doffing my hat to her decisive influence in the success of the mission of St. Augustine of Canterbury. The morning sun was scaling the city walls. The array of flowers in the War Memorial Garden stood erect and presented themselves like the colored tips in a crayon box left open. The cathedral tower, transept, and Trinity Chapel, like the prow of an immense ship breaking water, came in full view across the churchyard.

Brian's historic commentary fell silent as we walked along the cathedral's south side. The mind strains to appreciate the vastness of this structure which, as medieval pilgrims were wont to say, was "like three churches, built one on top of the other." When amid such enormous mass there is a sense of lightness and uplift, the architects have triumphed. The whole concept of a cathedral is filled with glory and romance. Those who labored on this sculptured masterpiece understood in some ways more about life than we do now. With their deep understanding of the spirit of nature—the meaning of stone and glass—and bursting to create a physical expression of their desire to glorify God, they built this cathedral. The very nature of the place is to raise our eyes and minds to greater things, things of eternity and peace and beauty, and to project our souls into the realm of unearthly appreciation. It is a spectacular monument to human ingenuity and artistry, but much more: it is a monument to faith. Fourteen hundred years later Christians are still nurturing and expressing their faith within the walls of Christ Church Cathedral.

As we approached the southwest transept portal, I noticed Ian's name tag on the lapel of his coat and was reminded that we had been asked the night before to wear them during the week. "Oh, I forgot my name tag already," I remarked, brushing my left front shirt pocket as I crossed the threshold.

"Don't worry," Brian reassured me with a wink. "This is God's house and he already knows you." We entered and slowly advanced until the full view of the nave unfolded to our left. "Ahhh, this is a holy place," breathed Brian, to no one in particular.

It was here that Augustine had restored and enlarged the Roman church which was on this same piece of ground and dedicated it to Christ Jesus the Savior. He lived with some of his monks near the cathedral while the rest settled outside the city walls in a monastery dedicated to St. Peter and Paul, later to be known as St. Augustine's Abbey.

England had been converted by monks. The English Church had been organized by monks. So monasteries played an important part in all its early history. There is one monastery in particular which had a significant role in the development of Christianity in England. Ironically, it sits in a peaceful valley across the English Channel in Normandy. Two of the greatest men to ever sit in the Chair of St. Augustine were monks who came from the Benedictine Abbey of Bec-Hellouin in Normandy, France. Today Bec is a place of pilgrimage for many Anglicans, symbolizing the unity of history and inspiration between the Church of England and the Church of Rome.

In the rear of the chapel at Bec, an inscription stone given by the former archbishop of Canterbury, Michael Ramsey, reads: "From the Cathedral of Canterbury to the Abbey of Bec-Hellouin in communion of destiny and hope. That all may be one."

The first monk from Bec to sit upon Augustine's chair was an energetic and enterprising Italian who, according to his contemporaries, was the most cultivated man of his time. His name was Lanfranc. Advisor to William the Conqueror, the builder and abbot of the cathedral church of Saint-Etienne of Caen, and subsequently archbishop of Canterbury, he became in England the reorganizer of the Church and stamped the cathedral and monastery with a character it was never to lose in all the medieval centuries. An ardent believer in the monastic life, a great statesman, a jurist, an architect, a man of piety and charity, Lanfranc was a bulwark of the kingdom.

Lanfranc's successor (1093), Anselm, was also his disciple, and an even greater scholar and saint than his master. A dialectician and mystic, the questing of his highly individual mind was to lead to the freeing of intellect in its own sphere of activity and thus prepare the way for the prodigious advance of culture in Europe. His famous reference to "Fides quaerens intellectum," the faith which seeks to know, or the faith seeking understanding, precisely defines his attitude of mind. His influence was more personal and intimate than that of Lanfranc and likewise deeper and more lasting. He was an awakener of people's minds.

The rebuilding of the cathedral church, initiated by Lanfranc, continued during Anselm's time under the scrutinizing eye of Blitherus the Saxon, a master mason described in a contemporary document as "the very distinguished master of the craftsmen." The Norman cathedral and its priory must have been one of the most imposing foundations in England, but Anselm did not live to see this magnificent prayer in stone consecrated. He died in 1109 and was buried in the apse of the chapel of St. Peter and St. Paul, later named St. Anselm's Chapel. His bones, placed in a copper shrine, became an object of veneration to pilgrims, although his canonization did not take

place for more than three hundred years. The official consecration of the church took place on May 4, 1130. King David of
Scotland and King Henry I of England were present, and the
chronicler monk who described the ceremony wrote that "so
famous a dedication has never been heard of on the earth since
the consecration of the temple of Solomon." Shortly thereafter, the third of the Bec men to serve as archbishop of Canterbury, Theobald, crowned King Stephen and Queen Matilda on
Christmas Day in 1142. The three men from Bec were dedicated to prayer and in search of an Ultimate. They managed to
live and to transmit a culture which is impregnated with the
principles of Christianity, open to everything truly human and
equipped to enrich humankind and their world. It was in
Theobald's household that a young man named Thomas Becket was trained for the great offices that were to come to him.

After a brief look around the choir, at the head of which
stood the main altar and, on a landing several steps above it,
the Chair of St. Augustine, we resumed our movement across
the length of the transept to the Place of the Martyrdom. I followed Brian down the steps into the northwest transept where
his outstretched arm guided my eyes toward the inscription
set into the floor:

Thomas Becket
Archbishop Saint Martyr
Died Here
Tuesday 29 December 1170

In the Middle Ages men thought differently than they do
now. In the west of Europe, at least, power over others was
considered as something for which everyone would strive. The
Middle Ages saw a great struggle between the authorities of
Church and State, each of them trying to gain a decisive influence over people's minds and actions. In modern times such a
struggle would seem to be a repudiation by the Church of its
proper spiritual function, but in those days there was no
thought of distinguishing between spiritual and temporal power; both were inextricably mixed together. Moreover, whatev-

er the faults of the Church or of its leaders, their ability to resist the secular powers was in practice the only means by which freedom could be safeguarded. Without this resistance, the secular powers would have been dictators without opposition, and the ordinary people would have suffered severely as a result. Although Church leaders were not intending it, they were in fact defending human liberties against the state. The same may be said of the state against the Church.

When Lanfranc was made archbishop of Canterbury in 1070, the city had within it three different sources of control: the king, the archbishop and the abbot. The clergy, it must be remembered, were the only people who could read and write, and they therefore filled all the posts, whether in Church or state, which required these skills. They were also the largest property holders and were inevitably and naturally engaged in trade and commerce. They were only displaced with the spread of education and the rise of a new commercial class at a later stage of history. Among the privileges which they enjoyed was that of being tried in Church courts instead of those of the king, an arrangement which was a constant cause of strife between the two. The landed properties of the Church and its wealth were often the envy of royal eyes, and disputes about property, about the legal rights of clerics, and about the investing of bishops in their office by the king gave rise to generations of disputes. Anselm was forced into exile over the issue, and the quarrels were to come to a head in the most famous event of Canterbury's history.

Thomas Becket was the king's closest confidant and advisor in matters of state. One can imagine the groan that rumbled throughout the realm when the news reached the streets that the king had constrained the monks of Canterbury to elect his chancellor as archbishop. Thomas Becket was a skillful diplomat, a dashing and successful soldier, but his life had been more secular than religious and he was, moreover, only in deacon's orders.

But he was not the man to do anything by halves. Instead of continuing to follow the king's wishes, he transferred all his efforts to trying to establish the claims of the Church. Now that he was a bishop he did with vehemence all that the ideal bishop of those days was expected to do. He rose before dawn. He practiced mortification by boiling his food to tastelessness and wearing a hairshirt. Above all, he became an unbending champion of the rights of the Church. King Henry II was striving to reorganize justice after Stephen the Feeble's anarchy, and the chief obstacle in his way was the existence of the ecclesiastical courts which claimed to decide not only Church questions including marriage and wills, but also all criminal cases in which a cleric was concerned (a term which included door-keepers and singing-men and all in minor orders). Punishments in Church courts were generally lighter. A convicted thief, for example, could expect death from a secular court or life imprisonment on bread and water from a bishop's court if he could prove "benefit of clergy." If the convicted man had money or influence, a life sentence might be shortened to a few years (or even months) by using a much abused practice called "compurgation." The bishops had prisons, but they preferred not to use them, as they naturally disliked the expense of maintaining prisoners. The usual penalties were penance or excommunication. The judges reported that in nine years a hundred murderers had in this way escaped punishment, and Henry made the demand that clerics found guilty in the Church courts for offenses against the criminal law should be deprived of their orders and handed over to the king's judges to be dealt with as laymen. The real problem with Church courts was not the criminal side so much as that they claimed jurisdiction over areas like marriage settlements and inheritance disputes which affected everybody, not just the clergy. And if a property case got transferred to Rome (a standard method of appeal) it took years to settle and cost a fortune in bribes. The Church amassed a huge amount of revenue through the judicious manipulation of such cases.

Becket declined to surrender a single privilege of the Church. Most of the commoners were probably in agreement with him, for the king's judges were everywhere hated for the ferocity of their sentences. Three meetings were held, at each of which the dispute grew more bitter. Then news came (1164) that Becket had been driven from the king's presence as a traitor. For the next six years Canterbury was without an archbishop.

When, in 1170, a peace was patched together, Becket crossed the channel from France and was led in triumphal procession from Sandwich to Canterbury. But his years in exile had by no means mellowed his mood. Before leaving France he had excommunicated the archbishop of York for presuming to crown the Prince of Wales in his absence, a privilege which he declared belonged exclusively to the see of Canterbury. When the king heard of this new dispute, he cried out in a mixture of anger and exasperation, something along the lines of: "What sluggard knaves I have in my court that they suffer me to be bearded thus by one low-born clerk!" On December 29 Thomas Becket was murdered in the cathedral by four knights who thought themselves to be carrying out the king's wishes to get rid of a traitor.

The event horrified Christendom, for a greater sacrilege than the murder of an archbishop in his own cathedral could hardly be imagined. He was immediately regarded as a saint. It is worth noting that such canonization had nothing to do with the holiness of his life. In many ways Becket was a difficult character, by no means free of faults. But from the earliest days of the Church those who were martyred for their faith were at once numbered among the "saints," quite apart from the character of their lives. It was this tradition that Becket shared when, three years later, the popular verdict was confirmed by the Pope and Becket was declared St. Thomas of Canterbury. For the king it was not only a crime but a blunder, and he knew that his cause was lost. Becket on earth had been a formidable opponent. Becket in heaven was unconquerable.

Fasting and in pilgrim's clothes, Henry came to Canterbury and knelt with bared back at the martyr's tomb while the monks scourged the king. The abuses of the ecclesiastical courts were yet to remain unchecked, for nothing could now induce the clergy to give up one jot of the claims for which St. Thomas died. If it was the worst thing that could have happened for the king, it was the best thing that could have happened for the city. The present cathedral and the development of the city of Canterbury during the Middle Ages sprang from the murder of Becket, for it occasioned vast pilgrimages from which both cathedral and city were enriched. Canterbury became the second most popular shrine in Europe after Rome and multitudes of visitors poured into the city for centuries until the Reformation. The choir of the cathedral was burnt down in 1174 and it was rebuilt to a design especially conceived to have as its high point the shrine of the martyr. To this shrine the body of Becket was transferred in 1220. From that time pilgrims of all ranks (witness the group represented in Chaucer's *Canterbury Tales*) came to the city either especially to visit the shrine or to pay homage while passing to and from France.

We stepped from the Place of the Martyrdom into Our Lady's Chapel where people were gathering for Mass, some kneeling on the little floor cushions, others sitting in the wooden straight-back chairs. "Mass is held each day in a different chapel of the cathedral," Brian whispered to me as we stood for a moment in the rear, looking for three chairs together that were available. "This is the Becket Chapel. Tomorrow Mass will be in the Martyr's Chapel and the following day in the crypt where one kneels on the stones of the original structure. That is my favorite." Not seeing three places together, Brian and Ian went up and found two between a businessman and an elderly woman with an umbrella, to the front on the right. I slipped into an aisle seat on the left hand side, took the kneeling cushion from the chair, placed it on the floor and knelt. In a moment the presiding priest strode up the far aisle on the right dressed in alb, stole, cincture, chasuble, and something I hadn't seen since my altar boy days: a maniple—a small liturgical vestment that hangs from the wrist and which served originally as a kind of handkerchief for the removal of sweat from the face during the service. He genuflected, mounted the altar step, bowed and kissed the altar, and turned to lead us in prayer with the sign of the cross.

Midway through the first reading I realized that my mind was elsewhere, reflecting on the potential confusion that awaits a non-Anglican who might, for whatever reason, decide to join an Anglican congregation in worship every now and then. If the church of one's choice that particular day is Anglo-Catholic (tending more toward traditional Catholic ritual and practice) in character, one may observe holy water fonts, confessional areas, stations of the cross, statues, and a sanctuary lamp. The sermon might well concern the seven sacraments, fast and abstinence regulations, or the real presence of Christ in the Eucharist. And the priest would be vested in the traditional pre-Reformation Christian vestments, much like the priest before me now.

If the church were "Low" or Evangelical in its liturgical leaning it might well resemble a typical Protestant chapel in architecture, ecclesiastical furniture, vestments, and liturgy— little different from a Congregational or Methodist church. The minister would be vested in surplice and stole and the main worship service might be Morning Prayer rather than a Communion service or Anglican Mass. The congregation might be hearing a sermon on justification by faith alone or the sole sufficiency of Scripture or the two Christian sacraments as opposed to the seven sacraments of the Roman Catholic Church.

A third Episcopal church might resemble the first or second in appearance and liturgy. It is the "broad Church" tradition within Anglicanism which opts for some middle position that usually involves liturgical similarity (e.g., vestments) to normal Catholic practice. Doctrinally, it owes as much or more to German liberal Protestant scholarship. All three are representative of the three main "parties" in Anglicanism: the High Church or Anglo-Catholic, the Low or Evangelical, and the Broad or Modernist. Sharing in the worship in one of each on successive Sundays would be a marvelous inductive learning experience to bring one to the realization that the Church of England and its North American counterpart embrace a wider spectrum of doctrine and practice than any major Communion. There's even an official name for it: "Anglican comprehensiveness." Later, querying Brian about this theological elasticity, he responded: "Well, that depends on what you think of elastic. If it's what holds your trousers up, then it's a good thing, isn't it?"

"But Brian," I responded, "a Christian Church which is aware of a wide variety of diverse theological positions and which deliberately decides not to adopt one or other of them has to offer a more definite reason for doing so than 'if elasticity is what holds your trousers up, then it's a good thing, isn't it?' Toleration of diversity needs to be justified theologically if it is to be able to claim any kind of integrity. There is a point at which a natural desire to avoid a fuss shades off into an unwillingness to seek for any clarity."

"Well, there was something of that in the origins of 'comprehensiveness' in the Church of England," Brian replied. "It was at least in part to mitigate the sharpness of the exchanges between Anglicans of different persuasions in the nineteenth century that the theory of comprehensiveness of the Anglican Communion was raised to a key position in how we saw ourselves.

"Comprehensiveness, in the context of how the Anglican Church understands itself, simply means that there are many elements in the Church which in other Communions are regarded as mutually exclusive. Most often it is associated with the inclusion of Protestant and Catholic elements in the one fellowship. Some people think of it in terms of Catholic thesis, Protestant antithesis, and Anglican synthesis. But comprehensiveness is not to be taken to mean that plain contradiction is a normal expression of Anglican diversity. To be Anglican is not to be content with self-contradiction. Properly understood, comprehensiveness is the distinction between fundamentals and non-fundamentals. It's not so far from what the Roman Church described at Vatican II as the 'hierarchy of truths.' "

In 1968, the Lambeth Conference—the meeting held every ten years by all the bishops of the Anglican Communion—spoke of the comprehensiveness of the Anglican Communion:

> Comprehensiveness demands agreement on fundamentals while tolerating disagreement on matters in which Christians may differ without feeling the necessity of breaking

communion. In the mind of an Anglican comprehensiveness is not compromise. Nor is it to bargain one truth for another. It is not a sophisticated word for syncretism. Rather it implies that the apprehension of truth is a growing thing: we only gradually succeed in "knowing a truth." . . . It has been the tradition of Anglicanism to contain within one body both Protestant and Catholic elements. But there is a continuing search for the whole truth in which these elements will find complete reconciliation. Comprehensiveness implies a willingness to allow liberty of interpretation, with a certain slowness in arresting or restraining exploratory thinking.

The priest, now with his back to us, was preparing the offertory gifts. Though some were now sitting, Brian was on his knees.

When representatives from the worldwide Anglican Communion (confined largely to England and former English colonies) come together in an international conference like CANTESS, one of the questions that must be resolved with great sensitivity is the "how" of prayer. I had noted the night before in my orientation booklet that there were three services of Holy Communion planned during our stay in Christ Church College, and on each occasion a different Anglican rite would be used. The first would be the rite that has been in use for over three hundred years in Anglican churches: the rite of 1662. The first Holy Communion service to be used in English appeared in the first Prayer Book of Edward VI (son of Henry VIII) issued in 1549 and drawn up by Thomas Cranmer, archbishop of Canterbury. Cranmer crafted two prayer books, one in 1549 and another, much more Protestant in conception, in 1552. In one of its rubrics, the 1552 Holy Communion Service explicitly denies any real presence in the elements. It is the 1552 version (somewhat revised and toned down in 1559 when Elizabeth came to the throne) which forms the basis of the 1662 prayer book rite. It attempted to provide a balanced view of eucharistic theology, taking into account the Catholic and Protestant controversies of those days. The language is that of the sixteenth and seventeenth centuries, the days of Shakespeare, and perhaps represents the English language at its richest and loveliest moment.

From a Catholic viewpoint, however, it must be regarded as questionable or even defective doctrinally. The 1662 eucharistic prayer contains no calling down of the Holy Spirit (*epiclesis*) or remembering of the death, resurrection, and ascension of the Lord (*anamnesis*). The language may indeed be beautiful but it is celebrating penance and the cross in a liturgy which on the whole tends to be rather joyless and short on thanksgiving.

It was a desire to correct these defects, much more than the wish simply to update the language, which led to the modern Anglican liturgies. The new forms give the language a contemporary rendering (a sizable representation *wanted* a liturgy expressed in the language of today) and greater participation to the laity. A period of liturgical experiment and revision finally issued in the publication of the *Alternative Service Book 1980*. While the 1662 Prayer Book emphatically remains in use as the traditional Book of Common Prayer of the Church of England, many parishes have adopted the contemporary style liturgy for their main services. The publication of the *Alternative Service Book 1980* was hailed euphorically as "the greatest publishing event in the Church of England for three hundred years." In its preface the bishop of Durham writes: "Christians are formed by the way in which they pray, and the way they choose to pray expresses what they are. Hence, those who seek to know the mind of the Church of England in the last quarter of the twentieth century will find it in this book. . . ."

An educational companion volume, *Anglican Worship Today,* was published by the Group for the Renewal of Worship as a "comprehensive family resource book." It would be hard to find a book which so well and so imaginatively commends new forms of worship and new understandings of the relationship between liturgy and life to the general body of Church members, be they Anglican or not. It offers a rare and welcome middle ground between the highly technical and the often superficial devotional treatment of liturgy. It is meant for laypeople come of age. The companion volume vigorously advocates eucharistic worship as the norm for the Sunday assembly of believers. In two controversial areas it reflects the clear convictions of the Anglican Liturgical Commission: doctrinal conservatism and linguistic innovation ("the language of worship should be as immediately accessible as God himself"). Though there is a marked evangelical reluctance to rethink the Reformers' attitude to the doctrines of eucharistic sacrifice and real presence, *Anglican Worship Today* demonstrates the considerable measure of reconciliation that has come to pass between Evangelical and Catholic Anglicans.

"We do not presume to come to this thy table, O merciful Lord, trusting in our righteousness, but in thy manifold and great mercies." It was Communion time—time to brace myself once again for that only-one-left-in-the-pew-feeling. I didn't know what Brian's expectations were, but I hoped he would understand. "We are not worthy so much as to gather up the crumbs under thy table. But thou art the same Lord, whose property is always to have mercy. Grant us therefore, gracious Lord, so to eat the flesh of thy dear Son Jesus Christ and to drink his blood, that our sinful bodies may be made clean by his body, and our souls washed through his most precious blood, and that we may evermore dwell in him, and he in us. Amen."

The Anglican-Roman Catholic International Commission (ARCIC), created in 1965, was asked to examine differences which, in the controversies of the past, divided the two Communions. Their aim in starting off was to see if they could discover substantial agreement in faith on the Eucharist—"substantial," in this sense: Could the theologians representing each tradition come to unanimous agreement on essential matters where, in their consideration, doctrine admits of no divergence? In their Windsor Statement (1971) on eucharistic doctrine they answered, "We can," and they said that "if there are any remaining points of disagreement they can be resolved on the principles here established."

As people emptied their pews and formed a line in the

center aisle, I remembered some of those principles and recalled my own joy when the document came out. At the time I was spending the middle term of the school year at Virginia Episcopal Seminary on the exchange program offered by the Washington (D.C.) Theological Union where I was doing my theology studies. We had discussed, at table and in our residence hall rooms, the commission's statement: That there is one historical, unrepeatable sacrifice, offered once-for-all by Christ and accepted once for all by the Father. That it is the glorified Lord himself whom the community of the faithful encounters in the eucharistic celebration through the preaching of the word, in the fellowship of the Lord's Supper, in the heart of the believer, and, in a sacramental way, through the gifts of his body and blood, already given on the cross for their salvation. That his body and blood are given through the action of the Holy Spirit, appropriating bread and wine so that they become the food of the new creation already inaugurated by the coming of Christ. That some traditions have placed a special emphasis on the association of Christ's presence in the heart of the believer through reception by faith, and others have emphasized Christ's presence with the consecrated elements. That these two movements must be held *together* in eucharistic doctrine since in this sacrament Christ *gives himself* to his people *so that* they may *receive him through faith.* And that, with regard to reservation of the Eucharist, adoration of Christ in the reserved sacrament should be regarded as an extension of eucharistic worship—even though reservation of the Eucharist does not include immediate sacramental reception, which remains the primary purpose of reservation (e.g., for the sick).

In 1979 the Commission, responding to suggestions for clarification received in the wake of the Windsor Statement, added further comments in a reply entitled "Elucidations." One in particular, addressing the meaning of the much polemicized notion of "transubstantiation," was bound to be appreciated. "Becoming," they said, does not imply material change. Nor does the liturgical use of the word imply that the bread and wine "become" Christ's body and blood in such a way that in the eucharistic celebration his presence is limited to the consecrated elements. It does not imply that Christ becomes present in the Eucharist in the same manner that he was present in his earthly life. It does not imply that this *becoming* follows the physical laws of this world. What is here affirmed is a sacramental presence in which God uses realities of this world to convey the realities of the new creation: bread for this life becomes the bread of eternal life. *Before* the eucharistic prayer, to the question "What is that?" the believer answers: "It is bread." *After* the eucharistic prayer, to the same question, the believer answers: "It is truly the body of Christ, the bread of life." In the Eucharist the human person encounters in faith the person of Christ in his sacramental body and blood. This is the sense in which the community, the body of Christ, by partaking of the sacramental body of the risen Lord, grows into the unity God intends for his Church. The ultimate change intended by God is the transformation of human beings into the likeness of Christ. The bread and wine *become* the sacramental body and blood of Christ in order that the Christian community may *become* more truly what it already is: the body of Christ.

So I asked myself: If there is all this agreement, and the last two archbishops of Canterbury have repeatedly suggested intercommunion to the Pope, why am I still in my seat when I very much want to be up there with everyone else? In moments like this no answer tends to satisfy, but the ones that have to be given are: while the work of the theologians in the Agreed Statement has been formally accepted by the Anglican National Synods in the United States, Canada, and England, it has not yet been formally accepted by both Churches. Secondly, intercommunion also involves issues relating to authority and to the mutual recognition of ministry which, while they are being worked on, have not yet been satisfactorily resolved. In the end, Communion (eucharistic) means communion (ecclesial).

Brian understood. As we walked back across the church-

yard where modern pilgrims were now stirring in their sleeping bags, the tower carillon was ringing out over the city like
someone playing a quick do-re-me-fa-so-la-ti-do on the piano,
punctuating each terminating "do" with a deep bass gong before repeating the scale. Totally unsolicited, Brian said: "Tomorrow morning we'll go to your place, the Church of St.
Thomas." He pointed to a steeple stretching up above the rooftops on the other side of Christ Church Gate which serves as
the main entrance to the cathedral yard. "We'll have a per-
verse kind of brotherhood: just as you didn't communicate today, I won't tomorrow, but we'll be there with each other in
persevering anticipation of the day *when.* And in the mean-
time, we'll find a solidarity in the burden of sharing the abstention."

I was very touched by his sensitivity. We had only known
each other since yesterday, but where one encounters such respect, one also finds deep potential for friendship.

"I know how you feel," he said as we passed a French-
speaking family coming through Christ Church Gate in hopes
of catching the first morning tour of the cathedral. "I make frequent retreats and days of recollections in a Roman Catholic
monastery near me in Ireland and I've become very good
friends with the monks there. And every now and then they'll
tell me in so many words that I'm welcome to communicate.
But I say to them, 'There has to be universality of Communion
in this church, not just Communion between a small group of
like-minded individuals. What right do I have to come to your
table if I can't bring my people in here with me?' "

"With all respect for a certain validity in that point of
view," Ian interjected, "I think it has to be said that not all Anglicans would feel themselves represented by it. Our disciplines about intercommunion differ, both because of our
differences regarding ministry, and because of differing understandings of the relationship between eucharistic Communion
and the unity or communion of our churches. The Church of
England will welcome to Holy Communion a member in good
standing of another Church which professes a trinitarian faith,

whereas my impression is that the Roman Catholic Church—officially, that is—admits other Christians to Communion only in particular and carefully defined cases of spiritual need."

Ian's notion of Roman Catholic policy was quite right. Officially: when the other Christian has no access to the sacraments of his or her own Church for a significant time or reason, experiences serious spiritual need, has the proper dispositions, professes a faith in the Eucharist that is in accord with Roman Catholic doctrine, and freely seeks and has the permission of the local authority, intercommunion is permitted. In their twelve-year report entitled "Where We Are: A Challenge For the Future," the members of the Anglican-Roman Catholic Consultation (ARC) in the United States asked: "Must a close relationship and even sacramental sharing between us be delayed until all Anglicans and Roman Catholics throughout the world agree on every point that the other thinks is important, or is it possible that our growing together and sacramental sharing may be allowed to develop differently in different places?" The question, posed in 1978, has had no official response from the Roman Catholic side.

For Rome, eucharistic hospitality has certain parallels with meal patterns during courtship. When a relationship becomes somewhat serious, the young man is normally invited to a family meal. Later he returns the favor and brings the young lady to his house for dinner. Even though the closeness with each other and with the family grows through these experiences, it is only after marriage, after the public, formal covenant that he is considered part of the family and she is truly one of them. Then sitting down regularly and often at meals is accepted and expected.

We were going to be late for breakfast Ian thought, but Brian assured him there would still be plenty for everyone by the time we arrived.

Friday was the first full day of the summer school program, and we passed it in the reflective company of Cambridge's Regius Professor of Divinity, Rev. Dr. Henry

Chadwick. Most of his historical work has been on early Christianity, especially concerning its continuity and discontinuity with the Greco-Roman world into which it came. He spoke to us about St. Augustine. The following day, under the tutelage of Bishop John Moorman whose *History of the Church in England* has become a standard textbook, we turned our thoughts to Francis of Assisi. Moorman's seven books on St. Francis and the Franciscan Order make him an expert on the subject even among the men and women who wear the brown robe. The leader of the Anglican observers at Vatican II and a member of ARCIC, Bishop Moorman's very presence and work seemed to symbolize the revival of religious orders in Anglicanism and the growing appreciation of the approximately two dozen different orders for men and for women who seek to follow within that Communion the evangelical counsels of poverty, chastity, and obedience. Among the better known are the Holy Cross Order, the Society of St. John the Evangelist, Franciscans, Benedictines, and the Sisterhoods of St. Mary, the Holy Nativity, St. Margaret, St. Anne, and Poor Clares.

As part of our program on St. Francis, we walked across Canterbury after lunch to Greyfriars, the oldest Franciscan building in Britain. I fell into step with one of the friars in our company who was serving as a guide, and we talked about the coming to England of the Franciscans. In the early thirteenth century, when an agrarian problem was rapidly reaching a state of crisis in Britain because one-third of the land now belonged to the monks and honest men were asking themselves why so much land should be allowed to keep in comfort a relatively small number of landlords, the grey friars arrived. Arrested at Dover as lunatics, they were released the next morning as apparently harmless, barefooted, penniless beggars. As befitted followers of Francis, that young merchant from Assisi who eighteen years before had abandoned home and fortune in order to follow literally in the steps of Christ, they arrived with nothing but the one grey garment they wore, ragged and patched with sackcloth. Hence, they were called "Greyfriars." The contrast between friar and monk was not lost upon the people. The monk, to save his soul, withdrew from the world's wickedness. The friar, to save other people, threw himself into the world's wickedest places. The monks were governed on the feudal system of carefully graded obedience. The friars were a free democracy, organized by the citizens of a small republic. While the monk was chanting litanies in his stately chapel, the friar was listening patiently to the stories of Piers Ploughman in the village inn. And now nine members of the brotherhood had arrived in Canterbury. They were allowed to sleep on a schoolroom floor, and here five of them remained while four pressed on to London.

We turned left off High Street into Stour Street and passed through a great wooden portal, over a little bridge and down a dirt path. In front of us was the only surviving building among those put up by the Franciscans after their arrival in 1224. Built directly over the River Stour which is some twenty-five feet wide at this point, the building's sturdy stone walls rest in the middle on two thick, squat pillars implanted midstream in the river bed. It must have been wonderful for fishing in winter through a trap door in the floor. The friars' good temper, their homely spirit, and their cheerful self-denial soon turned the ridicule of the people of Canterbury to admiration. As soon as they learned the language, they preached up and down the countryside in the open air. Multitudes flocked to listen to their sermons. A wave of religious revival swept through the land, and recruits pressed eagerly into the brotherhood. In thirty years twelve hundred Englishmen became Greyfriars.

But their popularity ruined them. It is not easy to remain humble when all the world is flattering, or poor when queens and merchants, peers and peasants shower gifts upon you. When recruits are admitted by the score, the support system natural to a smaller band deteriorates, and scandals begin to creep in unchecked. Before long, "friar" was a short step in the popular mind from an idle vagabond, often lazy and sensual, fond of his food and drink, undermining the influence of the local clergy. Instead of saving the unhappy Church of England from its troubles, the friars frequently added to them. There were no great revivals after the followers of Francis. The general story of English medieval religious life in the fourteenth and fifteenth centuries, the monastic as well as mendicant, is one of steady decline.

Sunday morning was free for worship in the city. That, of course, meant the cathedral. "If I'm a member of the Supporters of the Cathedral Guild when I'm in Killamallock, you surely won't find me in some other church when I'm in Canterbury!" Brian declared. Besides, "Mr. Canterbury" himself, Canon Derek Ingram Hill, was mounting the pulpit this morning. His sermon was energetic and inspired; in fact, the whole service was worthy of the glory and romance of the soaring arches and gigantic pillars. Six of us were still at our places, talking in a small group, after the majority of worshipers had dispersed. Up the center aisle strode an elderly gentleman in grey tweed using his cane more after the fashion of a teacher's pointer than anything that was actually needed for walking. "Well now, there's a gaggle of clergy doing a post-mortem," he ventured with a humorous uplift in his tone, pausing a moment to eye us. "I've always said that parsons are like fertilizer: broken up and spread over the countryside they do marvelous things. But lumped all together in one place they tend to be offensive." With a slight wink and a punctuating tap of his cane, he turned on his heel and became a silhouette in the sunlight pouring through the cathedral's western entrance. In the light of the outing we were to take that afternoon, his words were ironically applicable to England's relationship with the Church.

The only item on the schedule for the afternoon was "Tea outings to local parishes followed by Evensong," which left us a good chunk of time to take a tour of the ruins of the Abbey of St. Peter and Paul founded by Augustine and now known by his own name. The ruins of his abbey, consecrated in 613 and for many years a more important center than the cathedral, now lie like the southern boundary of the Christ Church College campus. For the first two and a half centuries after Augustine, all the archbishops of Canterbury were buried in the abbey. The fact that a number of them were canonized undoubtedly helped make it a center of piety as well as ecclesiastical power and property. Throughout the early centuries there was rivalry and often enmity between the abbey and the cathedral, which increased as the power of the cathedral and its prior grew. Now both St. Augustine's abbey and the cathedral priory (so called because the cathedral monastery had no titular abbot, due to the fact that the archbishop was recognized as the spiritual father of the community while the *prior* was abbot in everything but name) lie in ruins. The visitor to England cannot help but be struck with melancholy upon seeing the remains of the great abbeys in some of the most romantic settings of the country standing in silent testimony to a bygone era. Lindisfarne, Tintern, Lacock, Fountains, Rivaulx, St. Edmundsbury, Castle Acre, and Mount Grace were some of the most remarkable. One could not begin to name them all. In April 1536, at the end of the twenty-seventh year of the reign of King Henry VIII, there were, scattered through England and Wales, more than eight hundred monasteries, religious houses, nunneries, and friaries. In them lived ten thousand monks, canons, nuns, and friars. Four years later, in April 1540, there were none. Their buildings and properties had been taken over by the crown and leased or sold to new lay occupiers. Their former inhabitants had been dispersed and were in the process of adjusting themselves to a different way of life. This major social and religious upheaval of these four years is called the dissolution of the monasteries.

Our tour group for the abbey ruins had expanded to four; three Americans and Brian. We paid our pence at the little white shed at the entry to the ruins and stepped onto the land given to Augustine by King Ethelbert. The foundations of the Church of St. Peter and Paul were lying under the ruins of the medieval Benedictine abbey before us. As we stood at an artist's sketch of the abbey in its glory, Charles, a Roman Catholic priest from Louisiana, mused: "What an impact Henry VIII's life had on the religious history of a nation!" Brian's normal voice modulation was soft, so soft that I usually had to strain to hear him over the hum of conversation in the dining room and often found myself studying his bottom crooked tooth in my effort to lip-read his words. This time I wasn't even looking and I heard him without any trouble at all. "Henry is a stick that Catholics like to beat Anglicans with," came Brian's rejoinder. "Henry's role in things is way overrated. He had a small part in the play that was on stage at the time. There was already a reform movement afoot—before Luther nailed his challenge to the door of Wittenberg, there was a vigorous movement in many parts of England attacking central doctrines of the medieval Church. And Henry was called 'Defender of the Faith,' wasn't he, for the refutation of Lutheran errors that he penned? What you see here goes well beyond our lusty king. Not even a Tudor could have effected all by himself such a change in the life of the country."

England was unique in its Reformation, unique in the Church established in consequence of the Reformation. The English Reformation was emphatically a political revolution, and its author King Henry resisted, for a time mightily, many of the religious consequences that accompanied the changes everywhere else in Europe. No one suggests that Henry severed the English ties with Rome and set himself up as head of the national Church for spiritual reasons. The crown was not by tradition anti-papal. With a fifth to a third of the land in the hands of churchmen, and with churchmen possessing special and independent rights in justice and in paying taxes, it was not possible for the king to rule effectively unless he used the theoretically supreme power of the Pope as a means of controlling his clergy. Cardinal Wolsey is an excellent example of this royal power.

Wolsey was Henry's chancellor from 1515 until his fall in 1529. During that time he seemed to wield all authority in the state. But he needed more than royal authority. To rule the state he needed papal authority to dominate the bishops and religious orders. So he obtained from Rome the powers of a papal legate on the grounds that he needed them for the reformation of the Church. His unpopular authority in the state, especially his exactions of money, enlarged the bitterness of educated laity against clerical power and therefore against the Pope. Control by the Pope in this new form was resented because it was making present and effective what had rarely been effective from a remote distance. To be free from papal interference became a goal desired by more laity and clergy than ever before in England.

Henry was validly married to the Spanish princess Catherine of Aragon, who had not been able to provide him with a male heir. With the memory of the War of Roses clearly in mind and the Tudor dynasty apparently so insecure, it was necessary for the unity and prosperity of England that a male and legitimate heir should be begotten by the king. Enamored of lady-in-waiting Anne Boleyn and anxious to marry her, the king asked for an annulment. The Pope put him off with delaying tactics and finally refused. Henry's archbishop of Canterbury, Thomas Cranmer, took it upon himself to declare the marriage to Catherine invalid and Henry announced himself to be the sole head of the Church of England in 1534. The Act of Supremacy stated: "The Bishop of Rome hath not by Scripture any greater authority in England than any other foreign bishop." Thomas More, the Lord Chancellor, among others, was beheaded for refusing to recognize the spiritual supremacy of the king. All of the English bishops except one, John Fisher, bowed to the king's wishes.

But even after rejecting the authority of the Pope, Henry VIII continued to resist attempts to turn the Church of England into a Protestant Church after the continental model. It was not until the nine-year-old Edward VI came to the throne in 1547 that the Protestant party in England gained the upper hand. In 1553 all clergy were required to give their assent to the Forty-Two Articles, which included the denial of transubstantiation and the sacrificial nature of the Mass. In 1550 and 1552 new rites of ordination were introduced which were compatible with the Protestant interpretation of the Eucharist. An important part of the ceremony in the Roman Catholic rite had been the handing to the new priest of the instruments of his calling, the chalice and the bread; in the 1552 rite he is handed only the Bible.

Henry VIII removed the English Church from obedience to the Roman see but never tampered with doctrine. For the common man, Catholic life continued much as before the administrative quarrel. England was in schism, not heresy. In the judgment of some readers of history, rather than being the first Anglican, Henry was a disobedient Catholic. That assertion, however, is open to question. In his last years Henry provided quite radical Protestant tutors for his children Edward and Elizabeth. In the end the question is murky because Henry, like all the Tudor monarchs, was more deeply political than religious. The preservation of dynastic power came first, with questions of faith subordinate to that aim. If Henry could raise support or gain political advantage from appearing to adopt a particular religious stance, he did.

The Anglican Reformation lacked the kind of doctrinal definiteness given, for example, to the Lutheran Church by Luther and the Lutheran confessional documents. The Anglican Church did not insist on the kind of formulated system of doctrine produced at the Council of Trent. But it would have astonished Cranmer or Hooker to be told that Anglicans had no doctrinal commitment. The explicit claim they were making was that the Church professed the identical faith of the apostles of the early Church. The present wide doctrinal freedom was not always characteristic of Anglicanism. It has come about in the past hundred years in response to the pressures of controversy (mid-nineteenth century) and subsequently (mid-twentieth century) of biblical and historical criticism. Relatively broad though its confessional commitment always was, the Anglican Church has progressively made it wider.

There are some Anglican writers today such as Stephen Sykes who, in response to this breadth of doctrinal tolerance unparalleled by that of other Churches with an Anglican structure, say that the Anglican Church has an urgent responsibility to articulate what it stands for as an institution. In ecumenical circles, for example, Anglicans often take pains to deny that they are speaking for the official party line of their own Communion. And precisely by doing so, they identify themselves as characteristically Anglican. "Englishmen," Hume once said, "have no distinguishing characteristics, unless that be the very characteristic which distinguishes them."

Not every Anglican would agree though that there needs to be something particularly distinctive about their Church, since many of them have no other desire than to be Catholic. "You Romans," Brian was saying as he moved amid the ruins of St. Augustine's Abbey, "you want to usurp the title 'Catholic' all for yourselves. We also consider ourselves Catholic. We accept the councils and creeds of the undivided Church of the first ten centuries. And any theologian who happened to be an Anglican would not describe his own work as Anglican but as Catholic theology. The teaching and practice of the undivided Church are his criteria."

Brian looked positively venerable in his thick white Irish wool sweater, clerical collar, and black slacks. "There doesn't need to be any specifically Anglican body of doctrine," he continued. "No Roman Catholic would regard his theology as less Catholic because it is Roman, or no Greek Orthodox would regard his theology as less Orthodox becaue it is characteristic of the Greek Church. 'Roman,' 'Greek,' and 'Anglican' are all verbal conventions useful for identifying the differing features of various accounts of Christian faith, not alternatives to the term 'Catholic.' These ruins are part of my tradition, too! Look at them. What a sight this monastery must have been at the height of its influence."

Eight times a day, he recounted as we stood in the middle of what was once the abbey choir, the community would gather in the abbey church to sing or recite the daily offices or to celebrate the daily Mass. The times of prayer were spread at intervals throughout the day, and even the hours of sleep were broken by the night office, Matins, which, where the rule was strictly kept, was timed for 2 A.M. The monastic day was therefore punctuated by the ringing of the abbey bell, the call to prayer, prayer for all according to their needs. This was the first responsibility of every religious community. The size and wealth of the benefactions which so many of them had received through the centuries of their existence are some measure of the importance which the Middle Ages attached to prayer. It could not be said with conviction that all was well with English monasticism in the early years of the reign of

Henry VIII. Even those who wished the orders well thought that a little pruning would not be amiss. Some of the smaller religious houses which had only a handful of inhabitants (the Black Death which had reduced the population in the mid-fourteenth century had affected the monasteries as well) might profitably be closed and accommodation found for their occupants in some of the larger houses, few of which held anything like their full complement. The buildings and lands set free could then be devoted to other and perhaps more useful purposes. Monasticism in England on the eve of the dissolution had the momentum of an established institution, but little real vitality.

Many of the larger abbeys, whose remains are so conspicuous a feature of the countryside today, had become ensnared in the toils of property-owning and found the cares of the world pressing hard upon them. The abbots and senior monks in such establishments found it very difficult not to be drawn into a very secular way of life, little to be distinguished from that of the country gentry who were their neighbors and social equals. A great abbey was usually a landowner on a very large scale, deriving its income from many sources, but chiefly from the rents and profits which came from the ownership of manors and other landed properties. The inhabitants of such religious houses found themselves inevitably deeply involved in problems of management and administration, supervising the affairs of tenants, or engaging in litigation in defense of the abbey's rights and privileges. The abbots of the more important houses also found themselves obliged, as were the important gentry, to serve the crown in a variety of capacities: land-drainage schemes, searching for hoarded foodstuffs in time of dearth, seizing the goods of aliens in time of war, or performing any one of a number of similar tasks which the government might choose to impose upon them. Thirty of the most important abbots sat in the upper house of Parliament.

Since, in the service of government, no very clear distinction was made between secular gentry and the heads of the larger abbeys, it is scarcely surprising that the latter had in many cases adopted a life-style scarcely to be distinguished from that of the former. As the ruins of St. Augustine's and the cathedral priory both indicate, the abbot or priory no longer shared the common dormitory and common refectory with their monks but had established for themselves a separate household in a separate lodging surrounded by their own servants. Even their recreation was secular in style, hunting and hawking being popular with many. But for the most part the monasteries were neither fervent nor disgraceful. They were pleasant, half-secularized clubs for common and comfortable living.

The dissolution of the monasteries was the brainchild of Thomas Cromwell, Henry's chancellor until his fall from grace and execution in 1540. When the dissolution proper began in 1536 with the Act for the Suppression of the Lesser Monasteries, it was also at first presented as a measure primarily of reform rather than of expropriation. However heavily disguised, it *was* clear and simple expropriation. Its principal effect was to transfer to the crown all the possessions of any religious house with less than two hundred pounds a year net income. The occupants were allowed to choose either to be transferred to a surviving house of their own order, or to receive dispensation from their monastic vows which would enable them to pursue a secular career. Compensation was given for all whose interests might be adversely affected by the suppression of the house—an early example, perhaps, of "nationalization with compensation." This first suppression was a limited operation which, on the whole, made no frontal assault on English monasticism and which could be defended as a reasonable and long overdue measure of reform and reorganization. It is difficult to avoid the conclusion, however, that the prime interest of the government in the dissolution was financial all along.

Sometime in the second half of 1537 there seems to have been a significant widening of government objectives. The second stage of the suppression began with the great Cluniac priory of Lewes which "voluntarily surrendered" or forfeited its properties to the crown. What marks a new development in government policy here is that, while the monks of that house were all retired on pension, they were not offered the alternative of moving to another abbey. All had to leave the cloister. This change in practice suggests that the government was now intent upon eliminating monasticism from England as a mistaken form of Christian life. The process, once begun, continued month by month, accelerating to a rate of nearly twenty a month by October 1538 until, in March 1540, the surrender of the last remaining abbey, Waltham, brought it to its end. It is clear that those who resisted the royal will too long or too blatantly might suffer severely for their obstinacy. The priors of Woburn and Lenton and the abbots of Glastonbury, Colchester, and Reading were hanged.

By 1540 the dissolution was complete. There were no religious houses left anywhere in England or Wales. The religious had been pensioned and dispersed. Their treasures, in the form of altar plate and richly embroidered vestments, had been gathered into the king's jewel house. Their bells had been taken down to be recast as cannons in the Tower foundry. The lead had been stripped from the roofs of the abbey churches for use as shot, and the timbers were used as fuel. Deprived of their protection from the weather, the great churches soon fell into decay, and the local people found in them a convenient source of building stone for their houses.

The crown's profit from the suppression was not great in the long run. It took on not only the properties of the monasteries, but also the obligation to meet a fairly extensive pension bill. The demands of the expensive war against France and Scotland in the 1540's forced the government to put the monastic estates on the market where they passed into private hands. An Anglican priest in England, whom I asked to review this manuscript, said with reference to this account: "I am the 'prior' of a priory purchased from the crown at the good office of a local nobleman of the royal court—for twenty pounds paid in two annual installments." The giving away of the confiscated monastic lands to the great noble families at bargain prices helped to keep the gentry off the king's back during a time of internal crisis. The dissolution staved off royal bankruptcy for perhaps a generation at most. In this case what was true of all the Protestant sovereigns of Europe was also true of Henry: in their need for money they missed a unique opportunity of converting these charitable resources to truly charitable ends like education, hospitals, or the relief of the poor. The charge against them would not be so severe if it could be shown that the endowments were diverted to truly national ends. The tragedy is that there is no more to show for the suppression of the monasteries than that it enabled a particular government to survive for a little while longer.

Probably the most notable social change associated with the dissolution was the ending of the practice of going on pilgrimages. Most of the famous centers of pilgrimages like the shrine of St. Thomas at Canterbury had been in the custody of the religious orders. In 1538 these shrines were attacked and destroyed on the grounds that the veneration of relics and the making of pilgrimages were undesirable superstitious practices which tended to divert people's attention away from more fruitful good works. The campaign against relics and pilgrimages ran hand in hand with that against the religious orders. The shrines and monasteries fell at the same time. The devotional practices of many Englishmen were, as a consequence, profoundly changed. The suppression of the monasteries thus contributed very significantly to that secularization of life and society which was so important a feature of the Reformation period.

We pulled the shroud of silence over the ruins of St. Augustine's Abbey as we left. It was the coldest, wettest summer in three hundred years in Britain, according to the newspapers. I had taken to sleeping in my jogging pants and pullover to keep warm at night. But this afternoon the sun had decided to reassure all doubting Thomases that it had not forgotten England. Ruins are somehow more agreeable to stroll among when warm splashes of sun draw golden hues from ancient stones. The four of us were quick to forgive and forget the unfavorable climate that visited us with day after successive day of rain and wet. Mid-July, it almost felt like a summer day. We were in a mood to lift a mug of English ale to the glory of short-sleeve shirts and the promise of drying puddles on tennis courts. Brian led the way around the city wall toward the Bishop's Finger, a hotel pub lying about two blocks up Northgate Street on the right, out of the North Gate.

The Irish gift of gab is most evident over a pint in the local pub, as Brian was about to demonstrate. "You Americans are hard to take," he commenced, placing his glass down on the table after an approving sample of its contents. "We Irish have a warm spot in our hearts for you naturally because you opened your arms to our people when we were starving. You took us in and gave us a new lease on life. But then our people came back and we didn't recognize them. After a couple of generations they came to see the motherland, talking in loud voices and wanting ice water. Like fools we got sucked in by the hypes of the tourist bosses and now we trot out some ale for you in singing pubs and offer you a poor apology for an American hotel. And you're so busy talking about Chicago and Boston that only as an afterthought do you ask us what our life is like. We sell out ourselves and who we are to what the tourist bosses say we should be like, and we drink in the images they feed us about ourselves over the media so we know how to act and what to say. And then when we have filled you with reasons to 'wow' and 'gosh-golly' all over the place we send you back home. I was talking to a lady once and asking her where she'd been, and in the middle of her reply she hesitated and said to her husband, 'Honey, did we do New Zealand?' And all of a sudden I felt depressed because all I could think of was: 'And now you're *doing* Ireland . . . ?' "

I had just been to Ireland the week before and found myself examining my conscience as to whether I'd "done" it. But Brian had already switched tracks, and no defense would be needed. "One of the reason's for Ireland's insularity is that it is simply an island," he expounded, leaning forward with a tilt of intensity. Now how, I wondered, could anyone make a statement like that and bring it off with a sense of significance and revelation? I began to focus on the magical rise and fall of Irish inflection and tones, looking for the secret. "There's no more desolate and lonely place in the world than the west coast of Ireland. If an Irishman has never been to Manhattan, it takes an act of faith for him to believe that there's anything out there after the sun has set into the sea and the clouds have come up in the West. He *has* to believe in a God to help him cope—even a God who threatens hellfire and damnation, a God who inspires fear and guilt, which is the only God most Irish know. It's no accident that that little island has given so many missionaries to the rest of the world and has had a far-flung spiritual empire through the religious vocations of so many of its inhabitants and descendants. There is something about Ireland that inspires wonder and the instinct to worship. It comes out of the very rocks. And it's for that reason that Ireland is a good place to grow up."

While the waiter was setting down another round, Brian's hand went under the thick white sweater to his shirt pocket and came back with a pen. He hurriedly jotted something to himself in green ink on the palm of his hand. Somehow, before the instrument had traced a letter, I knew it was going to come out green.

After trying to "do" Anselm on Monday, Luther on Tuesday, and John Wesley on Wednesday, a mid-week break seemed in order. Mary (whose acquaintance I had initially made in the taxi ride from the train station), Brian and I laid out a scheme over lunch for an excursion by bicycle into the rolling hills of Kent. The Canterbury Cycle Mart on Stour Street had just three bikes left to rent. We aimed them in the direction of Chilham which, our information booklet on the area said, was "an outstandingly pretty village with a fifteenth century church and a seventeenth century castle."

Brian was interested in hearing from Mary what kind of vibrations she had been receiving from the various Anglican clergy from different countries. Mary was the only ordained woman at the conference.

The Anglican Church of Canada and the Episcopal Church of the United States had not waited for the Anglican Communion to come to a worldwide consensus on women's ordination to the priesthood. The Lambeth Conference, which meets every ten years, is the Anglican Communion's primary consensus gathering assembly. But it is only a forum for the exchange of episcopal opinion. Its statements and resolutions are not binding on any individual Church. There does not exist, in fact, a body capable of taking a decision for the whole Anglican Communion.

The Canadian and American Synods, which are empowered to take decisions for their respective countries, gave approval in 1976. The Lambeth Conference ended its debate on the question a year later by producing a guarded statement which seemed to say: "Some Churches in the Anglican Communion ordain women and some do not. Let's respect each other and try to live together."

The Church of England General Synod, which can take decisions for the English Church, declared in 1978 that it saw "no theological objections" to the ordination of women. Nevertheless, when in 1979 legislation was introduced to change canon law and actually allow women's ordination, the synod elected not to pass it. Under synod rules if a bill fails to win approval it cannot be reintroduced for five years. The matter will no doubt come up again in 1984.

The Roman Catholic Church in its official dialogues had urged that Anglicans make a decision about the ordination of women that would be based upon their own convictions rather than upon the prudence of ecumenical politics, and that is exactly what the Anglican Churches of Canada and the United States did. No insult to the traditional discipline of the Roman or Eastern Orthodox Churches was intended, nor was the decision in any way a careless attempt to raise an unnecessary ecumenical obstacle. The subject has been under Anglican consideration for a great many years, several serious studies have been published, and many of the Episcopal seminary faculties have given their opinions in its favor. Faced with an urgent question of the highest priority for the lives of many Anglican Christians, and in the conviction that unity with either the Roman Catholic or Orthodox Church is still a long way off, the Anglican Synods of the United States and Canada made a difficult decision that their own independence compelled them to make by themselves.

To what extent does this action represent a problem for

future unity? Most Anglicans in serious dialogue with Roman
Catholics envision that the first phase of unity will be an official agreement of intercommunion or eucharistic sharing between the two Churches based upon a common faith in
essential doctrine, a common mission in the world, and the
benefit of an increasingly shared life. In such a union the present decision-making processes of both Anglicans and Roman
Catholics would have to be allowed to continue their independence at least for the foreseeable future. Thus, even if this sort
of intercommunion had been reached before the question of
the ordination of women had surfaced, there would most likely
have been a kind of agreement that would have left the Episcopal Church free to make (or free not to make) such a decision as it has now made. The hope is clearly that each Church
may conclude that, when placed in the total context of broader
ecumenical goals and the central doctrines of the Christian
faith, so many of which are already held in common, the ordination or non-ordination of women is not so high a priority that
sacramental sharing need be denied when there is divergence
of practice on this question.

At the Cantess Summer School, the whole range of reaction was represented. There were Anglo-Catholic traditional-
ists who felt that the action was not only wrong but impossible,
making the official Anglican Church apostate from Catholic
faith and practice. The more militant of these have moved
with the schism in the American Episcopal Church over the
question. Other dissenters were also present who remain loyal
to the official Church but who feel various degrees of malaise
ranging from "I'll go along, but I don't like it" to "I can't recognize the validity of women priests but I won't leave the
Church." Also represented were wholehearted supporters.

Mary was not much interested in talking about it. "Someone said to me at the table that he was looking forward to
talking with me and figuring out this whole women-and-men-
in-ministry-thing. I don't have anything to 'figure out.' I've
been living the reality of priestly ministry for five years now.
I'm not interested in discussing questions like 'What can wom-
en contribute to ministry that men can't?' I can contribute the

person that I am, and that's something no other person can contribute, whether male or female.

"I've been gradually leaving those categories behind. In the first couple of years after I was ordained, when someone would come to me for a wedding or counseling, I would think 'It's because I'm a woman.' I eventually learned it wasn't that at all. I was just perceived by the other as open. At other times I thought people were deliberately choosing my colleague because he's a man. But they were going to him because they wanted someone older with more experience.

"Early on when I was walking through our neighborhood, from time to time I'd hear a little child from the parish say to a playmate: 'There's a woman priest.' But now they just say, 'That's our priest.' The longer we live with it, the less people will look at it in terms of male-female."

About two miles out of Canterbury, we turned our bikes onto a country road and left the city's peripheral traffic behind. The weather was holding; the exercise and fresh air were a tonic. But Brian could not ride in silence. If Mary could not be drawn out further on the subject of women's ordination, he would apply the nozzle of his questions to me. His bike pulled abreast. I was ready for about anything but what came: the thorny question usually gingerly avoided because of the emotional, historical, and theological freight it carries with it—the validity of orders.

"How do you personally resolve the question of orders, Tom?" Only Brian could ask such a question while biking down a country road on a break between lectures.

"Brian," I said, "you're willing to risk a budding friendship to that hailstone?"

As we rode along, each of us contributed bits and pieces to the reconstruction of the background of the problem.

In 1896 Pope Leo XIII in a Bull entitled *Apostolicae Curae* declared that "ordinations performed according to the Anglican rite have been and are completely null and void." It was by no means the first occasion on which Rome concluded against the validity of Anglican orders, though the reasons given for the verdict have not always been the same. As early as

the reign of Mary Tudor (1553–58) Roman Catholics had decided that ministers ordained in the Church of England needed to be reordained if they "became" Catholics and sought
priesthood within the Roman Catholic Church. Since ordination, like baptism and confirmation, can only be conferred
once, this attitude implied the belief that the earlier Anglican
ordination was no ordination at all.

When Edward died in 1553, his half-sister Mary set about
restoring Catholicism in England. By the end of her reign in
1558 the hierarchy was in communion with Rome once again.
Mary had made herself and her brand of Catholicism disliked
by marrying a Spaniard, by fighting an unsuccessful war with
France, and by burning heretics in unprecedented numbers,
including big "show trials" of bishops like Cranmer, Ridley,
and Latimer. Still, for Elizabeth, with a treasury impoverished
and a land undefended, with the French claiming the English
crown through Mary Queen of Scots, with a Spanish army in
the Netherlands, and with two-thirds of England Catholic, it
was imprudent to be Protestant. But by birth, education, and
conviction a Protestant Elizabeth was to be. Under Mary she
had suffered for the Protestant cause. She was hailed by the
Protestant party as their champion. When she took the throne
the exiles hurried back from the continent. The usual historical
reconstruction of Elizabeth's first Parliament of 1559 puts Elizabeth somewhere in the middle between a conservative Cath-
olic-minded House of Lords and a radical Calvinist House of
Commons.

Later in her life, Elizabeth said that the Protestants had
driven her farther than she wanted to go. She was, after all, the
daughter of Henry VIII, and it is certain that she was personally attracted to a religious settlement like that of her father, at
least considered in generalities. A Catholicism without the
Pope, the royal supremacy, a preferably celibate clergy, the
real presence in the Eucharist. In 1559 she told the Spanish
ambassador (in what was probably truth as well as diplomacy)
that she was resolved to restore religion as her father had left
it. This was not a practicable program, because no one in the
country wanted it. The reigns of Edward VI and Mary had

made the Catholics more Roman and the Protestants more Reformed. She was ruling a divided people, among whom some
wanted the Pope and the others the Prayer Book for which
Cranmer, Ridley, and Latimer had died. Whatever Elizabeth's
real religious convictions, the only way of ensuring political
stability was to produce a "half-reformed" compromise which
left large areas of doctrine and practice deliberately vague. It
is precisely here that many locate the beginning of "Anglican
comprehensiveness."

There can be no historical doubt that it was the intention
of the architects of the Elizabethan settlement to provide a
context in which people of widely differing theological conviction could co-exist. There was, of course, no disguising the fact
that the Church of England denied the papal claims. But given
that denial, the "golden mediocrity" commended by Archbishop Parker, the first Elizabethan bishop, was supposed to be in-
clusive of conservatives in doctrine and polity as well as those
who had learned much from their lives in exile in the Reformed lands of the continent. The Church of England was, in
the most obvious sense, Protestant; but the important sense in
which it was not merely Protestant was contained in its hospitality to conservatism in doctrine and polity—a conservatism
the importance of which grew with the years.

For all her diplomatic talent Elizabeth had no dealings
with the Pope and she withdrew the English envoy in Rome
without ceremony. She abolished the Mass and reintroduced
the oath of supremacy although she called herself the supreme
governor rather than the supreme head of the Church. She sta-
bilized what has become known as Anglicanism, and she could
more logically be considered the founder of the Church of England than her notorious father. The Thirty-Nine Articles,
trimmed from forty-two, formed the doctrinal standard for the
national Church, now decidedly in the Protestant camp.
Queen Elizabeth and all members of the Church of England
were excommunicated by Pope Pius V, an action which Cardinal Newman and other Roman Catholic writers have considered a blunder which only bolstered anti-Catholicism in the
nation.

When, in 1559, Parliament passed the Acts of Supremacy and Uniformity constituting the Queen supreme governor in both spiritual and temporal matters and reimposing the Prayer Book, all the diocesan bishops with one probable exception refused to comply and were deprived of their sees. It was not anticipated that the Acts of Supremacy and Uniformity would be the permanent settlement they actually became. Everyone generally assumed that when the queen married, the situation would change again. The Spanish king, Philip II, long cherished hopes that Elizabeth would marry him. It was largely as a result of Spanish pressure on the papacy that Elizabeth was not excommunicated until 1570.

Elizabeth did not marry. The Acts remained. And the Church of England urgently needed new bishops.

Between 1892 and 1896 discussions took place on the continent and in England between Roman Catholics and Anglo-Catholic members of the Church of England. Among the leading participants were Abbé Portal on the Roman side and Lord Halifax on the Anglican. Pope Leo was asked to set up a new investigation into the question of Anglican orders. His totally unfavorable response in *Apostolicae Curae* begins by showing in considerable detail that as early as 1554, and several times afterward, Rome had studied Edward VI's Ordinal, and on every occasion had found that ordinations performed according to it were invalid. The Roman Catholic position has been that the sacrificial element of the priesthood had been excised from the Anglican rite of ordination for an extended period of years. By the time it was restored in the seventeenth century, the last of the validly consecrated Anglican bishops had died.

Many historians and theologians, Roman Catholic as well as Anglican, believe that the 1896 verdict failed to take into account a number of considerations which might have changed the papal stand. Many years after the papal announcement, it was revealed that only four of the eight members of the commission had voted to declare Anglican orders invalid. Of these four votes three were cast by English representatives who were sent to Rome with the express purpose of guaranteeing a negative decision. No Anglicans were invited to present their cases before the commission and almost all students of the question agree that the Anglican case was poorly presented by the continental Roman Catholics assigned to the task.

In any event the decision on Anglican orders cannot be used today to deny the validity of the orders of any particular Episcopalian priest or bishop. The participation in Anglican consecrations of Old Catholic and Polish National Catholic bishops for many decades has changed the *de facto* situation. Old Catholics are a loosely associated group of communities under the presidency of the Archbishop of Utrecht. Formerly within the Roman Catholic Church, their independent existence derives from their refusal to accept papal primacy of jurisdiction or infallibility as defined at Vatican I. Since 1931 intercommunion with the Anglicans has existed, and Old Catholic bishops (whose orders are recognized) have participated in many Anglican ordinations. A majority of the bishops of the worldwide Anglican Communion are now in the Old Catholic succession; they can trace their orders not merely to Anglican sources, but to bishops recognized by Rome as being validly consecrated. Churches of the worldwide Anglican Communion prize the apostolic succession and maintain that their bishops trace their commissions to apostolic times.

A Catholic understanding of the Eucharist has returned to the center of Anglican worship in most parts of the world. As it was precisely the understanding of the Eucharist (in its sacrificial aspect) that historically was at the heart of the question of the validity of orders, the convergence in eucharistic theology has been a key development. The Windsor Statement of 1971 indicates that the common Anglican understanding of the Eucharist is in harmony with that of the Roman Catholic Church. Consequently, even if the words of the ordination service, taken out of context, do not with sufficient precision denote the priesthood, within the context of the Anglican Church today their eucharistic meaning is plain and adequate.

Mary had fallen behind a bit, and seemed to be struggling with a malfunctioning of the gears on her three-speed, but it seemed to correct itself. Brian and I pushed off and started to pedal again as she slowly passed us by, preoccupied with the chain on her bike. We all rode in silence for a while, waiting to see if the thread of discussion would be picked up again. When Mary spoke up a fleeting sensation of inner chagrin betrayed my secret hope that the subject would be left behind. "Today," she said, "the Anglican-Roman dialogue hasn't approached the subject of ministry at all from the perspectives of Leo's bull. They begin by looking at what the Churches themselves affirm *now* about their understanding of ordination. It has gone well. The essential aspects of ordination and the broad sweep of functions which the ordained ministry serves in the Church were all agreed upon. If you insist on going back into history and trying to find a solution in what the Edwardian ordination rite did or didn't say, and what the intention was of those who used it—it's a dead end and will remain unsolved."

There was something else unsolved, of a considerably more practical nature. It had little to do with the validity of orders but much to do with the common needs of the faithful. Mary's bicycle chain was making threatening sounds. Each attempt to shift the gears increased the metallic protests. We all pulled off on the side of the road. A lovely rolling valley speckled with sheep lay below us. I overcame my sense of incompetence with things mechanical and proceeded to ponder the chain and get some grease on my hands.

There, amid grease and chain and upturned bicycle, the subject of holy orders seemed more incongruous than ever. The entire discussion had been too ponderous for a recreative bike hike and needed some levity. "Brian," I said, "I know how we could end this whole thing. Why don't you and Mary just submit to some form of reordination out of regard for Roman misgivings?"

Brian studied my face for the hint of a smile. He *thought* I was joking, but he wasn't sure. Mary didn't even look. "Ha!" she yelped in a mock-laugh.

"Tom," Brian responded, confirming my suspicion that he couldn't be insincere if he tried, "that might take more humility and generosity than I could muster. Besides which, it wouldn't be honest."

"Why don't *you* revoke the bull?" Mary countered. "It never was *infallible.*" She tobogganed down the last word, indicating that she had clearly caught on to the game. "In fact, there were politics mixed up in it. Leo's advisors thought that conceding the validity of Anglican orders would discourage a reconciliation between the two Churches on Rome's terms. If after all these years the case for *in*validity of orders is still not proved, why don't *you* just go one step further and say that validity is presumed?"

I tried to imagine the Pope revoking the judgment of the Bull, but Brian didn't wait for a response; he sensed the momentum created by Mary's question and moved with it. "Would you be accepting the presupposition of Leo's bull?"

"What's that?" I said, sensing a trap.

"That the only way in which valid orders can be conferred is by a bishop who can trace his orders through an unbroken chain of succession back to the Lord's commission to the apostles?"

I wasn't going to fall for that. First, that assumption could not even be proved from history to be the case in the Roman Church. It's known that in the Middle Ages ordinations were occasionally performed by priests, not bishops. Second, there is another way of interpreting apostolic succession which I sensed he was working up to. The second way of interpreting it is as the effort of a community to be faithful to the apostolic teaching. This consists more in a conformity of mind and heart and life to Christ than in an unbroken succession of bishops in history. Both, according to Roman Catholic teaching, are necessary. When succession of bishops is broken, it needs to be "repaired" through ordination conferred by bishops in valid orders.

I dodged Brian's question by putting one to him: "Let's suppose that an unbroken succession of bishops in the Anglican tradition is *not* there and that this 'defect' has not been 'repaired.' But let's also suppose that the conformity of mind and heart and life to Christ *is* there—faithfulness to the apostolic tradition. Is the 'defect'—a 'broken' succession of bishops—sufficiently serious to invalidate orders in that case?"

258 TALES OF CHRISTIAN UNITY

The chain was feeding nicely onto the sprocket wheel.

"Go on," Brian said. "You're only halfway home with it."

"Oh, you guys are awful!" Mary interjected. "Enough is enough!"

"Hang on, Mary," Brian persisted. "We're on the verge. . . . There are two elements in the ordination of a bishop: ordination by bishops from other sees—Old Catholic, Roman Catholic, Orthodox—as a link with the universal Church, and the call coming from the new bishop's own Church as a link with the origins of his own see—in this case, the Anglican Church. Granted: both should be there. But in the absence of the first link, can the second suffice to keep the episcopacy and the priesthood 'alive'?"

"You know where he's going with that, I hope," Mary said matter-of-factly as she sat down under a tree. "If you say 'yes,' then we are not dealing with a reunion situation where Anglican clergy would come seeking ordination as if for the first time. If you say 'yes,' we have a situation in which valid priests and bishops—Roman Catholics as well as Anglicans—come to receive the fullness of the sacramental sign. As long as the Church is divided, the fullness of the sign of catholicity doesn't exist anywhere, including in the Roman Catholic and Orthodox Churches."

"Mary," I declared, flipping her bicycle into an upright position, "your bike is fixed and so, I think are we!"

We were off and rolling again toward Chilham. Under an oak tree in the yard of its fifteenth century village church, we sketched the service in which it would all happen. The accent of "recognition" would not be used. That would be too Church-oriented, where somebody "wins" and somebody "loses." More appropriate would be the language of "a reconciliation of ministries." Representatives of our Churches would come before God together, asking God to give to *all* our ministries what they are lacking. It is God, after all, who does the reconciling.

We sat in the shadow of the village church of Chilham. It had been constructed at the inception of the turmoil leading to the Reformation in England. While it seemed old, it should not, Brian declared, be allowed to blind us to the fact of fifteen centuries of common history.

Though we are all but small voices, there are situations of dialogue where, whether in a living room or over a back fence, we feel as though we *are* the Church in microcosm. On one level we were just two Anglicans and a Roman Catholic on a bike ride. Yet, on another level, we *were* our respective Churches incarnated there on the hillside in Kent. And if *we* could find a conscientious way through the historical and doctrinal tangle with which we could all live in peace ... well, surely then, all that stands between the convictions of honest Christians and the consensus of Vatican synods and Lambeth Conferences is time.

John Henry Cardinal Newman. Karl Barth. Teilhard de Chardin. CANTESS was in its last lap. Before taking our leave, however, our hosts were eager to give us a look at story-book England via a whole day excursion to (we could take our choice) Kent Castles and Gardens, or Windsor Castle and Eton, or Brighton. Brian decided in favor of Windsor. Since I had been there just before the conference began, I climbed on the coach for Brighton. My traveling companions for the day were Canons Robert Winters of St. Saviour's Vicarage in London and Milton McGregor of Townsville, Australia. I took particular relish in calling Robert "The Vicah." Always impeccably dressed in white shirt, tie, and grey tweed sport coat, his distinguished white hair brushed straight back, he so reminded me (and I loved to tease him about it) of the characterization of the Anglican establishment by the German Church historian von Dollinger: "There is no Church that is so completely and thoroughly as the Anglican the product and expression of the wants and wishes, the modes of thought and cast of characters, not of a certain nationality, but of a fragment of a nation, namely, the fashionable and cultivated classes. It is the religion of deportment, of gentility, of clerical reserve." The Anglican Church has succeeded in recent years in broadening its appeal to people far removed socially from society's leaders. Formerly, however, it was once labeled "The Conservative Party at prayer," an appellation which strikes the visitor to Westminster Abbey in London as historically substantiated. In the Musicians' Aisle are the graves and memorials of famous musicians like Henry Purcell, Orlando Gibbons, and Ralph Vaughan Williams. In the Statesmen's Aisle are the graves and memorials of many renowned British politicians including Prime Ministers Pitt, Palmerston, Disraeli, Gladstone, Peel, and Asquith. In the opposite transept is the Poets' Corner with graves and memorials of most of the major English poets: the tomb of Chaucer, and memorials to Shakespeare, T.S. Eliot, W.H. Auden, and Gerard Manley Hopkins. Dr. Samuel Johnson, Charles Dickens and George Frederick Handel are also buried there. And in front of the high altar is the Lantern, where all but two of the English kings and queens have been crowned since 1066.

In one visit to the abbey that summer, I entered the great west door behind two university students hefting well-worn backpacks. After advancing twenty paces into the nave, past the memorial to Winston Churchill, the portrait of King Richard II and the graves of David Livingstone, David Lloyd George, Clement Attlee, Ramsay MacDonald and Isaac Newton, one of them paused and, reaching for his guidebook with a puzzled expression on his face, whispered to his companion: "Where are we—is this a Church or a museum?"

"It's a family affair," was Brian's homely way of explaining it. "The tablets and monuments are one way of reminding us of the communion of saints; we remember these people with great affection. It should be looked upon in the context of a parish keeping alive the memory of those who have lived and died in it." Westminster Abbey, he had granted me, was another question: "That's a national shrine. The size and grandeur of some of the monuments make the altar look like a kitchen table. Family pride gets out of hand at times."

The day had dawned sparkling and clear, a veritable pearl in a month's string of wooden beads. Such weather on the day of our outing was enough to restore faith in the ultimate graciousness of Reality. We mounted the spacious coaches at 9:00 A.M. After a couple of weeks of seeing signs in restaurant lots reading "No Football Coaches Permitted Here," it had finally broken upon me that the nation was not demonstrating any particular antipathy for the instructors of its soccer players; it simply called its buses "coaches." Our red and white marvel had a continuous window all around the upper half of the siding, and see-through panels in the ceiling as well. Robert, Milton and I made our way to the rear where we could appreciate the view from left as well as right, up as well as behind. We drove southwest out of Canterbury in the heart of the Weald (read: ups and downs) of Kent, England's garden.

Robert was recounting with enthusiastic commentary a liturgy he had attended in Canterbury: "We used the 1662 Prayer Book—what a delight! That phrase 'true and lively sacrifice' which, in the new Communion service has been changed to 'living sacrifice'. . . . Someone once asked me what the difference was, and I said, 'Well, I'll tell you: if I go to visit an old folk's home, they're all *living,* but they're not all *lively,* are they?' Certainly not! Beautiful word that, 'lively.' " He repeated it to himself, tenderly savoring each syllable.

Milton nodded in agreement. "I'll give you an example of what the controversy of the Prayer Book has been like among us," he said to me. "It's like a Roman Catholic neighbor of mine who came up to me after Vatican II when the Mass was changing from Latin to English. 'Oh, Milton,' he sighed, 'there's a movement afoot and I hope to God it only lasts a short time because I want to die a Catholic.' For some Anglicans, changing the language of the Prayer Book to some modern language version isn't dying an Anglican."

The ride passed quickly, and we soon arrived in Brighton. The most distinguished of all the British seaside resorts, it once was known as "London by the Sea," a description which applies particularly to the number and variety of shopping areas. Limited to an afternoon as we were, the choice was difficult. "The Lanes" were a "must." After that, given the amount of time remaining, a decision would have to be made among the chic shops in Brighton's East Street and adjoining Regent Arcade, the Gardner Street Junk Market, and the open market at The Level. First on the agenda, however, was the conducted tour of the Brighton Pavilion planned for the whole group.

The rich history of Brighton stems from that handsome, wayward, gifted, spendthrift character, George, Prince of Wales (later Prince Regent and finally King George IV). The prince first visited Brighton in 1783 and by 1822 his Royal Pavilion was completed in the style of the Moghul palaces of India, and it deserved its title of the most bizarre and exotic palace in Europe. With its onion-shaped dome, tent-like roofs, numerous pinnacles and small minarets, the Oriental exterior is only surpassed by its still more amazing Chinese interior. Milton and Robert were vying with one another for the best image: Milton: "The prince's own little Kremlin." Robert: "Table laid for dinner with too many pepperpots." Milton: "Looks like St. Paul's came down from London to Brighton and 'popped.' "

During the tour Robert had decided that in view of our lectures on John Henry Newman and the nineteenth century Tractarian Movement in England, it was very important for me to see the Church of St. Bartholomew's in Brighton as a symbol of the Anglo-Catholic element in the Church of England which grew out of that era. We chose a path through the Lanes' narrow red brick alleyways in which are clustered a fascinating collection of antique shops, pubs, and cafes.

Robert led us to Ann Street with the confident step of a scout who has been over the path many times before. There, on Ann Street, towering above the neighboring houses, is the church which was dubbed by some as "The Barn" and by others as "Noah's Ark." St. Bartholomew's is one hundred and seventy feet long and claims to be the tallest parish church in the British Isles, rising even higher than Westminster Abbey. When it was being built, there were objections to its height and scale; householders complained that it caused downdrafts and made their chimneys smoke. It is the "cathedral" of what used to be called "The London-Brighton South Coast Religion" with its incense, ritual, embroidered vestments, and candles. After the coming of the railways in 1841, the population of the town increased rapidly and more churches were needed. Fr. Arthur Douglas Wagner, the curate of St. Paul's in Brighton, inherited a considerable fortune which gave him the means to

St.
Bartholomew's
Church

finance the building of new churches. He belonged to a generation of priests who were imbued with the Tractarian revival which was both evangelistic and sacramental, and he built churches in which the liturgy could be performed with grandeur and the people could experience it in all its richness. The architectural style of the South Coast Religion was as atypical of English churches in general during this period as its liturgical style.

"The Tracts for the Times," a publication that appeared from 1833–41, gave its name to the Tractarian Movement. The Tracts originated and ended with John Henry Newman. The

Oxford Movement, which was sparked off by the Tracts, continued to grow and expand long after the Tracts had ceased. The basic conception of the Oxford Movement is that of the Holy Catholic Church as a visible body upon earth, bound together by a spiritual but absolute unity, though divided into national and other sections. This conception drew with it the sense of historical continuity, of the intimate and unbroken connection between the primitive Church and the Church of England, and of the importance of the Fathers as teachers and guides. It also tended to emphasize points of communion between those different branches of the Church which recognize the doctrine of apostolic succession. Newman was the guide, the philosopher, and the martyr of this great religious revival in England.

The Tractarian Movement succeeded after his time in planting among the varieties of Anglican religious life a Catholic party. It did not succeed in uniformly giving a pre-Vatican II continental style, but it left a virtually uniform sacramental life that had not existed before.

In the final analysis, Newman's work had a lasting impact: he resuscitated the Fathers, brought into relief the sacramental system, and paved the way for an astonishing revival of long-forgotten ritual. Among the literary stars of his time, he is distinguished by the pure Christian radiance that shines in his life and in his writings. He is the one Englishman of that era who upheld the ancient creed with a theologian's knowledge, a Shakespearean force of style, and a fervor worthy of the saints.

The interior of St. Bartholomew's compresses the issues brought into focus by the Tracts during the Oxford Movement into so many coded messages of religious conviction.

The high altar and pulpit are designed with a proportionality that reflects the conviction of the equally important dual thrust of word and sacrament in the liturgy.

The panels in the high altar represent the crucified Lord in the center; to the left are Our Lady, St. Joseph, and St. Peter, and on the right are St. John, St. Bartholomew, and St. Paul. In contrast to the more Protestant positions of many of their Anglican brethren, the Anglo-Catholics stress their Catholic heritage. The question is still real today: while the Roman and Anglican Churches agree about the doctrine of the communion of saints, they differ regarding the proper place of the saints in Christian devotion. The saints are examples, but are they intercessors?

One of the large stained glass windows in the nave pictures the Madonna and Child. Directly beneath it is the Lady Altar.

There is agreement in venerating Mary as the Virgin Mother of God, but difference regarding her place in Christian devotion and in the doctrine of the Church as to her relationship to the work of redemption and to the Church itself. The two Roman Catholic "Marian dogmas" (the Immaculate Conception, defined in 1854, and the Assumption, defined in 1950) occasion difficulty to Anglicans. Some cannot accept the doctrines themselves; others, while willing to accept them as possible opinions, do not accept Roman Catholic claims to an authority to define such doctrines as "of faith."

In the rear of St. Bartholomew's, with their Oriental-looking onion-shaped domes, are the confessionals. The Anglican Communion gives a special place to the sacraments of baptism and Holy Communion. The Thirty-Nine Articles speak also of "those five commonly called sacraments" that is to say, confirmation, penance, orders, matrimony and extreme unction. It does not deny to these latter the name "sacrament" but differentiates between them and the "two sacraments ordained by Christ" described in the catechism as necessary to salvation for all. Roman Catholics accept all seven as sacraments in the full sense of the word. Since the Second Vatican Council, various Agreed Statements now show a general acceptance of the sacramental and grace-giving nature of orders and matrimony. Confirmation has a very important place in Anglican practice (indeed, the Anglican Communion, unlike the Roman Catholic Church, does not admit of exceptions to the law that a bishop is the minister of this sacrament). Anglican practice varies as regards penance (called absolution) and the anointing of the sick.

In the sanctuary, a great baldachino in Byzantine style is

supported by white alabaster capitals with interlaced vine patterns. On either side of it stand two giant candlesticks surmounted by a bronze ornament and, nearer the altar, six large brass candlesticks. The tabernacle door is of beaten silver. Stations of the cross are carved in stone and wood set in the brick piers along the aisles. In the back is a holy water font. With one sweep of the eye, in other words, the visitor is presented with several reasons why the average Anglican viewed the Anglo-Catholics, until recently, with a mixture of suspicion and amusement. Many of them were quite unaware of the nature of Anglo-Catholicism and may not have even heard that religious orders in Anglicanism were revived after a lapse of three hundred years.

In the last twenty years, however, the liturgical lines between the various parties in the Anglican Church have blurred. The liturgical renewal within the past two decades has exerted a strong sacramental influence across the board within the Church. The low, broad, and Anglo-Catholic traditions are no longer as distinguishable as was the case from 1890 to 1960. The particular parish that guards a clear identity as "low Church," for example, would be today the exception and perhaps even a curiosity. Vestments, used only by the Anglo-Catholics twenty years ago, are now used widely and as a matter of course by the majority of Anglican priests.

The performance of liturgy is, while subject to regulation, astonishingly various. There is a considerable contrast of styles to be seen, corresponding, it may be, to a different conception of worship: a traditionally formal Prayer Book service and a modern informal liturgy.

It was too glorious a day to linger indoors, especially with the sea and a magnificent beach within walking distance. We returned to the midtown area and walked along the beach past the King's Esplanade and Lawns, the Brunswick Lawns, and turned left at Brighton Centre on West Street to pass a second time through The Lanes on our way back to the Pavilion and our coach.

Supper was a little later than usual at Christ Church College to accommodate all travelers. By the time we finished it was 8:30 P.M., and the afterglow of a bona fide summer day still lingered in the air. Brian and I found each other in the dining room and decided to take a walk. I recounted the visit to St. Bartholomew's and how in many ways it served as a microcosm of the Tractarian Movement and several of the issues which Newman addressed.

"Ah, but there's one issue which Newman took up with which we still have to deal," Brian remarked softly. "And that's the Pope. Authority. We still have to deal with authority. Newman believed that the Church has an infallible teaching office inasmuch as the Church has been entrusted with an eternal revelation which must be safeguarded and never lost. 'Which is the Church which takes this seriously?' he asked. The chair of Peter is the only place which claims to exercise what Newman thought the Church must possess in lieu of what had been given to it. And so he joined the Church of Rome, because it had the nearest family resemblance to the Church of the Fathers which he sought. He actually knew very few Roman Catholics, but he was converted to the *idea* of what the Church is. He was worried by Vatican I because the kind of infallibility he endorsed had to be exercised pastorally as well as collegially, with consultation of the laity as an important part of its exercise. He backed infallibility, but a minimalist infallibility. And, today, we Anglicans are still worried by Vatican I."

Many Anglo-Catholic moderates would be more blunt and say that the notion of papal infallibility is explicable only in terms of nineteenth century Roman triumphalism.

Anglicans and Roman Catholics agree that an authority attaches to the Church as a whole as it speaks God's word to the world. But within the Church, doctrine and discipline are the particular responsibility of the bishops, who have received at their ordination a special commission to discern and give expression to the insights of believers into the teaching of the Gospel. There is a growing agreement between the two Churches that in a united Church a special ministry of unity would be exercised by the Bishop of Rome as a focus of communion, although agreement has still to be reached on the precise nature, scope and mode of exercise of his authority, particularly as a teacher of the faith.

In the first centuries there was a clear development as bishops came together to consult in council, saw their responsibilities toward the whole Church as well as toward their individual dioceses, and recognized a special ministry and authority in one bishop. Roman Catholics see this as Christ's express will for his Church summarized in the Petrine texts (Matthew 16; Luke 22; John 21). Anglicans see these facts as an historical development, possibly providential, but ask whether this is really of the essence of the Church. They likewise question some traditional Roman Catholic interpretations and applications of the Petrine texts and ask whether St. Peter's special functions are necessarily continued in the Church of subsequent ages. In particular they query the Roman doctrine of the Pope's universal jurisdiction. In their 1982 Final Report, the Anglican-Roman Catholic International Commission reached a consensus on authority in the Church and in particular on the principles of primacy: "We can now together affirm that the Church needs both a multiple, dispersed authority . . . and also a universal primate as servant and focus of visible unity in truth and love."

The basic question is: What is involved in acceptance of the universal ministry of the Bishop of Rome? Would this mean, at most, a form of universal presidency in charity when essential matters of faith are at stake? What relation, then, would the Vatican have to the various synods of the Anglican Communion? There are some questions about the Anglican acceptance of a universal primacy which cannot be answered until Anglicans and Roman Catholics have come to some consensus on what acceptance actually involves.

Our walk past St. Martin's Church, down Longport Street into Burgate and around the cathedral yard, had now come full circle. Brian suggested that we stop by the campus pub. David, an Episcopalian professor of theology from Massachusetts, was in the process of ordering a glass of ale from the bar. "Make that two more," Brian directed the bartender. I spotted a free table along the wall and moved to reserve it for us. Brian and David arrived momentarily.

"One of the things I've enjoyed most about this summer school," David reflected, "has been the informal exchanges outside of the lectures. Nothing like a few jars of ale to make all of us pub-stool theologians."

"Same here," Brian contributed. "Tom and I were just having a go at cracking the authority-nut."

"Ah, yes," David nodded knowingly, with an air of resignation. "We closed the pub down on that one the other night. We were determined to solve it before going to bed. Too bad you weren't there for that one, Tom. Can't deal with that one without bringing in your man there, the Pope. We Anglicans and Romans are of one mind that the Church will not fail in truth in the long run. The problem is how the Church or the bishops in council or the Pope is preserved from error in particular cases when speaking to essential doctrines of faith and morals. The fundamental question is: *Can* the Church speak definitively on moral and ethical issues?"

"Ethics," Brian grunted, "the 'ecumenical ghetto.' If we think that reaching agreement on baptism, the Eucharist, and ministry has been difficult, we haven't seen anything yet. In the realm of Christian ethics we're entering a more perilous path. And there's no way around it either. The project of unity has to pass by here, too: the use of sex in marriage, contraception, abortion. Even when our Churches agree on the principle of responsible parenthood or on the principle of the rights of human life from its very beginning, in practice we tend to apply them differently—mainly because the relationship between the individual conscience and the authority of the teaching Church is not viewed in the same way."

"But do you think some kind of organic unity between our churches needs to wait until agreement on all those issues is reached?" I asked. "As far as ARCIC is concerned, substantial agreement exists on the essential issues. Its final report is expected to say that we are essentially united in faith. Do the areas of disagreement that remain have to be seen as grounds for keeping our Churches apart? Why couldn't we argue them out in a united Church? Not all Roman Catholics are in the same place on those issues. There are even various interpretations among Roman Catholic theologians as to what papal infallibility actually means."

"In general, I'm very sympathetic to that approach," David replied. "But when you move in on that notion of a 'united Church,' it's like reaching into a rose bush: you're after the flower and you discover the thorns. There's a big difference in structure between our two Churches. An Anglican bishop is accountable to no one except God—certainly not to the archbishop of Canterbury. Anglican parish priests are also much more independent of their bishops than their Roman counterparts are. It's next to impossible to dislodge a vicar from his parish except for reasons of moral turpitude."

Brian was nodding in agreement. "To us," he continued, "the Roman system seems oppressively authoritarian and overly centralized. There's the top-heavy curial bureaucracy, with the consequent conservatism in matters where the Church needs to be open to change."

"There's a difference in atmosphere, too," David observed.

"Right you are," Brian affirmed again. "The Roman Catholic parishes which I know well in England and Ireland—even the best of them—seem to be clergy-dominated with little official encouragement for lay initiative or leadership. The Church of England puts a much higher value on lay participation at all levels of decision making."

"All of that adds up," concluded David, "to a fairly significant divergence in attitudes, even if the ARCIC statements show substantial agreement on crucial doctrinal questions such as sacraments and the nature of the ministry. Agreement at the level of faith is not always evident in visible expression. The Episcopal and Roman Churches differ somewhat in their forms of worship, their traditions of spirituality, and their styles of theological reflection. On the one hand you have Rome-centered, definitive documents, and, on the other, you have government by synods, less definitive documents and fewer laws about matters of Christian obligation—like Sunday worship. Over the past few centuries each of the Churches has continued to grow and develop in its own separate way without the benefit of close contact with the other."

Brian was beginning to fear that he and David were sounding too negative. "In the last decade or two," he observed in a conciliatory tone, "thanks to a movement of change that is difficult to explain apart from the providence of God, we've grown to understand one another more deeply. There's no question but that we're closer now than at any time since the English Reformation. It will be interesting to see whether the authorities in both Churches are prepared to give ARCIC's work the massive endorsement it needs if it is to have any practical effects."

"The Anglican Communion already has, to a considerable extent," David added. "The last Lambeth Conference, in 1978, endorsed the statements of agreement and said it hoped that they would provide a basis for sacramental sharing between our two Communions. Since then the synods of the various Churches making up the Anglican Communion have studied them, and some have formally accepted them. It's still unclear whether a Roman response can be made which will be officially representative of Roman Catholic opinion throughout the world. In the United States and Canada the rapprochement has had a fairly good exposure. Much of that is due to the American and Canadian Anglican-Roman Catholic dialogue groups. There was a recent news release in which the U.S. group said that, after about twenty joint consultations, the two Churches share so profound an agreement on the level of faith that they are in fact 'sister Churches' in the one Communion which is the Church of Christ. I don't know how much more can be said by the theologians than that."

"Aye," Brian said, "they've constructed the frame; now what we need are the plumbers and the electricians of unity— the practical people who can make what's on paper workable. That may be where we Anglicans have something special to contribute. We've never had a very tidy house. The way things go forward in the Anglican Church baffles neatness and logic. And that, it seems to me, is the kind of spirit that needs to mark our move toward unity—a willingness to keep things going forward even if every 't' is not crossed nor 'i' dotted."

David signaled to the waiter for three more ales. "There's a lot to what you say, Brian," he said, reaching into his pocket to pay for the next round. "There's something about Anglicanism that makes it specially qualified to work for greater unity. Anglican theology is true to its genius when it is seeking to reconcile differing systems. For all the mud in the face we take on behalf of 'comprehensiveness,' it is precisely what enables us to reach out in different directions. It seems to me that there's a special vocation there to be an instrument for the restoration of visible unity. The Anglican Church that I know has never commended itself as the best type of Christianity. Its credentials have been its incompleteness. As Michael Ramsey said, 'Its vindication lies in its pointing through its own history to something of which it is a fragment'—the universal Church."

"There have been many moments, haven't there, in the history of Anglicanism where there was a call to rule out one attitude or another," said Brian, looking over our heads as though his eyes were fixed upon a parade of historical events off in the distance. "But the Church has always chosen to endure the tension." He seemed to have rejoined us once again. "If our Churches were to enter into some kind of organic unity, Tom, based on substantial agreement in essentials, you can bet your eyes that there'd be tension. But the point is: it could be a *creative* tension, with lots of cross-fertilization of ideas and insights.

"Like right now, for instance, a lot of Anglicans think we need more worldwide organization, for all kinds of reasons: doctrinal and liturgical cohesion, to help the Church's work of evangelization, and so forth. Well, now, it's no secret, is it, who has the genius in that area?"

"And some Roman Catholics," I chimed in, "are increasingly concerned to recognize and protect a greater degree of local self-government and theological expression within various regions. And we know who has the genius there, don't we?" I raised my glass in their direction. They met the gesture and three glasses clinked in a toast of mutual respect.

I made a move to head back to my room. There was some writing I wanted to do. Brian decided that he'd walk back in that direction with me. We said good-night to David and emerged from the pub to find that the evening air had only mellowed.

"What a delightful evening. I could be lured into staying outdoors a little while longer," I hinted, eyeing the bench outside our residence hall that faced the illuminated cathedral tower.

"Why don't we sit out here and pray Compline together?" Brian suggested.

"Fine! I'd like that."

And so we prayed there in the fading light, close by each other in the middle of the bench, both using Brian's breviary. When we reached the closing prayer he said, lifting his hand in my direction, "Let's absolve one another as we pray this." I did likewise, and together we prayed: "May Almighty God have mercy on you, forgive you all your sins through our Lord Jesus Christ, strengthen you in all goodness, and by the power of the Holy Spirit keep you in eternal life."

"Amen," we said, with one voice.

Further Reading

Alan C. Clark and Colin Davey, *Anglican-Roman Catholic Dialogue, The Work of the Preparatory Commission,* London, Oxford University Press, 1974.

Anglican-Roman Catholic Marriage, The Report of the Anglican-Roman Catholic International Commission on the Theology of Marriage and Its Application to Mixed Marriages, Church Information Office, Church House, London, SW1P 3NZ, 1975.

*ARC Marriages: A Study of U.S. Couples Living Episcopal-Roman Catholic Marriages.

*Educating for Unity: A Survey Concerning Diocesan Ecumenical Leadership.

*The Lived Experience: A Survey of U.S. ARC Covenants.
        *The above studies can be obtained from:
                17500 Farmington Rd.
                Livonia, Michigan 48152

Steven W. Sykes, The Integrity of Anglicanism, Seabury Press, New
    York, 1978.

The Final Report: Anglican-Roman Catholic International Commis-
    sion, Office of Publishing Services, U.S. Catholic Conference,
    1312 Massachusetts Avenue, N.W., Washington, D.C. 20005, or
    Forward Movement Publications, 412 Sycamore St., Cincinnati,
    Ohio 45202.

Epilogue

A few years ago, when I was struggling to decide between two paths that were before me—ecumenism or formation work with seminarians—I consulted with friends to ask their opinions as to where they saw me being more suited. From my married friends, active members of parishes, came the consistent reply: "Ecumenism? Christian unity? It's not even an issue in our experience of Church life!"

That response had the reverse effect upon me. The more I heard it, the more clearly my decision began to take definition. The fact that the scandalous division between Christians "is not even an issue" for so many of us is a large part of the problem. Most of us who have grown up in our divided Churches and denominations unconsciously assume that this is the "normal" situation. Ecumenism, then, becomes "abnormal." The fact that we Christians have lived for centuries with our divisions and antagonisms does not make these phenomena normal, even though they may be widely accepted and familiar. The unfortunate fact is that we are reasonably comfortable with the way things are, and that we feel very virtuous if we take a few tentative steps toward uniting with other Christians. The tendency is to identify only Beirut and Belfast as intolerable situations, because there disunity erupts into violence. But there is a similarly intolerable situation in Winnipeg or Spokane or Houston or New York where Church disunity mostly takes the form of peaceful coexistence. The abnormality, the deformity, of a divided Church has become normal, and we are not necessarily unhappy with or disturbed by it.

The dynamics of institutional loyalties tend, at times, to cast the work for Christian unity in the role of an unpopular minority movement. Ecumenism is then forced into a counter-cultural role. It may be true to say that few Christians are really against Christian unity today. But how many are truly informed and positively in support of it? It is easier to accept division than to work at ending division.

We simply cannot experience a stronger ecumenical future nor be loyal to the Gospel unless we stop accepting the prevailing ecumenical pessimism and start creative programs in education toward unity. In the final analysis, we live in a pre-ecumenical age, not a post-ecumenical retreat.

Significant movements often pass through several stages and are subject to change in a way consistent with their own dynamic. The ecumenical movement is now in a stage where learnings are being internalized by the Churches. New lessons will be learned in new stages of the movement. At the present time, after the initial post-Vatican II euphoria, we are like a tree in winter. To many, it appears that there is no life in the tree and that nothing is happening. Inside it, however, the vital forces are being gathered for a new bursting forth in yet another springtime.

Two buds that have been maturing over a long period of time have recently blossomed and promise much fruit. In January 1982, the World Council of Churches' Faith and Order Commission, the most comprehensive theological and ecclesiological forum in Christendom, unanimously accepted a major text on "Baptism, Eucharist, and Ministry." The careful preparation has taken over a half-century for its maturation. It is being given to the Churches for their appropriate study and action and will hopefully serve as a basis for unity. The agreement is, in the words of one of the commission's core group members, "nothing short of a miracle."

Then two months later, in March 1982, the Final Report of the Anglican-Roman Catholic International Commission was received by Pope John Paul II and Archbishop of Canterbury

Dr. Robert Runcie. It signaled the accomplishment of a dialogue agenda initiated in 1968 which focused upon the persisting theological differences between the two sister churches. Besides Agreed Statements on Eucharistic Doctrine, Ministry and Ordination, and Authority in the Church, the Final Report contains a common vision on the very difficult issues of the universal jurisdiction of the Pope, papal infallibility, divine right as applied to the Roman primacy, and the meaning of the scriptural texts concerning Peter's role.

Though the members of the Commission unanimously propose the Report as an articulation of their faith, they offer it to their fellow Roman Catholics and Anglicans as an aid to them in judging whether or not Roman Catholics and Anglicans are in fact one in their faith. The Commission has designated the Report as a Final Report only in the sense that it believes the Report has concluded the initial phase of official international dialogue between the Roman Catholic Church and the Anglican Communion. It is offered by the Commission to both Churches in the hope that it may be studied by the members of both Churches, win their approval, and become, if not the basis, at least the catalyst for fuller cooperation between them so that as sister Churches they may mutually assist one another on the road to unity.

The visit of Pope John Paul II to England, May 28–June 2, 1982, was a critical moment. If he and Archbishop of Canterbury Dr. Runcie had made no reference to the Commission's work, it would have indicated that it had been politely received but that nothing much was intended to be done about it.

On the eve of Pentecost, the two leaders issued a common declaration in Canterbury Cathedral in which they publicly committed their two Communions to effective follow-up.

The completion of this Commission's work bids us look to the next stage of our common pilgrimage in faith and hope toward the unity for which we long. We are agreed that it is now time to set up a new international Commission. Its task will be to continue the work already begun: to examine, especially in the light of our respective judgments on the Final Report, the outstanding doctrinal differences which still separate us, with a view toward their eventual resolution . . . and to recommend what practical steps will be necessary when, on the basis of our unity in faith, we are able to proceed to the restoration of full communion. . . . We are well aware that this new Commission's task will not be easy, but we are encouraged by our reliance on the grace of God and by all that we have seen of the power of that grace in the ecumenical movement of our time.

. . . Once more then, we call on the bishops, clergy and faithful people of both our Communions in every country, diocese and parish in which our faithful live side by side. We urge them to pray for this work and to adopt every possible means of furthering it through their collaboration in deepening their allegiance to Christ and in witnessing to him before the world. Only in such collaboration and prayer can the memory of the past enmities be healed and our past antagonisms overcome.

Our aim is not limited to the union of our two communions alone, to the exclusion of other Christians, but rather extends to the fulfillment of God's will for the visible unity of all his people.

One could not have hoped for much more. Besides anything that is said in such encounters, the very sight of two Church leaders kneeling in prayer together provides people with a vision of unity which until that moment seemed out of the question. An intangible of inestimable value is released in people's hearts and imaginations: hope springs up. It is this melting of the heart's cynicism, this thawing of disinterest, that provides the foundation for a future unity. The way through the door to unity is on our knees. Conversion of hearts is at the very center of the journey.

Never has the ecumenical movement had such excellent signposts to mark the extensive convergence taking place as it has in the Final Report and the WCC Faith and Order Commission's "Baptism, Eucharist, and Ministry." Never have there been such excellent tools to work with as these for local level, grassroots education. They should not only be preached about but be the objects of study in colleges, seminaries, adult education programs and joint-parish study groups.

The question that will inevitably come up is: What kind of unity are we seeking?

The unity sought does not mean uniformity. It does not mean absorption of smaller Churches by bigger ones. It does not mean reduction to a common minimum. It does not mean that anyone's essential doctrines will be watered-down. It does not mean a loss of one's identity.

The unity we seek is a unity of faith in those doctrines commonly deemed essential, agreement on which is required and would suffice to bring us together into an organic union. Disagreements on things that are important but not among the "essentials" can be worked out within the family along the way. An organic union finds its proper expression when all the Christians of a locality appear as a single visible fellowship, united in truth and holiness, displayed in love, service, and worship (especially at the Lord's Supper), and active together in evangelism. Within this union there will be a rich diversity of tradition and practice in the oneness of Christians in each place. This union will also have a universal dimension, offering a sign of hope for the unity of all humankind. It will, in any case, be the work of the Lord and his Spirit. Beyond that, for the moment, we must say with the evangelist John: "We do not yet know what we shall be" (I Jn 3:2). One can see, then, how the past twenty years, for all their advances, have been a mere prelude to the more mature ecumenism now emerging.

In the new ecumenism there will be greater realism in expectations, no minimizing of the doctrinal and sociological issues which divide the Churches, and a conscious effort to deepen the individual's understanding of and attachment to his or her own faith community.

Every Christian needs a vital home-community experience where faith is deepened, hope is rendered more vibrant, and love is more far-reaching. It is those who are at the center of their parishes' life, not at the periphery, who are the most engaged in and greatest assets for Church unity. The ecumenical movement thrives in an atmosphere of mutual hospitality.

But to receive another means that there is a place (Church community) where I live, a home wherein I open the door *from the inside* to welcome another.

Similarly, to be received by another means that while I have a home, I accept the invitation to go where the other lives. Mutual hospitality requires both knowing how to receive and how to enter into the home of another without moving in and quitting my own domicile.

Mutual hospitality calls for each of us to know where we live and to be knowledgeable about why things are done in our house as they are. Comfortable and secure with that, we can enter into, appreciate, and be enriched by the different style or modes of self-expression in our neighbor's home. When we come to appreciate, perhaps to love, what others value, we shall automatically support them in wanting to preserve it, and we shall learn in practice what is meant by unity without uniformity.

This opening of our doors on the local level and learning to share our lives has now become more important than anything else in the ecumenical movement. In the last five years the theologians and Church leaders who participate in high-level conversations have been pointing to the practically-more-important level of the parish and congregation as the truly vital, essential area for ecumenism. Without local-level work for unity the other levels (of official talks and documents) are rendered fruitless and left without soil for their implanting.

It is groups of people, not sets of doctrinal or theological propositions, communities of belief, not systems of belief, which primarily need to be reconciled. And this is a task which theologians alone cannot accomplish. It is love even more than truth that makes us free and enables us to overcome our estrangements. Theology alone cannot hope to cope with the host of social, cultural, historical, political and psychological factors involved in the disunity of the churches. Only people being Christ to one another can heal those wounds.

"I pray every day for unity," John Paul II has said. "Christ prayed for unity and we know the Father listens to his prayer.

Christ's prayer is the reason for our hope, and we know that 'hope does not disappoint us' " (Rom 5:5).

If we could all say as much—that we pray daily for unity—what would the cumulative transforming power of that prayer be?

Fr. Paul Couturier, the French priest who made universal The Week of Prayer for Christian Unity, believed that prayer for unity demands and forms men and women of energy so moved by the tragedy of Christian division that they can no longer rest in peace. The prayer he bequeathed us divests us of our own interests and puts us at the service of God's will with abandonment and trust: "For the unity of the Church of Jesus Christ, as he wills it, and when he wills it."

"Neither Catholic prayer, nor Orthodox prayer, nor Anglican prayer, nor Protestant prayer suffices," he declared. "All of them are necessary—and all of them together!"